Nine Talmudic Readings
by Emmanuel Levinas

Nine
Talmudic Readings

by Emmanuel Levinas

TRANSLATED
AND WITH AN INTRODUCTION
BY
Annette Aronowicz

Indiana University Press
BLOOMINGTON & INDIANAPOLIS

First Midland Book Edition 1994

Manufactured in the United States of America

Library of Congress Cataloging-in-Publication Data
Levinas, Emmanuel.
[Quatre lectures talmudiques. English]
Nine Talmudic readings / by Emmanuel Levinas ; translated with an
introduction by Annette Aronowicz.
p.   cm.
Translations of: Quatre lectures talmudiques; Du sacré au saint.
ISBN 0-253-33379-2 (alk. paper)
1. Talmud—Criticism, interpretation, etc.   I. Levinas, Emmanuel.
Du sacré au saint. English. 1990.   II. Title.
BM504.2.L4413   1990
296.1'206—dc20   89-46329

ISBN 0-253-20876-9 (pbk.)

2 3 4 5 98 97 96 95 94

CONTENTS

Acknowledgments

I want to thank Franklin and Marshall College for the two grants that have enabled me to complete this project. The first, in the summer of 1986, allowed me to meet with Emmanuel Levinas and to research some of his earliest writings on matters Jewish in the Bibliothèque Nationale. The second, awarded for the academic year 1987–1988, made it possible for me to hire an assistant to prepare this manuscript for publication. I am very grateful for the college's support.

Secondly, I want to thank my assistant, Scott Feifer, who typed many drafts with great care. Without his attention to detail and great loyalty to the cause, the manuscript might never have seen the light of day.

Then, there are a number of people who have helped me think through certain matters, concerning the translation as well as my own interpretive essay. Foremost among them is Jacques Rolland, who directed me to some of Levinas's early essays in the Bibliothèque Nationale. Our many conversations were also of great assistance with regard both to details and to general principles. I want, too, to thank Susan Handelman, whose generous spirit and very good questions were a much-appreciated stimulus to my own thoughts. Lastly, I want to thank the many friends who read parts of my manuscript attentively and offered helpful suggestions, most especially Kees Bolle, Michael Kerze, Eric Lane, and Leon Galis.

Translator's Introduction

> The true goal of the mind is
> translating: only when a thing has
> been translated does it become truly
> vocal, no longer to be done away
> with. Only in the Septuagint has
> revelation come to be at home in
> the world, and so long as Homer
> did not speak Latin he was not a
> fact. The same holds good for
> translating from man to man.
>
> —Franz Rosenzweig[1]

Translating into "Greek"

These Talmudic commentaries are, as Emmanuel Levinas tells us himself,
an attempt at translating Jewish thought into the language of modern
times. That is, they are simultaneously an attempt at letting the Jewish texts
shed light on the problems facing us today and an attempt at letting modern
problems shed light on the texts. Levinas sometimes refers to this approach
as translating the Jewish sources into "Greek," Greek being his metaphor
for the language Jews have in common with other inhabitants of the Western world.[2]

These Talmudic commentaries, then, can be viewed as a mark of the
secularization of the Jewish tradition, for today the majority of Jews live
not in a world apart but in the world at large. They too need to worry about
the State and nuclear war, revolutions and the relation between the sexes,
all the burning issues of the times; and, what is more, they are used to
expressing these issues in a language derived from sources other than the
traditional Jewish ones. As a result, the Jewish texts' way of posing
problems—in particular, the Talmud's way of posing problems—is no
longer intelligible or meaningful to a large majority of Jewish readers. The
very polemic Levinas wages in every one of his commentaries against people
for whom the Talmud is but a disjointed folkloric remnant or a dated discussion is a sign of its lack of transparency, its inability to communicate to
most contemporary Jews.[3]

The impenetrability of these texts is due not so much to a different historical context as to the Talmud's allusive, elliptical, seemingly incoherent
style, so different from the expository logic that Western, university-
educated readers expect. Translating the Talmud into a modern idiom,
translating it into the problems of the times, means, then, for Levinas, presenting its teaching in an expository, conceptual language that would be

accessible to any educated, even if uninitiated, listener. This attempt at utter intelligibility, at clarity, at an exposition that aims at every human being
regardless of background or prior assumptions, in "un langage non-
prévenu" is also what Levinas means by translating into "Greek."[4]

But if the fact of translation can be read as a sign of modern Jews' distance from the language of their own tradition and from their own spiritual
resources, as a sign of secularization, it is also for Levinas the sign of a secularization in a very different sense, for he claims that the texts *always* need
to be translated into secular language, into the language of contemporary
issues, into the language that strives to be understood by all, into the language of prose and demystification. The very distance we might feel with
respect to these traditional sources is, in a sense, a gain for these very
sources, for it allows their universal import to manifest itself in yet another
of its aspects. For Levinas, the capacity of these texts to signify is infinite,
and only successive "secularizations," translations into the language of the
times, can bring these infinite meanings to light.[5] Translation, and thus secularization, is here not a sign of regret for a lost past but the very life of a
tradition. It is, no doubt, in this context that we should understand his
comment that "the translation of the Septuagint is not yet complete, [and]
that the translation of biblical wisdom into the Greek language remains
unfinished."[6]

But why should modern Jews, at home in Western ("Greek") intelligibility and Western ("Greek") wisdom, go back and attempt to translate these
obscure Jewish sources? Levinas addresses this question often in his Talmudic commentaries; but beyond the answers he suggests explicitly, the very
richness of meanings his readings bring to light has its own eloquence. But
what made *him* decide to undertake the task of translation, when there
were no commentaries such as his available to persuade him? Here, a brief
sketch of his life, with special attention to the tension of "Greek" and Jew
within it, might provide us with a clue.

The "Greek" and the Jew

Emmanuel Levinas was born in Kovno, Lithuania, in 1906, into a Jewish
community in which, as he put it, "to be Jewish was as natural as having
eyes and ears."[7] The first language he learned to read was Hebrew, at home,
with a teacher, but it was also part of his formal education at the Hebrew
Gymnasium he attended after the family's return to Kovno in 1920. During
World War I they had moved to Kharkov, in the Ukraine, and while there
Levinas was one of a small number of Jews admitted to the Russian
Gymnasium.

While the Jewish influences in his childhood and early youth were very
much present, so much so that one can hardly speak of "mere influences,"
we can also see that other cultures were already exercising their strong pull.

His parents knew Yiddish, yet Russian was spoken at home. In the Jewish *Gymnasium*, he developed an abiding love for the great Russian classics, which he credits with the awakening of his philosophical interests. And there he learned of Goethe and yearned, as he put it, to know the cathedral of Cologne.[8]

In 1923, at the age of seventeen, Levinas went to France to study at the University of Strasbourg, and for the next decades it would seem that it was the non-Jewish cultural influences that aroused his passion and commanded his time. He became particularly engrossed in the thought of Husserl and Heidegger, both of whom he studied with in 1928–1929 at the University of Freiburg. His was the first complete work on Husserl in France, and it was Levinas who introduced Heidegger into the French intellectual world.[9] As he once put it humorously: "It was Sartre who guaranteed my place in eternity by stating in his famous obituary essay on Merleau-Ponty that he, Sartre, 'was introduced to phenomenology by Levinas.' "[10] Levinas's career in the French intellectual world culminated with his appointment as professor of philosophy at the Sorbonne in 1973, an appointment preceded by two other university positions (Poitiers and Nanterre) and by many and frequent contacts with the great figures of French intellectual life.

It would seem that during these years—a good part of his adult life—"the square letters," as Levinas calls Hebrew and the Jewish sources with which he had become acquainted in his childhood and early youth, had receded completely. Indeed, there is little evidence of a living encounter with Jewish texts in the 1920s and 1930s. It should not be forgotten, however, that soon after his arrival in France, Levinas joined an organization of considerable importance in the world of modern Western Jewry, the Alliance Israélite Universelle.

The Alliance was established in France in 1860 by a group of Jews prominent in French life. Inspired by the ideals of the Enlightenment, they wished to promote the integration of Jews everywhere as full citizens within their states, with equal rights and freedom from persecution.[11] While the eagerness of the Western Jews in the nineteenth century to enter into their host cultures has subsequently been criticized as an abandonment of the vital core of the Jewish tradition and as self-serving, Levinas underscores the religious nature of this move toward emancipation.[12] For nineteenth-century Jews it was not a mere desire to shirk their Jewish identity in order to make life more comfortable. They were also spurred by a vision of the unity of humankind, a sense of coincidence between Jewish and modern European values, and an ardent desire to participate in movements promoting this unity.

One of the many goals of the Alliance Israélite Universelle was to establish schools in areas where Jews were not receiving the kind of education that, members of the Alliance believed, would make them fit to enter the modern world as productive citizens. The Alliance thus saw itself as having a "civilizing mission," the regeneration of its brethren in the Mediterranean Basin who were not educated in the Western tradition.[13] This "civilizing mission" expressed itself in the creation of a curriculum that would train the Jewish youth of North Africa and the Middle East in modern languages, French taking a chief place, and in secular disciplines such as mathematics, (European) history, and science. These schools also taught Hebrew and some Jewish subjects.[14] However, the status of these latter subjects was lower than that of the "secular" curriculum. They were taught by local teachers who were not trained by the Alliance and who were very poorly paid, and the number of hours devoted to these subjects was small in comparison to the hours devoted to the others. Much tension often arose between the Alliance teachers and the local community over how, what, and by whom these subjects should be taught.[15]

The history of these Alliance schools reveals what nineteenth- and twentieth-century Western Jews (the Alliance had members outside the French community, as the word "universelle" in its title indicates) perceived to be the relation between European culture and the Jewish heritage. It seems clear that the Alliance took it for granted that there was a coincidence of ideals between the two traditions. As a result, anything in the Jewish sources or way of life encountered in the communities of North Africa or the Middle East that pointed in a direction other than that of modern French culture was not deemed worth transmitting.[16]

Levinas's membership in this organization soon after his arrival in France would seem to imply that he too saw the relation of Jewish and Western traditions as primarily one of a coincidence of ideals. But if this were so, events of the 1930s punctured this assurance. With the advent of fascism and all it brought in its train, Levinas, in a number of essays written for, among others, the journal of the Alliance, began to reflect upon the necessity of discovering the specificity of Judaism.[17] If we are being forced to admit our difference, what does this difference really amount to? In one of these essays he wrote:

> Modern Jewish consciousness has become troubled. It does not doubt its destiny but cannot calmly be witness to the outrages overwhelming it. It has an almost instinctive nostalgia for the first, limpid sources of its inspiration. It must once again draw its courage from it and again rediscover in it the certitude of its worth, its dignity, its mission.[18]

There is a groping in these essays for a return to one's own inner resources, reminiscent of the Talmudic injunction (which Levinas discusses in "Damages Due to Fire") to withdraw into one's home, "rentrer chez soi," in a time of epidemic.

It was the failure of emancipation, then, the refusal of admittance to the City, that led Levinas back to a rethinking of the relation between the Jewish and the European, or "Greek," traditions. But it would be altogether inaccurate to see in this rethinking, which was eventually to lead to a "return,"[19] any sort of closing oneself off again into a purely Jewish world, even if that were possible. For Levinas, the rethinking of the relation of Jewish to "Greek" sources would have to include the vision of *universality*, of *one* humanity in which all related as equals and in which all participated responsibly, the ideals of the Alliance.[20] The difference now was that in order for this *one* humanity to come into being, Western sources of spirituality, Western wisdom, would no longer suffice. In order for a genuine human community to emerge, it was *Jewish* wisdom, the *Jewish* vision of the human being, which must be understood and made available to everyone else. In one of his many essays on this subject, he insists

> upon the remarkable role that devolves upon the actuality of Israel, in its very exception, as formation and expression of the universal; but of the universal insofar as it unites persons without reducing them to an abstraction in which the oneness of their uniqueness is sacrificed to the genus; of the universal in which oneness has already been approached in love.[21]

Levinas's return to the specificity of Judaism, its difference, is thus not merely an attempt to retain some sort of identity in the homogeneity of modern life. It is not an ethnic loyalty. Rather, for him, *the return of the Jews to Judaism is necessary for the weal of the world.* Perhaps it is because of the immense obligation that Levinas sees devolving upon the Jewish tradition, in addition to the intellectual riches that he has revealed within it, that a commentator has said that he has succeeded in giving back to Judaism its "lettre de noblesse," the stamp of nobility.[22]

Levinas's desire to rediscover and reformulate the specificity of Judaism, which is present in the essays of the 1930s, began to be fulfilled through his meeting with an extraordinary teacher, Mr. Chouchani, with whom he studied from 1947 to 1951. Chouchani is the master whom Levinas mentions frequently in the course of his Talmudic commentaries. He was apparently very learned, both in Western knowledge and in the Talmud, which he knew by heart. Levinas's studies with Chouchani were tremendously intense and provided a way of entering the text that left all parochialism far behind. The aura of mystery surrounding Chouchani is very pronounced in Elie Wiesel's account of him (for Wiesel also studied with him, although neither Levinas nor he was aware of having the same teacher) and apparent even in Levinas's descriptions.[23] Chouchani obviously did not fit into any categories, seems to have appeared and disappeared as he pleased, and commanded tremendous respect and affection. The *hiddenness* of Chouchani, the fact that, outside of a small circle, he remained completely unknown, the fact that his own history was not particularly clear to those who did know him, makes one think of the Talmudic passage in which Moses retires to his tent; Levinas's reaction to this passage is that sometimes Judaism remains alive only in one man and yet this suffices to ensure continuity. Perhaps it is not altogether without significance, then, that Chouchani died in 1968 during the publication of *Quatre lectures talmudiques*, the first collection of Levinas's Talmudic essays.

No doubt in great part because of his contact with Chouchani, Levinas realized that the discovery of the specificity of Judaism had to go through the Talmud and that it required a knowledge of the Talmud's original languages, Hebrew and Aramaic. The reader of his commentaries will note that Levinas does his own translations of the Talmudic passages he has selected for discussion. Translation into "Greek," into the language of the times, cannot happen without a prior contact with the original wording and ambiance of the text. In 1946, a year before his meeting with Chouchani, Levinas became the Director of the École Normale Israélite Orientale (ENIO), the school the Alliance established in Paris in 1867 to train teachers for its schools in the Mediterranean Basin. He eventually changed the curriculum to place a much greater emphasis on the Hebrew language and on the study of Jewish sources, taking charge, for many years, of the Talmudic lessons himself. The Alliance schools had always included these Jewish subjects in their curriculum but, as mentioned earlier, they were considered of lesser importance. By changing the emphasis of the curriculum, Levinas was not in the least changing the goals of the Alliance. Its aim remained an openness to the world at large and an integration into secular culture. However, in Levinas's eyes, this universality could not be accomplished without reentering into the particularity of the Jewish tradition.

Levinas remained Director of ENIO for several decades. During this time, he wrote a number of essays on the problems facing Jewish education and on the necessity and sense of a revival of Jewish spirituality.[24] These are among his most beautiful essays: They portray a vision of a Jewish renaissance at the same time that a complete openness to the world is being maintained. In his writings, the two are not to be found side-by-side, but one actually guarantees the vitality of the other. A complete openness to the world guarantees a revival of Jewish spirituality, while a revival of Jewish spirituality makes possible an openness to the world. In a sense, Levinas's own life during this period best illustrates the contents of these essays, for while he was heading a Jewish school, writing essays on the Jewish tradition, and, from 1960, giving Talmudic commentaries at the yearly colloquia of Jewish intellectuals in Paris, he was also writing his great philosophical works, the works that speak to all human beings in "Greek," *Totalité et infini* (1961) and *Autrement qu'être ou au-delà de l'essence* (1974), to mention the two generally recognized as his major contributions to the philosophical tradition. The Jewish subjects were fed by the philosophical work, and the philosophical work was fed by the contact with Jewish sources. The Jew and the "Greek" were in constant relation.

This brief *aperçu* of Levinas's trajectory may throw some light, then, on the background of the Talmudic commentaries, why and how they came into being. They are propelled by Levinas's search for the specificity of the Jewish tradition and represent not a culmination of that search but a perpetual renewal of the desire to search itself. "A true culture," Levinas said, "cannot be summarized, for it resides in the very effort that cultivates it."[25] Each essay in this volume addresses the following question: what teachings about the human being do the Rabbis convey that cannot be found anywhere else but here but which apply to the entire world? In the process of hearing how this question is answered, however, the reader of these commentaries may also expect to discover something else: *the manner by which this specificity of Judaism is to be brought to light—Levinas's hermeneutic.* In fact, the mode of access into the text is crucial, for, as I hope to make clear shortly, it is the living embodiment of its teaching. That is, Levinas's way of reading the Talmud incarnates the very message it brings to light. I will thus turn to a discussion of his hermeneutic, for it is the key to the center of the Jewish tradition that Levinas wishes to evoke.

The Hermeneutic: Subjectivity and Objectivity

I would like to pause at two features in Levinas's essays which I consider most revealing of his hermeneutic. The first is the humor present throughout his commentaries. The second is the manner in which Levinas approaches religious vocabulary, most especially the term "God."

The humor in the Talmudic commentaries is not in the least opposed to the seriousness of what Levinas is saying.[26] Rather, it is a sudden catapulting to the fore of his subjectivity, often in the form of irony, which reveals the distance, the heterogeneity, between the text and its interpreter at the same time that it reveals the relationship between the two. Examples of this kind of humor abound, and they depend on the sudden breaking of the rhythm of the discourse. For example, in "Promised Land or Permitted Land," Levinas comments on the story of the twelve explorers whom the people of Israel sent on a preliminary investigation of the Promised Land, as recorded in the Torah and reworked by the rabbinic sages. Ten of the explorers, feeling qualms about the conquest of Canaan, tried, upon their return, to dissuade the people from going further. Levinas calls these explorers "leftist intellectuals." The modern term, with its connotation of avant-garde thought and a university atmosphere, reverberates strangely in the context of events taking place in the Sinai desert in the second millennium B.C.E. A similar example is from "As Old as the World?" At one point, a heretic asks the Rabbis how they expect a husband and wife to refrain from sexual relations for a specified period each month if the Law does not require that they

be separated during that time. Levinas remarks that the heretic was "probably already a Parisian."

In each case, and there are many more, the juxtaposition of the modern
term to the ancient one is incongruous. Levinas does not attempt to soften
this incongruity but emphasizes it, vaunts it, in fact. It is as if he wishes to
draw attention to his own subjectivity and to the process of interpretation
itself rather than to conceal it. The prominence of his own subjectivity in
the text is not incidental to his hermeneutic but crucial. It reveals that the
text does not mean by itself but requires the specific person of the interpreter to bring this meaning to light. As he says often, within the text are
enclosed an infinite number of meanings that require a plurality of people
"in their uniqueness, each one capable of wresting meanings from the signs,
each time inimitable."[27] Or, as he put it elsewhere,

> It all happens as though the multiplicity of persons . . . were the condition for
> the fullness of "absolute truth," as though each person, through his unique-
> ness, ensured the revelation of a unique aspect of the truth, and that certain
> sides of it would never reveal themselves if certain people were missing from
> mankind. . . . "[28]

To put one's specific person into the act of interpreting, as interpretation
requires, is to use all that is at one's disposal, all the tools one has. Thus,
Levinas brings his rich familiarity with European culture to bear upon his
understanding of Talmudic passages. We find explicit references—such as
those to the Russian poets Esenin and Pushkin, to the French dramatists
Corneille and Racine, to the Greek Aeschylus, to modern philosophers like
Hegel or Heidegger—as well as implicit ones. For instance, in the section on
the café in "Judaism and Revolution," we find a paraphrase of a well-
known passage from Pascal's *Pensées:* "You know that all evils occur as a
result of our incapacity to stay alone in our room."[29] In fact, when we think
of Levinas's tools—his Western tools—in approaching the Talmud, we
could also name the phenomenological method, the putting in brackets of
all considerations outside the text and allowing the meaning of the text to
appear from the structure that arises. The very preoccupation with
method—the commentaries are strewn with remarks about the relation to
the text, as the text is being interpreted—is itself characteristic of phenomenology, although calling it such may not necessarily lead to a greater understanding of what Levinas is up to.

What is important, though, is that Levinas's references to European art-
ists and thinkers are not merely decorative. They are designed precisely to
put the text into a context which, although on the surface incongruous
with it, allows the original text to give off its own specific scent.[30] In the
process the Talmudic text is secularized, brought into the world at large, the
discourse of all people. Yet, in this changing of contexts or in this juxtaposi-

tion, the Talmud does not become merely another example of a universal truth. Rather, it seems to function as the center to which all the other expressions can be related. The procedure here is reminiscent of what Franz Rosenzweig called for in one of his essays on Jewish learning: "We all know that in being Jews we must not give up anything, not renounce anything, but lead everything back to Judaism. From the periphery back to the center; from the outside in."[31]

The use of one's own specific person in the task of interpretation does not make interpretation an easy matter. On the contrary, Levinas stresses that it is an exertion, a battle, a tearing or wresting of meaning from the text. The word he uses again and again to characterize this struggle is the French *sollicitation*. The English to "solicit" does not necessarily connote a great deal of motion or commotion, but, as one of the commentators on Levinas's Talmudic essays, David Banon, has pointed out, the Latin roots of the term have to do with a shaking-up, in reference to a whole.[32] The context in which we find the word in the commentaries (I have tried to put it in brackets following my translation, wherever it appears) suggested to me an equivalent such as "wresting," "teasing from," even "forcing," in one case. One of the images Levinas uses in the Talmudic essays themselves suggests this *force*, this *struggle*, very well, although the word *sollicitation* does not yet appear. In "The Temptation of Temptation," we hear of Raba, one of the Talmudic sages who, while studying the Torah, rubs his foot so hard that blood spurts out. Levinas comments: "As if by chance, to rub in such a way that blood spurts out is perhaps the way one must 'rub' the text to arrive at the life it conceals. . . . Raba, in rubbing his foot, was giving plastic expression to the intellectual work he was involved in." Another image Levinas frequently uses to suggest the exertion necessary to bring the meaning of the text to light derives from Rabbi Haim of Volozhin, one of the great Lithuanian rabbis of the late eighteenth century. Interpreting a passage from the *Sayings of the Fathers* in which rabbinic commentary is compared to "hot embers," Haim of Volozhin explains: "The embers light up when one blows upon them; the intensity of the flame that thus comes to life depends on the length of breath of the person who interprets."[33]

Levinas insists that this solicitation, this rubbing, this blowing upon, is not mere subjectivism, not a mere imposition of an individual's impressions upon the text willy-nilly, although he concedes that perhaps all search for truth cannot help but run this risk.[34] What does keep interpretation, then, from being merely subjective fancy? Levinas mentions a number of rabbinic principles that minimize the risk. For instance, according to the rabbinic hermeneutic, solicitation, the wresting of meaning from a text, has to be done by people "with ears and eyes on the look-out, attentive to the *whole* from which the excerpt is taken, open as well to life: the city, the street, other human beings . . . " (my italics).[35]

In the context of the commentaries, "eyes and ears on the look-out,

attentive to the whole" means not simply overviewing a text and skipping
passages but paying attention to every single detail present, much as the
Rabbis asked themselves why there was an extra *yod* in the word *vayitzer*
("And God Created Woman"). It also means paying attention to the way a
text like the Talmud is ordered. At many places in the commentaries
Levinas pauses to explain this particular order. In line with the injunction
that the interpreter must use his specific person to wrest the meaning from
the text—and Levinas's commentaries elicit as much interpretation as the
texts they themselves are interpreting—I refer here to Blaise Pascal's categories as a means of clarifying the order that Levinas perceives in the Talmud.

Pascal, in one of the *Pensées*, insists that the Bible has an order, that in
its arrangement of texts it is not just a hodge-podge. But to see this order
one must be able to make a distinction between the order of the mind,
"which uses principles and demonstrations," and the order of the heart,
which "consists mainly in digressions upon each point which relates to the
end so that this shall be kept always in sight."[36] For Pascal, of course, the
order of the heart is quite distinct from loose sentiment or fancy. It is a
structured whole but distinct in the manner of conveying its truth from
that of the order of the mind.

In the order of the heart there is an apparent unrelatedness between con-
tiguous parts because they do not relate to each other as principles do to
their demonstrations. But this unrelatedness is only apparent because each
of the separate parts points to "the end," the meaning toward which the
entire text is tending. Thus, each of the parts points to the whole, as does
the peculiar juxtaposition of parts, all of which reflect back upon each other
as they all reflect the central meaning in one of its aspects.

Levinas, in saying that the interpreter must have "eyes and ears on the
look-out, attentive to the whole from which the excerpt is taken," means
that the Talmud is organized on the order of the heart, just as the Bible is
for the Rabbis, that there is one web of meaning in it, expressed in a myriad
of ways through the specific parts. This does not at all diminish the presence of the order of the mind in the text. It means, rather, that the text
operates in several dimensions at once.

More specifically, then, to pay attention to "the whole from which each
excerpt is taken" means not only, in the case of Levinas, paying attention to
the *whole* psalm from which the Rabbis quote one verse (as he does so masterfully in his discussion of Psalm 104 in "Judaism and Revolution") but
also placing each passage or even segment of a passage into a *whole* of
which it is only a part, the entirety of the Talmud. Take, for instance, the
commentary in "The Youth of Israel," which is perhaps especially appropriate as an illustration in that the Mishna and the Gemara,[37] both in themselves and in their relation to each other, appear even more discontinuous
than most of the other passages Levinas has chosen to comment on.

The Mishna was concerned with regulations governing the nazirate.[38]

The Gemara, making no references to the nazirate, begins in the following way:

> Rab said to Hiyya, his son: Snatch (the cup) and say grace. And, similarly, Rav Huna said to Raba, his son: Snatch the cup and say grace. Which means: greater is the one who says grace than the one who answers *Amen.* But don't we have a *baraita!* Rabbi Jose taught: He who answers *Amen* is greater than he who says grace. I swear that this is so, Rabbi Nehorai answered him. Know that it is the foot soldiers who begin the battle and that the victory is attributed to the elite troops, who appear as the battle is finishing.

In the order of the mind, the text seems quite self-explanatory and, as Levinas remarks, trivial. It is an argument about who is more meritorious, the person who says the blessing (over wine) or the one who responds "Amen." In the order of the mind, there seems to be no particular reason for Rabbi Nehorai's choice of the image of foot soldiers and battles to indicate his position in favor of the greater merit befalling the "troops," the congregation that says "Amen." He could have chosen another image. In the order of the mind, it is his opposition to that of the previous position quoted which is the one point worthy of attention. Levinas will show, however, that the image of foot soldiers and battle is intrinsically connected to the meaning of the entire debate. But, in order to do this, he has to see the "whole from which the excerpt is taken."

He stops at the mention of saying grace to ponder at the meaning of the act of blessing. If one thinks about it, he says, to bless (food and wine) is to recognize that one is not in ultimate control of one's nourishment, that one receives it as a gift. Thus, this particular discussion about blessing is a part that points to an invisible orientation, present everywhere throughout the Talmud, a certain non-mastery vis-à-vis the world, vis-à-vis the other man. Levinas goes on to say that the recognition of non-mastery over the world in fact allows one to recognize the need of others for whom food is also a gift, but a gift that might somehow have gotten diverted one way or another. The image of the foot soldiers and battle is crucial, then, to the meaning of the passage, as it can be interpreted to mean that the performance of the act of blessing ensures a defense of the other's right to eat. The discussion among the Rabbis about who has the most merit, the sayer of grace or the respondent, is not forgotten in the least. But, now, the sense of the question appears. It is no longer a mere quibbling over the arithmetic of piety. Rather, Levinas shows that the Rabbis' going back and forth on this issue signifies their recognition both of the need of a community that lives by the orientation expressed by the blessing and of the need for someone to take the first step toward acknowledging his non-mastery, the acknowledgement of which is what the blessing signifies. Levinas claims, then, that the Rabbis are not just prescribing behavior, although they are very much also doing that, but that they are reflecting upon what it *means* that the act be done.

By the end of his commentary, Levinas has shown the profound unity which articulates not only this portion of the Gemara but the relation of all of the Gemara to all of the Mishna. He does it through painstaking attention to each rabbinic saying. But, as indicated above, he locates each in the order of the heart, in the whole it points to—this attitude toward the other person in its myriad of manifestations. It is in this way that he manages to deepen the logical link between each passage. The entire section is as if bathed in the meaning which permeates the Talmud in its entirety. For Levinas the Talmud is a text that functions symbolically. Not only does each of its specific parts reveal a spiritual orientation but also the *whole* Talmud reveals one symbolic orientation toward which the entire text is tending, through its multitude of particular statements, each capable of reflecting upon the others.

This symbolic ordering may explain why it is impossible to summarize the argument of any of these Talmudic commentaries. They, like the texts they follow, aim not at a systematic comprehension of a problem based on principles and demonstrations, but at glimpses into a whole that one cannot make completely present as an argument from principles can be made present. The very mode of a commentary, broken up by the articulations of the passage and forced to derive its continuity from them, rebuts attempts to make a beeline for "the end." Thus, the interpreter, while bringing his or her entire person to bear on the text, must also pay extreme attention to the specificity of the text, which includes paying close attention to the way it is ordered, to its *symbolic* dimension. The subjectivity of the reader requires as its corollary that intense attention to the *object*, not only in what it manifests but also in what, through its manifestations, it hides. It must take this double dimension, this order, the spirit in the letter, into account.

The other rabbinic principle that Levinas felt cautioned against mere subjectivism is that the reader must be open to life: "the city, the street, other human beings."[39] This no doubt means that the interpreter must have experiences that can be used to illumine the sense of the texts, as in the statement that such and such an experience has suddenly made me understand this or that passage in a great author. But, more important for our emphasis here, it also means that one needs to be aware of issues of concern to the *polis*. It should not be forgotten that each of these Talmudic essays was originally delivered as a response to some questions the French-speaking Jewish community felt it urgent to address: attitudes to take toward the Germans, the land of Israel, the place of Judaism in the world at large. This too helps to make the relation of the interpreter to the text something other than mere whim, for it forces him out of his private universe into the life he shares with others.

But the third, and probably the most important, principle of rabbinic hermeneutic that Levinas emphasizes as most crucial to maintaining the authority of the text free of merely arbitrary impositions is the obligatory recourse to Oral Law, especially as it has been set down in the Talmud. One must go through the tradition of commentators on the text that precedes one's own commentary. It is this passage through the tradition that curbs, trains, molds one's own subjectivity. He says this in many places:

> What allows one to establish a difference between a personal originality brought to the reading of the Book and the pure play of amateurs' (or charlatans') illusions is a necessary reference of the subjective to the historical continuity of interpretation, is the tradition of commentaries that cannot be ignored under the pretext that inspirations come to you directly from the text. A "renewal" worthy of the name cannot circumvent these references, just as it cannot circumvent the reference to what is called Oral Law.[40]

Thus, the subjectivity called into play by the act of interpretation is always an extreme attention to what is outside itself. In fact, for Levinas the primary connotation of "self" is not an interiority closed in upon itself. When the self is true to itself it is nothing but that which is established by its response to the Other. It is the other person who disrupts our complacency, our sameness, our self-sufficiency, and, in the attention he or she commands, establishes the self that we are in reality, a face without any rear area, an occiput, to conceal itself, a complete exposure. These few lines certainly cannot do justice to Levinas's very complex notions of subjectivity, touched upon in the Talmudic commentaries, but carved out masterfully in his great philosophical works, such as *Totalité et infini* and *Humanisme de l'autre homme.* However, they should suffice to suggest that for him the primary sense of subjectivity is not a private universe, a sealed interiority, but an unparalleled attention, a response to what is outside, the most outside of which is the other human being. Thus, when Levinas talks of the necessity of the specific person of the interpreter in the act of interpretation, the lines we are accustomed to draw between subjectivity and objectivity blur. His is a redrawing of the lines in which a total subjectivity is at the same time a total attention to the object.

This may explain the humor we noted at the beginning of this section, for it expresses the tension between two specificities—the self and the other—awareness of the irreducibility of the text to his one interpretation and yet a real relationship, a profound, though unexpected, link between the two, in which the text is brought very close and yet kept very far. As such, the hermeneutic is also a living embodiment of what Levinas feels to be the specific content of the Jewish tradition, as conveyed through the Talmud. As he tells us in every essay, it is the special vocation of the Jews to remind the world of the obligation to the Other Man, which can only be accomplished through an attention to his specificity that requires all of my own and which is the essence of my inalienable responsibility. Perhaps because the hermeneutic, the way of entering the text, is *already* an incarnation of precisely that for which it is searching, the peculiar question Levinas sometimes asks: "Am I reading the text into a preexistent framework or do I derive the framework from the text?" becomes unanswerable. The question must be asked, however, because it indicates an awareness of one's own presuppositions, formed by tradition, without which the proper distance toward the object could not be maintained nor could the proper comprehension of its hidden sense be accomplished.

Perhaps, also (and here we may be taking liberties with Levinas's own understanding, or are we merely "rubbing the text?") the humor that we detect throughout the commentaries reflects the fact that the Talmudic text, even in its translation into "Greek," has the capacity to "make the hands impure." Levinas discusses this concept in a more-recent Talmudic commentary, which is not included in this volume.[41] It is a term the Rabbis apply to the Bible when discussing the validity of translating the Pentateuch into other languages. A valid translation is one that retains the text's capacity "to make the hands impure," to preserve its sacred status. Levinas interprets this to mean that the meaning of the Bible cannot simply be possessed by the individual grasping hand, which he analogizes to a desire to possess as such,[42] but that this will to power must be curbed, deflected, through the prism of tradition, which, by shaping one's vision, prevents blind appropriation. Besides, the long line of interpreters must manifest to the newcomer in that line that the text exceeds any one interpretation and will always be incommensurate to his grasp. Thus, the text always remains inviolate, no matter how much wresting of meaning is carried on by individual interpreters. It is always full. Anyone who would want simply, directly, to contain it once and for all, bypassing tradition, would desacralize the text and thus also himself. Therefore, when Levinas refers to the twelve explorers in Deuteronomy as leftist intellectuals, he is making it clear, because of the irony of the analogy, that the text and his interpretation do not coincide in any direct way, thus freeing the text, maintaining its power "to keep the hands impure."

The Hermeneutic: Time and Eternity

The other major feature of Levinas's hermeneutic to which I would like to draw attention is the manner in which he approaches religious vocabulary, especially the term "God." One might think that this word does not require translation into "Greek," that it is perfectly understandable to everyone. But Levinas insists on translating it, interpreting it as he does everything else. The translation he offers is not an allegorization. God does not become equivalent to Reason or to Society. That is, the key to the meaning of the term cannot come from the outside but must rely on the context, the place in the text, in which the term appears.

   The translation of the term occurs in many places throughout the commentaries. For instance, in "Toward the Other," following a discussion as
to what God does or does not forgive on the Day of Atonement, Levinas
concludes that "God is perhaps nothing but this permanent refusal of a
history that would come to terms with our private tears." It is a peculiar
sentence as God here is not some dimension of the psyche, an entity of our
inner life—a translation we might be used to—but a stance taken toward
the sufferings of human beings. God "is" the refusal to acquiesce to the
judgment of the State, of history, at the expense of the person whom this
history or this State crushes in order to arrive at its goal. He is, as he puts it
in the same passage, a refusal of a universality that ignores the interhuman
order, the refusal of the realization of a unity that would not have been
arrived at through the respect for persons. God, then, is a term whose
meaning comes to light through an *ethical* stance, a defense of the specificity of the human being, the other man, in the face of reasons of state or
abstractions about universal happiness. Later in the same commentary,
Levinas adds: "The respect for the stranger and the sanctification of the
name of the Eternal are strangely equivalent."
   Once again, we see the process of secularization that Levinas's translation involves, but this secularization, this bringing into the world, into the
times, is by no means intended as an elimination of transcendence. Rather,
it aims at its *relocation* in the midst of interpersonal exchange. "God" disappears as a reality one can have access to outside human activity. However, human activity reveals itself as pointing beyond itself. An act such as
the protection of strangers, for instance, conceals within it a dimension of
reality for the indication of which the use of the word "God" comes to
mind. What the text teaches, according to Levinas, is that it is through *action*, not through the fixing of the idea of God in our mind, that the wholly
other, transcendent dimension is made accessible. Thus, the content of the
text, its teaching, is parallel to the hermeneutic by which this teaching is
uncovered. The hermeneutic required, as we recall, that the word "God" be
understood on the basis of the context, the human interactions, in which it
appears in the text. But that is also how the presence of God is to be
glimpsed in daily life itself, in the exchange between people. In both cases, it
is the *embodied* truth—the truth in action—that conveys meaning. In both
cases, there is a fight against a merely abstract knowledge, a desire to penetrate reality through the concrete and particular, through the *act*. The hermeneutic is, once again, symbolic of the very content of the tradition it
searches to understand.
   However, the particularity of the act through which any translation of
the word "God" must pass also opens into a universal perspective. Levinas
is quite aware that there are people in the audience for whom the presence
of this term would indicate a split, a "they" and a "we," the they who
believe in God and the we who do not, thus relegating the teaching of the

text to the time in which it was written or to the group that still believes. Levinas's translation of the term into secular language bespeaks his confidence in the transcendence of the text, its ability to communicate across time and across such things as "belief," which is not a way of establishing anything like one's relation to God:

> I do not wish to talk in terms of belief or nonbelief. *Believe* is not a verb to be employed in the first person singular. Nobody can really say *I believe*—or *I do not believe* for that matter—that God exists. The existence of God is not a question of an individual soul's uttering logical syllogisms. It cannot be proved. The existence of God, the *Sein Gottes*, is sacred history itself, the sacredness of man's relation to man through which God may pass.[43]

The willingness and effort to translate the word "God," to make it burst the bounds of individual belief or non-belief is thus an act proclaiming the universality and also the eternity of the text, its capacity to speak to all human beings at all times.

The eternity and universality of the text, for Levinas, do not mean that it somehow floats above history, that it is not a product of historical forces, like everything else. He knows very well, for example, that there were Greek influences on the Jewish tradition—note his reflections on the Sanhedrin in "As Old as the World?" Its eternity is that it can time and again illuminate varying historical contexts. In one of his essays of the 1930s, "L'actualité de Maimonides," he said that the eternity of a great author is precisely his ability to become intermingled with the issues of the day.[44] To be timeless is thus an infinite capacity to enter history. It is this that, at least in part, Levinas refers to as the paradigmatic quality of the text. Without losing any of its specificity, it means in a myriad of contexts.

Levinas's Talmudic commentaries are themselves soaked in the present historical context. On nearly every page there are references to World War II, to the specter of Nazism, and to the philosophical outlook which might have led to it. There are also many references to the members of the contemporary French Jewish community, the participants of and contributors to the Colloquia. Often Levinas will address Rabi or Baruk, or Misrahi or Memmi, people often not very well known outside the French intellectual world and sometimes unknown outside the Jewish community in Paris. Thus, in their references, the commentaries are as particularized, localized, as the texts they are commenting on. But this immersion in the times is the very way to testify to the *eternity* of the Jewish sources, for it clothes them in actuality, in the present. The Talmudic commentaries are, Levinas tells us, this generation's testimony to the way it has understood its own tradition when it sought from it "food for thought and a teaching concerning what is fundamental"[45] and, as such, a link to the eternity of the texts.

But the eternity of the text, for Levinas, involves not only fitting into the present but also *judging* it. The teaching of the tradition reveals a standard of measurement by which current outlooks can be evaluated. The commentaries are full of digs against people who would measure the teachings according to how well they correspond to our cherished "modern" ideas. Thus, for instance, the Talmudic lesson on the creation of woman challenges our accepted notions of what constitutes liberation, and "Judaism and Revolution" challenges the identification of Judaism purely and simply with revolutionary action.

The capacity of the Talmudic text to judge the present can be well illustrated by the story of Rab in "Toward the Other." In the Talmudic passage, Rab has insulted his teacher, Rav Hanina, by not starting his lesson over when his teacher enters the room. Hanina refuses to forgive him, although Rab asks it of him thirteen years in a row, before the Day of Atonement. Hanina is not an unbending man. Why, then, does he refuse to forgive? Levinas adduces several reasons, including the possibility that Rab himself was unaware of the nature of his fault and thus could not properly ask for forgiveness. But at this point we are suddenly jerked into the present:

> One can, if pressed to the limit, forgive the one who has spoken unconsciously. But it is very difficult to forgive Rab, who was fully aware and destined for a great fate, which was prophetically revealed to his master. One can forgive many Germans, but there are some Germans it is difficult to forgive. It is difficult to forgive Heidegger. If Hanina could not forgive the just and humane Rab because he was also the brilliant Rab, it is even less possible to forgive Heidegger. Here I am brought back to the present, to the new attempts to clear Heidegger, to take away his responsibility—unceasing attempts, which, it must be admitted, are at the origin of this colloquium.

It is not the particular reading of this story which is crucial here, but the way Levinas makes the story a source of standards for measuring the present. This, needless to say, requires that the interpreter give the text this authority to judge, and, as we find out in "The Temptation of Temptation," this authority must be given before we know the content of the text. In that lesson, Levinas comments on the Talmudic discussion of how the Israelites came to accept the Torah. One of the most striking features of this acceptance is that they agreed to accept the commandments *before* they had even heard what they were. At least, that is the way that the odd ordering of the biblical text "we will do and we will hear" is understood by the Rabbis and pondered, in turn, by Levinas. The authority given to the Torah and to the standards embedded in it must precede the actual discovery of these standards, if they are to come to light at all.

This brings to mind the introductory paragraphs of nearly all of the Talmudic essays, in which Levinas expresses his inadequacy before the passages he has selected to comment on. To be sure, this acknowledgement of the mastery of the text refers to the infinite layers of meaning in it, which make all interpretation recognize its schematic nature. It is also Levinas's acknowledgment of his own late start in Talmudic studies. Yet, beyond this, the demurral of the introductory paragraph expresses the *necessary* presupposition of the text's power to teach. Otherwise, it cannot. Levinas does not bow to the superiority of the text, its power to teach and judge, *after* the fact of reading but *before* the fact of reading. There is a certain prerequisite attitude in which the text must be interpreted.

In many respects, the main service of these Talmudic commentaries is to provide a living portrait of the authority given to the text at the same time as one continues wresting and wrestling with its meaning. For Levinas insists that it is this very willingness to be judged by these sources that has maintained the Jews as the eternal people. It is eternal in that it has not allowed the judgment of history, the judgment of the powers-that-be, to determine the truth or reality of a situation. It is the relation to the texts that has allowed this. But why would Jews continually want to remain outside the times? The answer is *freedom*, the difficult freedom of having an inner life that can rise above the pressures of the hour. In his *Humanisme de l'autre homme*, Levinas gives us an image of Léon Blum in 1941. While in prison, he finished a book in which he refused to accept the present, horrible, reality of World War II as final: "A man in prison continues to believe in an unrevealed future and invites one to work in the present for the most distant things, of which the present is an irrefutable negation. . . . There is a very great nobility in an energy freed from the stranglehold of the present."[46] Blum, while Jewish, did not derive his spiritual sustenance from traditional Jewish sources, and Levinas never claims that only the Jews have this power to rise above the present. It is a fundamentally human trait. Yet what singles out the Jews, what constitutes their particular service to mankind, is that they remind others of a source of truth outside history, of a dimension outside time, through their separatedness, their insistence on a way of life embodying the truths of their texts. This way of life, which maintains its own standards despite the course of universal history, functions as a symbolic reminder of what it means to be completely human.[47] Jewish separatedness is at once its incomparable particularity and its universal calling.

This brings us back to God. The term "God," Levinas reminds us, is always referred to in the Talmud as The Holy One, Blessed be He: "Holiness in rabbinic thought evokes most of all separation (like our word 'absolute'). This term therefore names—and this is very noteworthy— a mode of being or a beyond being rather than an essence."[48] If we bring everything we have said together, the very separatedness the texts refer to when they speak of God is reflected in the Jewish people when they translate the term "God" into a language that permits judging the times. God's separatedness requires the medium of a hermeneutic before it can be *embodied* in the people's separatedness, in their refusal of the judgment of history. Again, the herme-neutic is not outside the text it is interpreting but already an essential part of its teaching.

This examination of Levinas's hermeneutic reveals, then, that learning *how* to read a rabbinic source is already learning what these sources pre-scribe. The order can also be reversed. Learning what these sources prescribe also teaches the proper approach for deriving this teaching. The act of inter-preting, as we see it in these Talmudic readings, is both an entryway into the Jewish tradition and an already-being-there. But, here, we come upon the tension between the specificity of the Jewish tradition and its universality. For while the Talmudic commentaries provide us with a glimpse of what is at the heart of the Jewish tradition, they also provide us with a glimpse of the religious dimensions as such. I would like, in a few broad strokes, to suggest something of this religious dimension, as it appears in Levinas's thought, and to reflect upon some of the questions it may raise for us.

The Religious Dimension: The Struggle with the Angel

What strikes me as central to Levinas's perception about the nature of reli-gion is his insistence upon the utter *ordinariness* of what we are accus-tomed to call the transcendent. We have just seen this in Levinas's translation of the word "God," which always derives its meaning from or-dinary human activity, as, for instance, in his statement in "Judaism and Revolution" that the love of God reveals itself in the employer's negotia-tions about the wages and working hours of his employees.

> As little as I have ever understood the exact meaning of the expression "the opening up of the soul in its love of God," I ask myself, nonetheless, whether there isn't a certain connection between the establishment of working hours and the love of God, with or without the opening up of the soul. I am even inclined to believe that there are not many other ways to love God than to establish these working hours correctly, no way that is more urgent.

This statement should certainly not be taken to mean that one's love of God *results* in moral or ethical behavior. Rather something else is going on. "The ethical is not merely the corollary of the religious but is, in itself, the element in which religious transcendence receives its original sense."[49] In other words, it is *in* our interactions with our fellow human beings as such, quite independently of any love of God these individuals may or may not profess, that the love of God may appear or lie hidden. The remark "Man would be the place through which transcendence passes"[50] should remind us that the ordinariness to which Levinas draws our attention, the ordinari-ness of saying "after you" as we sit at the dinner table or walk through a door,[51] is, in the end, not that ordinary, for it is the potential passageway of that which is most extraordinary.

Unlike Rudolf Otto, the famous theologian and historian of religions, whose *Idea of the Holy* has had tremendous impact on our perception of religion in this century, Levinas refuses to situate the transcendent, what Otto called the "Wholly Other" in some realm apart from our daily interactions, in a privileged experience accessible only to a few. For Levinas, the transcendent is part and parcel of our most taken-for-granted activities. It is not something "extra" that occasionally intrudes upon our world. Levinas quotes Franz Rosenzweig (whose view of religion is reflected in all Levinas's Talmudic commentaries, as well as in his philosophical works) as saying that "the division of men into those who are religious and those who are not does not go far. It is not at all a question of a special disposition that some have and others do not. . . . "[52] Rather, for Rosenzweig, as indeed for Levinas, religion is a matter of the *living* relations that all human beings engage in.[53]

I have italicized the word "living" because Levinas here and in his second essay on Rosenzweig associates life with the moment in which the specific person overcomes "the immobility of concepts and frontiers"[54] to come into relation with what is other, infinite, and transcendent. This happens when he interacts with other human beings in their specificity, without the grid of a system. Thus, "life in this precise sense, living—is religion."[55] The realm of religion, then, is "neither belief, nor dogmatics, but event, passion, and intense activity."[56]

Levinas's formulation of the religious dimension may seem to many to be irreligiousness itself, for here, as elsewhere, his approach is thoroughly *secular.* There is no "other" world besides the one we all live in, and there is no eternity outside time. Yet one cannot emphasize enough that this secularization is not a claim that, in the end, there is "merely" the world and "merely" history. For this world and these times contain, in Levinas's view, a *hidden* dimension, something infinitely more than we might expect, which remains hidden even when it reveals itself, and the relation to which makes human life what it is. It is this play between the ordinary and the extraordinary—or, perhaps better put, this ability to extract the extraordinary from the ordinary and to point to the ordinariness of the extraordinary—that the reader can expect to see in the Talmudic commentaries.

In this redefinition of religion, Levinas is, of course, not alone. Various thinkers of the last centuries—Pascal, Kierkegaard, Barth, Bonhoeffer, Buber, and Rosenzweig himself, to mention just a few well-known names —have, each in his own way, sought to convey the full scope of the religious dimension. Levinas resembles some in this list more than others, but all, I think, share in the effort to redraw the lines separating sacred from secular and, thus, to point to the relation with that which is transcendent in the midst of our most banal activities, even if this relation is not immediately visible to an eye interested only in surfaces or, as Levinas often says, in the letter.

This way of viewing religion as "la trame de l'être,"[57] the warp of being, should not be taken to mean, however, that for Levinas, it is sufficient to be a human being in general and that the positive religions are unnecessary. The Jewish tradition, at any rate, is quite necessary. Despite their emphasis on aggadic texts and their relatively few forays into Halakhah,[58] nearly all of these commentaries have something to say about the centrality, the importance, of Jewish ritual. This theme is most explicit in "As Old as the World?" in which the *mitzvot*[59] are seen as the hedge of roses that, by interposing a distance between us and natural spontaneity, keep us from evil, making possible a community in which justice, responsibility to the other, becomes a reality. We see it also in "Toward the Other," in which the ritual acts necessitated by the tradition to obtain forgiveness are those which form conscience: "Originating communally, in collective law and commandment, ritual is not at all external to conscience. It conditions it and permits it to enter into itself and to stay awake. It preserves it, prepares its healing." We come across it again in "Youth of Israel," where the regulations pertaining to the nazirite form and inform a spirituality that breaks the spell of narcissism and orient one toward service to all. Ritual acts have such a great meaningfulness for Levinas that he often reminds his readers that, without them, the sense of justice so often associated with Jewish consciousness will not last.

One may very well ask why, given the fact that the religious dimension is, in any case, present in our ordinary life, there would be any need for institutions such as the traditional Jewish *mitzvot*. For Levinas, however, the universal dimension is inaccessible to us unless it passes through a concrete, particular people, for only through the way of life of such concrete particulars does what is true for all human beings shine through. Without this embodiment, the universal dimension runs the risk of evaporating or becoming mere idea. Thus, while we can meet with individuals from all nations who enact the responsibility toward the other person, there nonetheless had to be a specific people who, in their teachings and doings, were chosen to express it. If not, our orientation as human beings would be lost; the sense of a human life would dissipate.

We see this movement between the universality and specificity of Judaism in many of the Talmudic commentaries. We can observe it, for instance, in "Judaism and Revolution," in the discussion of the meaning of the expression the Rabbis used, "the descendants of Abraham, Isaac, and Jacob." In the Talmudic passage in question the employer was told that he had an infinite obligation toward his workers, "for they are the descendants of Abraham, Isaac, and Jacob." This, of course, could be taken to mean that Jews deserve a special treatment, but Levinas makes the following remark:

Each time Israel is mentioned in the Talmud one is free, certainly, to understand by it a particular ethnic group which is probably fulfilling an incompara-

ble destiny. But to interpret in this manner would be to reduce the general
principle in the idea enunciated in the Talmudic passage, would be to forget
that Israel means a people who has received the Law and, as a result, a human
nature which has reached the fullness of its responsibilities and of its self-
consciousness.

... The heirs of Abraham—men to whom their ancestors bequeathed a difficult tradition of duties toward the other man, which one is never done with,
an order in which one is never free. In this order, above all else, duty takes the
form of obligations toward the body, the obligation of feeding and sheltering.
So defined, the heirs of Abraham are of all nations: any man truly man is no
doubt of the line of Abraham.

The coincidence of the Jewish tradition with our basic humanity is clear
here. To be Jewish, to be a descendant of Abraham, Isaac, and Jacob is to be
no less than a human being, if by this is meant a responsibility for the other
such as Abraham demonstrated toward the strangers who passed by his
tent. But the need for the specificity of the Jewish tradition does not suddenly evaporate, for it is precisely because Israel, the specific community,
has received the Law and enacts it, that the sense of what it means to be
human has been revealed. Levinas often says that the only particularity of
Israel is that of election.[60] It is the people chosen to make concrete through
its institutions the responsibilities to which all human beings are beholden.

Levinas once characterized the perpetual tension between the universal
and the specific, a movement which finds no resting point, as the struggle
with the angel, referring to the famous story of Jacob in Genesis 32. An
angel is that which has no body. It is pure spirit or pure interiority. The
genius of the Jewish tradition, Levinas says, is its awareness of the danger of
such disembodied truths.

> The great power of Talmudic casuistry is to be the special discipline which seeks
> in the particular the precise moment in which the general principle runs the risk
> of becoming its own opposite, which watches over the general from the basis of
> the particular. This preserves us from ideology. Ideology is the generosity and
> clarity of a principle which did not take into account the inversion stalking this
> generous principle when it is applied or, to come back to the image mentioned a
> moment ago: The Talmud is the struggle with the Angel.[61]

The universality that Levinas has in mind, then, is not a homogenous unity
but a respect for each particular, a particular from which a universal must
be wrested or in which a universal must be embedded, each time anew. It is
for this reason that Rav Eliezer, in "Desacralization and Disenchantment,"
is honored, for he dies, not in the contemplation of disembodied notions
about life or afterlife, but with a concern with such particulars as the purity
or impurity of a certain kind of shoe.

Levinas may, at this point, have convinced us of the necessity for the

Jewish tradition, always in tension with a universal dimension, but another question arises here, born from this very dialetic. What about other positive religions? Are they too needed in the global spiritual economy? With this question we fall out of the text. It is not within Levinas's purview, although it suggests itself naturally, given his emphasis on a community based on the recognition of specificity. It is thus a question we must answer on our own.

Although Levinas does not address the question of the place of other traditions directly, he nonetheless presents us with a hermeneutic which makes proper access to these traditions possible. For, while he derives his hermeneutic from the Rabbis and applies it to make rabbinic wisdom speak, it is also admirably suited elsewhere, wherever human beings have expressed their experience. Why should we not interpret terms referring to divinity in the Hindu epics, for instance, by paying attention to the human interactions in which these terms occur? Why should we not solicit texts, whenever we interpret, be they Bemba ritual or Lakota mythology? That is, why should we not search for that hidden whole in which each visible part is half-concealed, and for the revealing of which our entire personality must come into play? Why should we not ferret out the universal from the particulars of a given document?

At this moment, one might ask how the hermeneutic can be put into practice unless we have solved beforehand the problem of the One and the Many and answered systematically the question of whether traditions other than the Jewish one are indeed necessary to the spiritual economy of the world, and if so, how? But, here, one must point to the key of Levinas's hermeneutic: *the conviction, before one knows what the teaching amounts to, that a teaching exists in the texts to be interpreted, that the "warp of being" is somehow concealed there.* This is the whole paradox of "doing before hearing," of which Levinas talks in "The Temptation of Temptation" and of being chosen by the Good before choosing it, mentioned in "The Youth of Israel."

This paradox seems to me exceedingly valuable and exciting with respect to the implications of Levinas's hermeneutic for our approach to other traditions. We must learn to assume *beforehand* that the other man is master, that he has something to say, that the relation to him points us in the direction of that which is true. Later, we can sort out, as indeed we *must* do, again and again, the problem of the One and the Many, what and how all the different specificities do indeed contribute to mankind. But we cannot wait to have it all sorted out before we start. We must *already* know that the other is master before we have experienced the content of his mastery. The hermeneutic answers the question of the necessity of other traditions before we even have time to ask it.

I realize that, in reading Levinas this way, I am "rubbing the text." If one were to take him literally, one would not necessarily come to the conclusion that other traditions are worth exploring. This is not as representative of these Talmudic commentaries, where the topic does not come up except in brief glimmers, as of some of his other statements, where he proclaims himself resolutely "Europocentric,"[62] that is, holding to the centrality of European culture, as that which has achieved a language striving to express the universal. It would thus be, if one wants to read his work in a narrow way, the only culture that Judaism needs to confront, all the others not yet having reached the proper level or having already been translated into "Greek." However, Levinas's way of speaking of the relation to the other man is such that one does not have to do much "rubbing of the text" to see it as an opening unto that which is outside, that which is other, not in the exotic sense, but as that which we cannot contain in our terms once and for all.

In any case, reading Levinas the way we have just done, as opening us toward other traditions, does not diminish one iota the specificity of the Jewish tradition, does not make it just one out of many, whose difference no longer counts. For it is through the Jewish tradition that our very openness to other spiritualities gains its sense and its purpose. In the midst of multiplicity, it would still be the Jewish tradition that would orient us, allow us to see. At the same time, it would continually expose itself, be forced to confront the wisdom outside itself. Thus the tug between the universal, our openness toward all, which must, in order to be true openness admit the mastery of the other, his claim to Truth, and the specific, our rootedness in a Truth that cannot be made simply one among many, is the struggle with the Angel that will occur every time we interpret.

In the end it is my estimation that Levinas's greatest contribution in these Talmudic commentaries is his hermeneutic, which is not just a set of discrete principles, although it is also that, but an ethics, a vision of the interaction between specific persons, from which the principles derive or which the principles embody. This hermeneutic, though, opens up in two directions simultaneously. The first is toward the Jewish tradition itself, of which it is one expression, and which, in the present day, is sorely in need of a rediscovery of itself that is neither a closing itself off to the world nor an equation of itself with ready-made humanitarian principles. The other direction is that of the religious dimension as such, in whatever form it presents itself, an openness to the world at large and the multitude of specificities within it. These two directions are not really divergent but should operate as a perpetual to and fro. The greatness of these Talmudic commentaries is precisely that they invite us to this movement, the movement between a *chez-soi*, into which one can withdraw, and a tent open on all sides to which one beckons passersby.

A Word on This Translation

This volume comprises the four commentaries published in *Quatre lectures talmudiques* (1968) and the five that appeared in *Du sacré au saint: Cinq nouvelles lectures talmudiques* (1977). Both of these volumes included a preface or introduction by Emmanuel Levinas.

These nine commentaries were also published in the proceedings *(Actes)* of the Colloques des intellectuels juifs de langue française. It was at these colloquia, held annually in Paris since 1957, that Levinas first presented these readings. The colloquia proceedings deserve a study themselves, as they embody a certain period in the history of modern Jewry. The topics raised reflect both the intellectual and the political debates of the times, and since the colloquia have a tradition of some thirty years, it should be possible to detect changes in emphasis. But the *Actes* also convey something of the flavor, the texture of a particular segment of the French Jewish community. The list of participants, at the beginnings of the first few volumes, is revealing, primarily for the diversity of the intellectuals themselves: There is a preponderance of university professors, but there are also doctors, lawyers, rabbis, composers, and directors of institutes and schools. The very way they chose to identify themselves is also significant. Levinas, for instance, identified himself as the Director of the École Normale Israélite Orientale in the early volumes.

There is both a set format to the colloquia—morning and afternoon sessions, presiding officers, opening and closing addresses—and an informal atmosphere due, no doubt, to the fact that many of the people who participate have come to know each other's positions in the course of these yearly meetings, if they did not know them beforehand.

From the beginning, Levinas's commentaries evoked a great deal of admiration from his audience. The debates following the presentations, which are also recorded in the *Actes*, are lively, sometimes affectionate. But responses to Levinas were never free of challenges of various sorts. For example, Wladimir Rabi, who identified himself as "un homme de lettres," wanted to know how Levinas could possibly derive what he derives from the text when the text diverges so greatly from what it is itself interpreting. Levinas's answers to these queries are often sharp, but not without humor. The source note at the beginning of each commentary locates the transcription of the debate in the volumes of the *Actes*. Here the reader can get a good sense of the intellectual atmosphere in which Levinas's readings were and are being received.

The words "autrui" and "autre," key terms in Levinas's vocabulary, have presented translation problems. Both words mean "other," the difference being that "autrui" can only mean another human being, while "autre" means other in general, although it too can refer to other human beings. In the commentaries Levinas uses the two terms interchangeably; that is, I have detected no difference in meaning between "autrui" and "autre" in the vast majority of instances. In both cases the reference is always to the other human being. In my translation of these terms, then, I have done the following: for "autrui" I preferred to say "other person," "other man," "other human being," although when the context was sufficiently clear, I have translated it simply as "the other." I have tended to translate "autre" as "other," except when I thought there was a chance of not seeing what the term specifically refers to, the other person. As a result, the two terms often get translated the same way.

There has been a tradition, since Alphonso Lingis's translations of Levinas, to render "autrui" as Other and "autre" as other. In the philosophical works, where these terms are intensively elaborated, there may be good reason for proceeding in this manner. In the Talmudic commentaries, which speak a precise but nontechnical language, I did not want to risk mystifying the straightforward meaning of the text. "Autrui" and "autre" are both the other human being, of flesh and blood. I am aware that "other person" lacks the directness of "autrui" or "autre." It is cumbersome. But to my mind, it renders the overwhelming emphasis of Levinas's thought less ambiguously than do the alternatives.

As previously mentioned, Levinas made his own translations of the Talmudic passages from the Hebrew or Aramaic into French. I have thus translated them directly from the French, as his commentary depends on his wording, but not without consulting the English translation of the Talmudic passage in question (*The Babylonian Talmud*, translated into English under the editorship of I. Epstein [London: Soncino Press, 1935–48]). Wherever it was possible to adopt the English translation I did so, but most often, Levinas's commentary forced me to stick to his own word choice. Wherever there were biblical quotations, I relied on the English translation, *Tanakh* (Philadelphia: Jewish Publication Society, 1985), except, again, when Levinas's commentary necessitated a departure.

I have tried to provide a context for some of Levinas's references that might be unfamiliar to American readers. I have also, very occasionally, pointed to a difficulty in translating by providing the French original. These remarks appear in notes marked (Trans.). All other notes are Levinas's own, as they appeared in the French original.

NOTES

1. Nahum Glatzer, ed., *Franz Rosenzweig: His Life and Thought* (New York: Schocken Books, 1961), pp. 62–63.
This statement was picked as an epigraph because its contents seemed particularly relevant to Levinas's task in his Talmudic readings; but it is also important that its author is Franz Rosenzweig, whose influence Levinas has acknowledged in an oft-quoted passage in *Totality and Infinity* (Pittsburgh: Dusquesne University Press, 1969), p. 28: "We were impressed by the opposition to the idea of totality in Franz Rosenzweig's *Stern der Erlösung*, a work too often present in this book to be cited." Rosenzweig's influence on Levinas's work, I think, is also clearly discernible in these

Talmudic commentaries. It is to be noted that Levinas's first presentation at the yearly Colloquia of French-Speaking Jewish Intellectuals was a paper on Rosenzweig, "Entre Deux Mondes" (Between two worlds), in *La conscience juive: Données et debats* (Paris: Presses Universitaires de France, 1963), pp. 121–137. The Talmudic commentaries came later than that exposition.

2. This is the broadest usage by Levinas of the expression "translating into Greek." In a later commentary, "La traduction de l'écriture," in *Israël, le judaisme et l'Europe* (Paris: Gallimard, 1984), the expression is defined more precisely (see below, note 4).

Levinas's usage of the term "Greek" in the course of his writings is discussed by Robert Gibbs, " 'Greek' in the 'Hebrew' Writings of Emmanuel Levinas," paper delivered May 15, 1988, Jewish Philosophy Conference, Philadelphia. The relationship of "Greek" to Jew in Levinas's work is also considered by Catherine Chalier, "Singularité juive et philosophie," and David Banon, "Une herméneutique de la sollicitation—Levinas lecteur du Talmud," both in *Emmanuel Levinas: Les cahiers de la nuit surveillée,* no. 3, edited by Jacques Rolland (La Grasse: Editions Verdier, 1984).

3. The reader may obtain a better sense of the general climate in which Levinas delivered his commentaries by perusing the various *Actes* of the colloquia, in which all the proceedings were recorded, including, most often, the discussion following the oral presentations. The source note at the beginning of each commentary in this translation gives the bibliographic reference in which these debates can be found.

4. The above is a paraphrase from Levinas's "La traduction de l'écriture," in *Israël, judaisme et l'Europe,* p. 361. The original is worth quoting: "Je me suis avancé tout seul, bien entendu, en attribuant le parler grec à l'ordre, à la clarté, à la methode, au souci de la progression allant du simple au complexe, à l'intelligibilité, et surtout à la nonprévention du langage européen; ou, du moins au langage universitaire tel qu'il doit être, à la langue qu'un maître européen cultive, et qu'il parle, même quand il dénonce le langage universitaire et quand il réhabilite la 'pensée sauvage.' Je le dis encore un peu autrement . . . langage du déchiffrement. Il démystifie. Il démythise. Il dépoètise. Le grec, c'est la prose, c'est la prose du commentaire, de l'exégèse, de l'herméneutique. . . . "

5. For the necessity of translating, see Levinas, "La traduction de l'écriture," especially pp. 352, 358. For the infinite aspects of the text that require ever new interpretations, see "La Révelation dans la tradition juive" in Emmanuel Levinas, *L'au-delà du verset* (Paris: Les Éditions de Minuit, 1982). Several other essays in this collection stress this theme, including the Preface to *Du sacré au saint.*

The term "secularization" is mine, not Levinas's. It is my own "translation" of his insistence on demystifying, demythologizing, and, most especially, on confronting the problems of the times.

6. Richard Kearny, "Dialogue with Emmanuel Levinas," in Richard A. Cohen, ed., *Face to Face with Levinas* (Albany: State University of New York Press, 1986), p. 19.

7. "Emmanuel Levinas se souvient . . . ," interview with Myriam Anissimov, *Les Nouveaux Cahiers* 82 (Automne 1985):30.

8. Ibid., p. 31.

9. Levinas's first book on Husserl is *La théorie de l'intuition dans la phénoménologie de Husserl* (Paris: Alcan, 1930; Paris: Vrin, 1963, 1970). It was translated into English as *The Theory of Intuition in Husserl's Phenomenology,* by André Orianne (Evanston: Northwestern University Press, 1973). The seminal article on Heidegger was entitled "Martin Heidegger et l'ontologie," *Revue philosophique de la France et de l'étranger* CXIII (1932), 57ᵉ année, no. 5–6 (mai–juin):395–431. Levinas also

translated Husserl's *Cartesian Meditations* into French with Gabrielle Pfeiffer (Paris: Armand Colin, 1931).

10. Cohen, *Face to Face*, p. 16.

11. The two standard histories of the Alliance treat the founding of the organization at length: Narcisse Leven, *Cinquante ans d'histoire. L' Alliance Israélite Universelle (1860–1910)* (Paris: Librairie Felix Alcan, 1911–20), pp. 63–92; and André Chouraqui, *Cent ans d'histoire. L'Alliance Israélite Universelle et la renaissance juive contemporaine (1860–1960)* (Paris: Presses Universitaire de France, 1965), pp. 15–41.

There are also two more recent case studies of the Alliance's activities in which the founding of the organization is discussed: Michael M. Laskier, *The Alliance Israélite Universelle and the Jewish Communities of Morocco 1862–1962* (Albany: State University of New York Press, 1983), pp. 31–37; and Aron Rodrigue, "French Jews, Turkish Jews: the Alliance Israélite Universelle in Turkey", Ph.D. diss., Harvard University, 1985, pp. 43–57.

12. Emmanuel Levinas, "Le surlendemain des dialectiques," in *Emmanuel Levinas: Les cahiers de la nuit surveillée,* no. 3, p. 323.

13. The 1860 appeal of the Alliance to the Jews of the world went as follows: "If you believe that a great number or your co-religionists, overcome by twenty centuries of misery, of insult and prohibitions, can again find their dignity as men, win the dignity of citizens, if you believe that one should moralize those who have been corrupted, and not condemn them, enlighten those who have been blinded and not abandon them, raise those who have been exhausted, and not rest with pitying them. . . . If you believe in all these things, Jews of all the world, come hear our appeal, give your membership, your help, the work is a great one." "Appel à tous les Israélites," in *AIU* (Alliance Israélite Universelle) (Paris, 1860), pp. 10–11; quoted in Rodrigue, *French Jews, Turkish Jews*, p. 1. Rodrigue also speaks of the "civilizing mission" of the Alliance on pp. 18–26.

14. For an example of the kinds of curricula instituted in the schools, see Laskier, *The Alliance and Morocco*, pp. 100–108.

15. Ibid., pp. 80–95.

16. Laskier gives an example of the contempt or impatience of the director of one of the Alliance schools, Gogman, for what he considered no longer worth transmitting: "Gogman found the rabbi [Samuel Nahon, the new chief rabbi of Tetuan, Morocco] to be superstitious and a believer in the Zohar. Certainly no fervent Talmudist himself, Gogman indiscreetly interpreted Nahon's beliefs in theosophical concepts as an anachronism and belittled him; when Nahon praised the Kabalist Shim'on b. Yohay as a great figure in Jewish history, the director impetuously accused the rabbi of ignorance." Laskier, *The Alliance and Morocco*, pp. 81–82.

17. The essays Levinas wrote between 1935 and 1939 on the situation of the Jews have been collected in *Traces* 5 (Automne 1982).

18. Emmanuel Levinas, "L'actualité de Maimonides," *Traces* 5 (Automne 1982):97.

19. Levinas does not like to have the word "return" applied to himself, for he feels he has never left the Jewish tradition. He says this specifically to differentiate himself from the contemporary generation of young Jews, who, he feels, start from a nearly total ignorance of Judaism and are just now evincing a desire to discover it anew. Levinas, by contrast, had been steeped in Jewish culture as a child and an adolescent and participated in Jewish community affairs throughout his life. (Personal interview, June 23, 1986.)

20. The first four Talmudic readings translated in this volume, published as *Quatre lectures talmudiques*, were dedicated to Jules Braunschvig, a former president of the Alliance. While the dedication is undoubtedly a sign of personal friendship, it

can also be read as a sign of the continuity Levinas sees between the stress in his Talmudic commentaries and the goals of the Alliance.

21. Emmanuel Levinas, "De l'éthique a l'exégèse," *Les Nouveaux Cahiers* 82 (Automne 1985):66.

22. David Banon, "Le Pharisien est parmi nous," *Les Nouveaux Cahiers* 82 (Automne 1985):29.

23. Elie Wiesel, *Legends of Our Time* (New York: Holt, Rinehart), pp. 87–109; and Wiesel, *One Generation After* (New York: Random House, 1970), pp. 120–125. Levinas speaks of Chouchani in several places: in the interview with Anissimov in *Les Nouveaux Cahiers* 82, p. 32; in the interview with Kearny in *Face to Face*, pp. 17–18; in the introduction to *Quatre lectures talmudiques* reproduced in this volume (p. 8).

24. Many of these essays have been reproduced in *Difficile liberté* (Paris: Albin Michel, 1963), a collection of Levinas's writings on matters Jewish. Besides the essays on Jewish education, the volume contains a wide assortment of observations on contemporary issues and figures. It also includes the first two Talmudic commentaries (1960, 1961) Levinas delivered, which are not included in this translation.

25. "Comment le judaisme est-il possible?" ibid., p. 277.

26. The humor I am referring to here is a category for which I am indebted to the work of Kees W. Bolle, *Freedom of Man in Myth* (Nashville: Vanderbilt University Press, 1968). Drawing on the analyses of Jean Paul, Bolle says that, in this specific sense, " 'Humorous' is not to be confused with 'funny' or 'hilarious' or any such word. Generally the Romantics who first made humor into a topic of great interest were not so much intrigued by laughter about good jokes as they were by profound reasons for 'the smile which liberates.' True humor always concerns matters of ultimate importance" (p. 36). Bolle speaks of four aspects in which this kind of humor may reveal itself. The aspect most pertinent to our discussion is what he refers to as "subjective reservedness," what Jean Paul called "humoristic subjectivity" (pp. 56–57). The humor of this particular aspect is occasioned by the fact that "on the one hand, the 'objectivity' or authority of the material is unquestioned. But, on the other hand, there is someone who conveys this 'objective' and authoritative material" (p. 58). Ultimately, Bolle tells us, subjective reservedness is a practical awareness of the mystery of communication and understanding. It is the opposite of fanaticism (p. 63).

27. Levinas, *L'au-delà du verset*, p. 136.

28. Ibid., p. 163.

29. Pascal's own words: "Sometimes, when I set to thinking about the various activities of men, the dangers and troubles which they face at Court, or in war, giving rise to so many quarrels and passions, daring and often wicked enterprises and so on, I have often said that the sole cause of man's unhappiness is that he does not know how to sit quietly in his room." Blaise Pascal, *Pensées*, translated with an introduction by A. J. Krailsheimer (New York: Penguin, 1976), p. 67, *Pensée* 136 (139).

30. I am purposely reproducing Levinas's own phrasing when referring to the Rabbis' ability to make a passage switch contexts. See, for instance, "Promised Land or Permitted Land," p. 55, in which he speaks of the secret scent a text reveals itself to have when it is juxtaposed to others.

31. Glatzer, *Rosenzweig*, p. 231. There is another way to understand Levinas's juxtaposition of biblical and "secular" literature as well. In his essay "De la lecture juive des Ecritures," in *L'au-delà du verset*, pp. 136–138, Levinas speaks of the relation to the book as a fundamental mode of being. Our relation to the Bible would thus embody our relation to inspired speech in a paradigmatic manner. It would

make clear what our relationship to all inspired speech is. Thus, there is a continuity between sacred and secular texts.

32. Banon, "Le Pharisien est parmi nous," p. 25.

33. Levinas, *L'au-delà du verset*, footnote pp. 135–136.

34. Ibid., p. 164.

35. Ibid., p. 136.

36. Pascal, *Pensées*, p. 122, *Pensée* 298 (283).

37. For an explanation of these terms, as well as for the construction of the Talmud as a whole, please see Levinas's Introduction, pp. 4–5.

38. *Nazirate:* an institution of ancient Israel in which the participants vow to abstain from alcohol, from cutting their hair, and from contact with all impurity, for a set period, usually thirty days. Such a person is called a nazirite. For a fuller description of this state, see "The Youth of Israel."

39. Levinas, *L'au-delà du verset*, p. 136.

40. Ibid., p. 164.

41. Emmanuel Levinas, "Pour une place dans la bible," in *La Bible au present* (Paris: Gallimard, 1982), pp. 313–339.

42. Ibid., pp. 327–329.

43. Cohen, *Face to Face*, p. 18.

44. Levinas, *Traces*, p. 97.

45. Levinas, *L'au-delà du verset*, p. 126.

46. Emmanuel Levinas, *Humanisme de l'autre homme* (Montpellier: Fata Morgana, 1972), pp. 43–44.

47. In Levinas's second essay on Franz Rosenzweig, "Franz Rosenzweig, une pensée juive moderne," reproduced in *Franz Rosenzweig, les cahiers de la nuit surveillée*, no. 1 (Quétigny, France: La nuit surveillée et les auteurs, 1982), p. 77, there is a most beautiful formulation of this point, which I would like to quote at length:

"It is quite an ancient ambition of Israel to claim the rank of the eternal people, existing outside events, that is, not asking of them the meaning of its Israelite existence. Freedom in regard to the apparent logic of events, the possibility of judging them—such is eternity. It is not because Israel has miraculously survived that it arrogates a freedom in regard to History to itself. It is because, from the first, it has known how to refuse the jurisdiction of events that Judaism has maintained itself as one conscience, one throughout history. Hegel wants the nations to be judged by an anonymous history. Rosenzweig's contribution has consisted in reminding us that the roles are reversed. And to want to be Jewish in our days is, before believing in Moses and the prophets, to lay claim to the position of a conscience that posits itself unconditionally, to be a member of the eternal people. But perhaps, in the last analysis, this conscience is not possible without Moses and the prophets."

48. Levinas, *L'au-delà du verset*, p. 146.

49. Ibid., p. 133.

50. Ibid., p. 175.

51. Cohen, *Face to Face*, p. 32.

52. Levinas, "Entre deux mondes," p. 125.

53. Ibid., p. 127.

54. Levinas, "Franz Rosenzweig, une pensée juive moderne," p. 69.

55. Ibid.

56. Ibid., p. 74.

57. Levinas, "Entre deux mondes," p. 127: "Religion, before being a confession, is the very pulsation of life in which God enters into relationship with man and man with the world. Religion, as the *warp of being* [my italics], is anterior to the totality of the philosopher."

58. For a definition of the terms "aggadah" and "Halakhah," see Levinas's Introduction (p. 4) and "Damages Due to Fire" (pp. 194–195).

59. *Mitzvah* (pl. *mitzvot*): Hebrew word meaning "commandment(s)." Refers to the specific laws the Jews have agreed to fulfil in their covenant with God on Mount Sinai.

60. Levinas, *L'au-delà du verset*, p. 152: "The notion of Israel in the Talmud, as my master taught me, must be kept separate from all particularity other than that of chosenness. But chosenness means a surplus of duties."

61. Ibid., pp. 98–99.

62. In the context of a debate around his Talmudic lesson "La traduction de l'écriture," in *Israël, le judaisme et l'Europe,* an interlocutor inquires whether it is not Europocentric to affirm that only through conceptual, thus Western, thought, could the sense of a text be fully understood. Levinas answers: "Europocentrism is not for me the domination of desolation, unless, of course, it consists in conquering the world with canons. But, in the end, 'savage thought' has been understood in Paris but not Parisian thought by savage thought" (p. 368). In this exchange, the assumption shared by both participants is that European, "Greek" thought and language have risen to a level of conceptuality or abstraction, and thus to an ability to universalize, which non-European traditions have yet to reach. In the Talmudic commentaries, there are occasional references to mythological and to primitive thought, which seem to operate on the basis of the same dichotomy.

Four
Talmudic Readings

INTRODUCTION

The four Talmudic readings brought together in this volume represent the texts of talks delivered between 1963 and 1966 at the Colloquia of Jewish Intellectuals that the French section of the World Jewish Congress has organized in Paris every year since 1957. Preceding each lesson is the translation of the Talmudic text of which it is the commentary.

It is possible to detect themes of a general nature in the subjects of these talks: the forgiving of an unforgivable crime; the value of unlimited freedom without any obligation toward anyone; the violence of political creation; the relation between justice and private morality. Asking questions of the Talmudic texts will permit, we hope, a transposition of these themes beyond the ephemeral present in which they concern us and will allow us to confront Talmudic wisdom with the other sources of wisdom that the Western Jew recognizes. The third lesson, about the birth of the State, precedes by two years the discussions generated everywhere by the Six Day War, which the State of Israel was forced to win in June 1967.

The program of the Colloquia of Jewish Intellectuals always envisioned a Talmudic commentary, next to a biblical commentary, to be related to the general theme suggested to its members. Neither in the thought of the organizers nor in actual fact was this study of a Talmudic text to take on the character of a religious exercise, such as a meditation or a sermon within a liturgy. This would in any case have been contrary to the real essence of the Talmud, which the intellectual has the right to seek out.

The Talmud is the transcription of the oral tradition of Israel.[1] It governs the daily and ritual life, as well as the thought—including Scriptural exegesis—of Jews confessing Judaism. There are two levels within it: The first, in Hebrew, consists of the sayings of the sages called *Tanaim*, selected by Rabbi Judah Hanassi, who put them into writing at the end of the second century of the Common Era under the name of Mishna.[2] The *Tanaim* most certainly had contact with Greek thought. The Mishna became the object of new discussions, often conducted in Aramaic by sages called *Amoraim*, who in their teachings made especial use of sayings of the *Tanaim* that Rabbi Judah Hanassi had not included in the Mishna. These "left-out" sayings, called *baraitot*, are compared to the Mishna and used to shed light on

This introduction was written by Levinas for the first volume of his Talmudic essays, *Quatre lectures talmudiques* (Paris: Les Editions de Minuit, 1968), which includes the first four commentaries in the present volume.

it. They open new horizons within it. The work of the *Amoraim* is in its turn recorded in writing toward the end of the fifth century and receives the name of *Gemara*. The sections of the Mishna and the Gemara, presented together, the latter as a commentary on the former and, in contemporary editions, supplemented by the more-recent commentaries of Rashi and the Tosafists,[3] constitute the Talmud.

The Talmud exists in two parallel versions. One, the Jerusalem Talmud, represents the work of the rabbinic academies of Palestine. The other, the Babylonian Talmud, dating from approximately a century later, records the activity of the very renowned academies established in Mesopotamia. All the passages commented on here are taken from the Babylonian Talmud. Talmudic texts can also be classified under two headings: Halakhah and Aggadah (without always belonging exclusively to either one or the other). The Halakhah comprises those elements which, on the surface, concern only the rules of ritual, social, and economic life, as well as the personal status of the faithful. But these rules have a philosophical extension often concealed beneath questions of "acts to do" and "acts not to do," which were seemingly of immediate interest to the sages.

It is certain that, when discussing the right to eat or not to eat "an egg hatched on a holy day," or payments owed for damages caused by a "wild ox," the sages of the Talmud are discussing neither an egg nor an ox but are arguing about fundamental ideas without appearing to do so. It is true that one needs to have encountered an authentic Talmudic master to be sure of it. To retrace one's steps from these questions of ritual—which are quite important for the continuity of Judaism—to philosophical problems long forgotten by contemporary Talmudists would indeed demand a great effort today. In the renewal of studies we hope for in this area, it is clear one cannot start at the end.

But "philosophy," or the equivalent of what philosophy is in Greek, that is, Western, thought, also presents itself in the Talmud in the guise of moral tales and adages. (If the Talmud is not philosophy, its tractates are an eminent source of those experiences from which philosophies derive their nourishment.) These are the passages found side by side with the Halakhah and which are referred to as Aggadah. The Aggadah has, at first sight, a less-severe aspect for the uninitiated or beginners and has the reputation, in part false, of being easier. In any case, it allows for interpretations on different levels. For our four lessons we have drawn almost exclusively from the Aggadah.

Thus, a Talmudic text does not in any respect belong to "edifying discourses," even though that literary genre is one of the forms its own nature can take when it degenerates. But one can rediscover its initial thrust even when it is enveloped and weakened by thoughts that want only to be pious. In itself, this Talmudic text is intellectual struggle and courageous opening unto even the most irritating questions. The commentator must carve out a path toward them without letting himself be deceived by what appear to be Byzantine discussions. In fact, these discussions conceal an extreme attention to the Real. The pages of the Talmud, mischievous, laconic in their ironic or dry formulations, but in love with the possible, register an oral tradition and a teaching which came to be written down accidentally. It is important to bring them back to their life of dialogue or polemic in which multiple, though not arbitrary, meanings arise and buzz in each saying.[4] These Talmudic pages seek contradiction and expect of a reader freedom, invention, and boldness. If this were not so, a reasoning rising to the summit of abstraction and rigor would not have been able to coexist with certain logical forms of exegesis which remain purely conventional. How could fanciful procedures, even if codified—supposed to link the sayings of the sages to biblical verses—exist side by side with a masterly dialectic? These "weaknesses" can be explained neither by the piety of the authors nor by the credulity of the public. Rather, we are in the presence of allusions made by hypercritical minds, thinking quickly and addressing themselves to their peers. They do not proceed in the manner of those who would justify their deductions by appealing to the authority of a revealed and forced [*sollicitée*] letter of the text.[5]

To evoke freedom and non-dogmatism in exegesis today means one of two things. Either it means being a proponent of the historical method or, if the text has some connection with religious matters, in which case it is immediately classified as mythological literature, it means to engage in structuralist analysis. No one can refuse the insights of history. But we do not think they are sufficient for everything. We take the Talmudic text and the Judaism which manifests itself in it as teachings and not as a mythic web of survivals. Our first task is therefore to read it in a way that respects its givens and its conventions, without mixing in the questions arising for a philologist or historian to the meaning that derives from its juxtapositions. Did audiences in Shakespeare's theatre spend their time showing off their critical sense by pointing out that there were only wooden boards where the stage sign indicated a palace or a forest? It is only after this initial task of reading the text within its own conventions that we will try to translate the meaning suggested by its particulars into a modern language, that is, into the problems preoccupying a person schooled in spiritual sources other than those of Judaism and whose confluence constitutes our civilization. The chief goal of our exegesis is to extricate the universal intentions from the apparent particularism within which facts tied to the national history of Israel, improperly so-called, enclose us. We have given an account of this rule of universalization or interiorization in the first pages of the readings reproduced here.[6] Our approach assumes that the different periods of history can communicate around thinkable meanings, whatever the variations in the signifying material which suggests them. Has everything already been thought? The answer must be made with some caution. Everything has been thought, at least around the Mediterranean during the few centuries preceding or following our era. Is the exegesis we are suggesting rash because of this postulate? It fully accepts the risk of this rashness. Perhaps our exegesis rests on a yet rasher rashness to which we cannot but continue to expose ourselves. For we assume the permanence and the continuation of Israel and the unity of its self-consciousness throughout the ages. Finally, we assume the unity of the consciousness of mankind, claiming to be fraternal and one throughout time and space. It is Israel's history which has suggested this idea, even if mankind, now conscious of its oneness, allows itself to challenge Israel's vocation, its concrete universality. Does not antisemitism, a phenomenon unique in its kind, attest to its translogical nature? Immortal antisemitism continues in the form of anti-Zionism, at the moment in which Jewish history wishes also to be a land upon the earth that its concrete universalism contributed to unite and upon which the rigidity of the alternative national-universal is weakening.

But the meanings taught by the Talmudic texts, whose permanence we wish to show, are suggested by signs whose material form is borrowed from the Scriptures, from its stories, its civil and ritual legislation, its preaching, from a whole stock of Old Testament notions. Their meaning is also constituted by a certain number of events or situations, or, more broadly, by certain points of reference contemporary with the Rabbis or sages who speak in the Talmud. Despite the variations of sense that the elements of this signifying inventory might have undergone throughout the ages, despite the contingency of the circumstances in which these signs are inscribed and from which they received their power of suggestion, we do not think that a purely historical approach suffices to clarify this symbolism. Even less does a formalist investigation of the structuralist type seem appropriate to us here.

Indeed, it is legitimate to distinguish two regions within the past. One belongs resolutely to history and does not become intelligible without the scholarly and critical intervention of the historian. It inevitably contains a mythological dimension. The other belongs to a more-recent period and is defined by the fact of being linked in an immediate way to the present and to the present's understanding.[7]

One can call this immediate link living tradition and thereby define a past as modern. Biblical thoughts and narratives belong to the first of these regions. Only faith allows immediate access to them. Modern men who have lost this route approach them as myths and cannot separate the events and characters of the Bible from mythology without having recourse to the historical method. But the Talmud, despite its antiquity and precisely because of the continuity of Talmudic study, belongs, as paradoxical as this might seem, to the modern history of Judaism. A dialogue between the two establishes itself directly. Herein, no doubt, lies the originality of Judaism:

the existence of a tradition, uninterrupted through the very transmission and commentary of the Talmudic texts, commentaries overlapping commentaries.

The Talmud is not a mere extension of the Bible. It sees itself as a second layer of meanings; critical and fully conscious, it goes back to the meanings of Scripture in a rational spirit. The sages of the Talmud, the Rabbis, are called *Hakhamim*. They claim a different authority from that of the prophets, neither inferior nor superior. Does the word *Hakham* denote a sage or a scholar or a rational human being? We would need an exact philological investigation here. In any case, the Talmudists themselves referred to the Greek philosophers as *Hakhmei Yavan*, the *Hakhamim* of Greece.

What Paul Ricoeur says about hermeneutics, in contrast to structural analysis, which would be inadequate to an understanding of meanings deriving from Greek and Semitic sources, is verified in the interpretation of Talmudic texts. Nothing is less like the structure of "savage" thought. In no way does the Talmud continue the "way" of the Bible, even if one wished to see the latter as mythical. The Bible furnishes the symbols but the Talmud does not "fulfil" the Bible in the sense that the New Testament claims to complete and also to continue the Old. That explains the dialectical, argumentative language of the Talmud, conveying the "biblical myth" by making matters worse, if one can express it thus, with an undefinable touch of irony and provocation. (The term "biblical myth" is more the result of an intellectual vulgarity than of impiety, a misjudging of the Talmudic tradition which has transmitted it to us.) Whatever structures one could very usefully extract from the Talmudic method, no thinking can do without them, not even the thinking of partisans of structuralism. Lastly, from the formal point of view, the use the Talmud makes of biblical givens in order to set forth its wisdom is very different from the "pottering around" of primitive thought. It does not have recourse to bits and pieces of what was used elsewhere, but to its concrete wholeness.[8] The power of suggestion is refused to none of the aspects of the object-symbol. As a result, the symbolic casing molding all its forms is invisible to the naked eye, even leading it to confuse this manner of referring to biblical "verses" with the idolatry of the letter. Actually, the literal meaning, which *completely* signifies, is not yet the signified. The latter is yet to be sought. The symbolism here does not consist of conventional elements superimposing themselves on the flesh of the symbol. Nor is it a choice favoring the symbolizing function of one or another side of the symbol. The concrete flesh of the symbol does not waste away under the symbolic casing that a convention or a circumstance lends it. It means in all its fullness and with all that its subsequent history adds to it. Commentary has always tolerated this enrichment of the symbol through the concrete.

The commentaries begin again in each generation from this wholeness, with all its practically inexhaustible possibilities, but opened to these possibilities by the nonetheless defined outline of these object-signs. The Talmud, according to the great masters of this science, can be understood only from the basis of life itself. This holds not only for the very teaching it brings, which assumes life experience (that is, a great deal of imagination), but also for the understanding and perception of the signs themselves. Concrete realities, these signs are this or that according to the context of the life lived. Thus these signs—biblical verses, objects, persons, situations, rites— function as perfect signs: whatever the modifications that the passage of time introduces into their visible texture, they keep their privilege of revealing the same meanings or new aspects of these same meanings. They are thus irreplaceable, perfect, and, in a purely hermeneutical sense, sacred signs, sacred letters, sacred scriptures. Never does the meaning of these symbols fully dismiss the materiality of the symbols which suggest it. They always preserve some unexpected capacity for renewing this meaning. Never does the spirit dismiss the letter which revealed it. Quite the contrary, the spirit awakens new possibilities of suggestion in the letter. Talmudic thought casts light upon the symbols that undergird it, and this light brings their symbolizing power back to life. But, in addition, these symbols, which are realities and often concrete forms and people, are given meanings which they themselves have helped to create, are given an illumination bearing on their texture as objects, bearing on the biblical stories in which things and beings are intertwined. In this sense, the Talmud is a commentary on the Bible. There is an unceasing back and forth. The historical method might lack the back and forth which constitutes Talmudic dialectic. It might risk attaching itself to the origin of symbols that have long ago gone beyond the meaning they had at the time of their birth. It could impoverish or disqualify them by enclosing them in the anecdote or the local event in which they began.

The possibilities of signifying tied to a concrete object freed from its history—the resource of a method of thought we have called paradigmatic— are innumerable. Requiring the usage of uncommon speculative abilities, these possibilities unfold in a multidimensional space. The dialectic of the Talmud takes on an oceanic rhythm.

The commentaries we have attempted here certainly do not answer the demands we have just outlined. In this respect, too, they remain rash. But a marvelous master, Mr. Chouchani, of whose death in South America we learned during the very publication of this volume, has shown us what the real method is capable of. He has made a dogmatic approach based purely on faith or even a theological approach to the Talmud altogether impossible for us. Our attempt must attest to this search for freedom even if it does not attest to a freedom already possessed. To this freedom, it would like to invite other seekers. Without it, the sovereign exercise of the intelligence recorded in the pages of the Talmud can change itself, too, into the litany or pious murmur of a consent given beforehand, a reproach that could be made to Talmudists whose familiarity with these pages is nevertheless to be envied.

Although educated since early youth in the square letters, we have come late—and on the fringe of purely philosophical studies—to Talmudic texts, which cannot be practiced in amateur fashion with impunity. Thus, we have taken certain precautions in the talks collected here, despite the risks. In the sea of the Talmud, we have preferred navigating close to the shores by choosing for our commentary passages allowing for a relatively simple exegesis. The reservations which we formulate at the beginning of each of these talks are thus not the protests of false modesty. Our greatest concern, despite all that might appear new in the mode of reading we have adopted, is to separate the spiritual and intellectual greatness of the Talmud from the awkwardnesses of our interpretation. (Our mode of reading, although it has a style of its own, is common to a movement which arose within French Judaism after the Liberation. Our regretted friend Jacob Gordin played an eminent role within it, and we sometimes playfully refer to it as the School of Paris.)

Our lessons, despite their weaknesses, would like to sketch the possibility of a reading of the Talmud which would limit itself neither to philology nor to piety toward a "precious but outdated" past nor to the religious act of worship. It suggests a reading in search of problems and truths and that, no less than a return to an independent political life in Israel, is necessary for an Israel wishing to preserve its self-consciousness in the modern world but that may yet hesitate in the face of a return that would see itself in purely political terms.

The sages of the Talmud contrasted the coming into possession of the land of Israel to the idea of a heritage. The latter transmits the patrimony of the fathers to the children. The former restores the estate of the sons to the patriarchs, the fathers of sacred history, the only ones with a right to possession. The history of this land cannot be separated from sacred history. Zionism is not a will to power. But a modern formulation of Talmudic wisdom is necessary also for those who want to remain Jews outside the land of Israel. Finally, it must become accessible to cultured human beings who, without adhering to the answers Judaism brings to the vital questions of the times, are eager to know about the authentic civilization of Israel.

To give to such a study all the breadth it requires, to translate into a modern idiom the wisdom of the Talmud, to confront it with the problems of our time devolves, as one of its highest tasks, upon the Hebrew University of Jerusalem. Is this not the most noble essence of Zionism? Is it not the solution of a contradiction dividing both the Jews integrated within the free nations and the Jews who feel dispersed? Loyalty to a Jewish culture closed to dialogue and polemic with the West condemns the Jews to the ghetto and to physical extermination. Admission into the City makes them disappear into the civilization of their hosts. In the form of an autonomous political and cultural existence, Zionism makes possible a Western Jew, Jewish and Greek, *everywhere*. Given this, the translation "into Greek" of the wisdom of the Talmud is the essential task of the University of the Jewish State; it is more worthy of its efforts than Semitic philology, to which task the universities of Europe and America are equal. The Judaism of the Diaspora and a whole mankind astonished by the political renewal of Israel await the Torah of Jerusalem. The Diaspora, stuck in its living forces by Hitlerism, no longer has either the knowledge or the courage needed for the realization of such a project.

We hope, however, that readers who might glimpse in our commentaries the sources and resources of post-Christian Judaism will also recognize the limits of our enterprise and not imagine, after closing this book, that they already know what they have only glimpsed. (Post-Christian Judaism had no need of the testimony of the Dead Sea Scrolls to know it was alive at the dawn of Christian teaching, alive in a totally different way, moreover, from the life reflected in these manuscripts.) We are dealing with a spiritual world infinitely more complex and more subtle than our clumsy analyses. Judaism has been living in it for centuries, even if it is beginning to forget its foundations. This was a world whose existence remained unsuspected by the surrounding society, which contented itself with a few summary notions about it. These kept it from asking itself questions about the secret of human beings it declared strangers in order to account for their strangeness. The four lessons to be read here merely evoke from a distance the great teaching whose modern formulation is missing entirely.

NOTES

1. The term "Israel" is used here to denote not the State but the Jewish community. The sense of the word can also refer to the human community as such, as Levinas explains in "Judaism and Revolution," for instance. The reader is advised to pay attention to the context in which the term appears. (Trans.)

2. The Hebrew of the Mishna, which is different in its structure from the Hebrew of the Old Testament, is one of the chief sources of modern Hebrew.

3. The Tosafists were medieval rabbinic commentators, originally disciples and successors of the famous eleventh-century commentator Rashi. (Trans.)

4. Dialogue is not easily brought to life again in its written remains. We have, at any rate, kept our commentary in the form of oral delivery it had at the colloquia, not even eliminating from it the addresses to this or that friend or interlocutor present in the conference room.

5. The word *solliciter*, so frequently used by Levinas to express a key aspect of his hermeneutic, does not yet seem to have acquired the meaning it will have in some of the later commentaries. Here it is used in a somewhat negative vein. However, the act for which Levinas will later choose the term *sollicitation* is present from the first of the commentaries. (Trans.)

6. See also *Difficile liberté*, pp. 95f., 114, and *passim*.

7. See Gerhard Krueger: *Critique et morale chez Kant* (French translation published by Beauchesne), pp. 26ff.

8. The French here leaves a doubt as to the antecedent of "concrete wholeness." The original reads: "Du point de vue formel, enfin, l'usage que fait des données bibliques le Talmud pour exposer sa sagesse est très différent du 'bricolage' dont userait la pensée sauvage: il ne recourt pas à des bribes de ce qui a servi ailleurs, mais *à sa plénitude concrète*" (my italics). My sense of this passage is that *sa plénitude concrète* (its concrete wholeness) refers to the Bible as a whole, what has served elsewhere. This is based on the statements Levinas makes frequently about the Rabbis' treatment of the Bible as one whole. I offer it here as a suggestion for understanding an arduous passage, written rather early in the history of the Talmudic commentaries. For a much later description of rabbinic hermeneutic, see "De la lecture juive des écritures," "Le Nom de Dieu d'après quelques textes talmudiques," and "La Révélation dans la tradition juive," in *L'au delà du verset* (Paris: Les Editions de Minuit, 1982). Also, David Banon's "Une herméneutique de la sollicitation," in *Emmanuel Levinas: Les cahiers de la nuit surveillée*, no. 3., edited by Jacques Rolland (La Grasse: Éditions Verdier, 1984), is very helpful for a possible understanding of this part of Levinas's introduction. Finally, I refer the reader to my own introduction, more specifically to the section on hermeneutics. (Trans.)

TOWARD THE OTHER

■ From the Tractate *Yoma*, pp. 85a–85b ■

Mishna   *The transgressions of man toward God are forgiven him by the Day of Atonement; the transgressions against other people are not forgiven him by the Day of Atonement if he has not first appeased the other person.*

Gemara   *Rabbi Joseph bar Helbe put the following objection to Rabbi Abbahu: How can one hold that faults committed by a man against another are not forgiven by the Day of Atonement when it is written (1 Samuel 2): "If a man offends another man, Elohim will reconcile." What does Elohim mean? The judge. If that is so, then read the end of the verse: "If it is God himself that he offends, who will intercede for him?" Here is how it should be understood: If a man commits a fault toward another man and appeases him, God will forgive; but if the fault concerns God, who will be able to intercede for him? Only repentance and good deeds.*

Rabbi Isaac has said: "Whoever hurts his neighbor, even through words, must appease him (to be forgiven), for it has been said (Proverbs 6:1–3): "My son, if you have vouched for your neighbor, if you have pledged your word on behalf of a stranger, you are trapped by your promises; you have become the prisoner of your word. Do the following, then, my son, to regain your freedom, since you have fallen into the other's power: go, insist energetically and mount an assault upon your neighbor (or neighbors)." And the Gemara adds its interpretation of the last sentence: If you have money, open a generous hand to him, if not assail him with friends.

. . . Rab Jose bar Hanina has said: Whoever asks of his neighbor to release him should not solicit this of him more than three times, for it has been said (when, after the death of Jacob, Joseph's brothers beg for forgiveness): "Oh, for

This reading was given in the context of a colloquium consecrated to "Forgiveness" held in October 1963. The proceedings were published in *La conscience juive face à l'histoire: le pardon,* Textes presentés et revus par Eliane Amado Levy Valensi and Jean Halperin (Paris: P.U.F., 1965). Levinas's commentary is on pp. 289–304 and the discussion following it on pp. 316–335.

mercy's sake, forgive the injury of thy brothers and their
fault and the evil they did you. Therefore forgive now the
servants of the God of your father their wrongs" (Genesis
50:17).

 . . . Rab once had an altercation with a slaughterer of livestock. The latter did not come to him on the eve of Yom
Kippur. He then said: I will go to him myself to appease him.
(On the way) Rab Huna ran across him. He said to him:
Where is the master going? He answered: To reconcile with
so and so. Then, he said: Abba is going to commit murder.
He went anyway. The slaughterer was seated, hammering an
ox head. He raised his eyes and saw him. He said to him: Go
away, Abba. I have nothing in common with you. As he was
hammering the head, a bone broke loose, lodged itself in his
throat, and killed him.

 Rab was commenting upon a text before Rabbi. When Rab
Hiyya came in, he started his reading from the beginning
again. Bar Kappara came in—he began again; Rab Simeon,
the son of Rabbi, came in, and Rab again went back to the
beginning. Then Rab Hanina bar Hama came in, and Rab
said: How many times am I to repeat myself? He did not go
back to the beginning. Rab Hanina was wounded by it. For
thirteen years, on Yom Kippur eve, Rab went to seek forgiveness, and Rav Hanina refused to be appeased.

 But how could Rab have proceeded in this manner? Did
not Rab Jose bar Hanina say: Whoever asks of his neighbor to
release him must not ask him more than three times? Rab,
that is altogether different.

 And why did Rabbi Hanina act this way? Didn't Raba
teach: One forgives all sins of whoever cedes his right? The
reason is that Rabbi Hanina had a dream in which Rab was
hanging from a palm tree. It is said: "Whoever appears in a
dream, hanging from a palm tree, is destined for sovereignty." He concluded from it that Rab would be head of the
academy. That is why he did not let himself be appeased, so
that Rab would leave and teach in Babylon.

The passage to be commented on has been distributed to you. Perhaps
you should not take it with you. The texts of the Oral Law that have been
set into writing should never be separated from their living commentary.
When the voice of the exegetist no longer sounds—and who would dare
believe it reverberates long in the ears of its listeners—the texts return to

their immobility, becoming once again enigmatic, strange, sometimes even ridiculously archaic. It is true that many in my audience are excellent commentators themselves. They will not take my translation, whose original they know, with them. Besides, I am relying on their help in a task I pursue only as an amateur. In any case, they will soon notice that in presenting myself as an amateur, I am not indulging in a display of false modesty. It should also be known that I have not had much time to prepare this lesson, although the forty-five minutes reserved to me would, in fact, have required a less-hurried exposition in order to be more substantially filled.

I wish to make yet another comment: the lines you are reading are about forgiveness. But this is only one of countless texts the Talmud devotes to this subject. Therefore, one should not think after hearing me that the Jewish intellectuals of France now know what the Jewish tradition thinks of forgiveness. This is the danger of sporadic explanations of Talmudic texts, like ours, the danger of a premature good conscience, nourished, in this case, by the very sources of Jewish thought!

Finally, I would like to take a last oratorical precaution. I ask myself with some uneasiness if the President of the Alliance Israélite Universelle,[1] Engineer General Kahn, who is receiving you here, will not be shocked by the impending return to what he referred to earlier as "the abstract and conceptual plane." Let him rest assured. Certainly we are not heading toward an area which is practical and concrete in an immediate way. But you need only peruse the text before you to realize that we are not dealing with empty abstractions. The text has a rather unusual style. How are we to read it?

Those present for the first time at this session of Talmudic commentaries should not stop at the theological language of these lines. These are sages' thoughts, not prophetic visions. My effort always consists in extricating from this theological language meanings addressing themselves to reason. The rationalism of the method does not, thank God, lie in replacing God by Supreme Being or Nature or, as some young men do in Israel,[2] by the Jewish People or the Working Class. It consists, first of all, in a mistrust of everything in the texts studied that could pass for a piece of information about God's life, for a theosophy; it consists in being preoccupied, in the face of each of these apparent news items about the beyond, with what this information can mean in and for man's life.

We know since Maimonides that all that is said of God in Judaism *signifies* through human *praxis*. Judging that the very name "God," the most familiar to men, also remains the most obscure and subject to every abuse, I am trying to shine a light on it that derives from the very place it has in the texts, from its context, which is understandable to us to the degree that it speaks of the moral experience of human beings. God—whatever his ultimate and, in some sense, naked meaning—appears to human consciousness (and especially in Jewish experience) "clothed" in values; and this clothing is not foreign to his nature or to his supra-nature. The ideal, the rational, the universal, the eternal, the very high, the trans-subjective, etc., notions accessible to the intellect are his moral clothing. I therefore think that whatever the ultimate experience of the Divine and its ultimate religious and philosophical meaning might be, these cannot be separated from penultimate experiences and meanings. They cannot but include the values through which the Divine shines forth. Religious experience, at least for the Talmud, can only be primarily a moral experience.

Above all, my concern will be to keep to this moral plane. I certainly cannot deny that the rational expositions thus brought to light rest upon set positions, that they refer to preestablished attitudes. I cannot deny that the attitudes here are prior to the philosophical categories in which they come to light. But it is doubtful that a philosophical thought has ever come into the world independent of all attitudes or that there ever was a category in the world which came before an attitude. We can thus boldly approach this religious text, which lends itself in a wonderfully natural manner to philosophical language. It is not dogmatic; it lives off discussions and debates. The theological here receives a moral meaning of remarkable universality, in which reason recognizes itself. Decidedly, with Judaism, we are dealing with a religion of adults.

Our text consists of two parts: an excerpt from the Mishna (the name given to the oral teachings collected in writing by Rabbi Judah Hanassi toward the end of the second century); and an excerpt from the Gemara (the oral teachings of the period following the writing down of the Mishna and themselves recorded in writing by Rav Ashi and Ravina, towards the end of the fifth century), which presents itself as the commentary on the Mishna.

The Mishna is about the Day of Atonement—*Yom Kippur*. This Mishna was talked about earlier this morning, and I was even fearful for a second that what would be said about it was what I myself had prepared to say. But with the Talmud, there always remains something "unsaid," to use an expression in fashion with the intellectuals.

> The transgressions of man toward God are forgiven him by the Day of Atonement; the transgressions against other people are not forgiven him by the Day of Atonement if he has not first appeased the other person.

A few quasi-terminological explanations are in order: The Day of Atonement permits the obtaining of forgiveness for faults committed toward God. But there is nothing magical about this. It is not sufficient that dawn break on *Yom Kippur* for these faults to be forgiven. The Day of Atonement is certainly a fixed date in the calendar, and forgiveness, that is, the freeing of the guilty soul, requires a set date in the calendar. For the work of repentance requires a set date: to enable this work to take place every day, there must also be a day reserved especially for repentance. At least such is Jewish wisdom. But the Day of Atonement does not bring about forgiveness by its own virtue. Indeed, forgiveness cannot be separated either from contrition or from repentance, or from abstinence, fasts, or commitments made for the Better. These inner commitments can become collective or ritual prayer. The interiority of the engagement does not remain at this interior stage. It gives itself objective forms, such as the sacrifices themselves were in the time of the Temple. This interdependence of inside and outside is also part of Jewish wisdom. When the Mishna teaches us that the faults of man toward God are erased by the Day of Atonement, it wants to say that the celebration of *Yom Kippur* and the spiritual state it brings about or expresses lead us to the state of forgiven beings. But this method holds only for the faults committed toward the Eternal.

Let us evaluate the tremendous portent of what we have just learned. My faults toward God are forgiven without my depending on his good will! God is, in a sense, the *other, par excellence,* the other as other, the absolutely other—and nonetheless my standing with this God depends only on myself. The instrument of forgiveness is in my hands. On the other hand, my neighbor, my brother, man, infinitely less other than the absolutely other, is in a certain way more other than God: to obtain his forgiveness on the Day of Atonement I must first succeed in appeasing him. What if he refuses? As soon as two are involved, everything is in danger. The other can refuse forgiveness and leave me forever unpardoned. This must hide some interesting teachings on the essence of the Divine!

How are the transgressions against God and the transgressions against man distinguished? On the face of it, nothing is simpler than this distinction: anything that can harm my neighbor either materially or morally, as well as any verbal offense committed against him, constitutes a transgression against man. Transgressions of prohibitions and ritual commandments, idolatry and despair, belong to the realm of wrongs done to the Eternal. Not to honor the Sabbath and the laws concerning food, not to believe in the triumph of the good, not to place anything above money or even art, would be considered offenses against God. These then are the faults wiped out by the Day of Atonement as a result of a simple contrition and penitential rites. It is well understood that faults toward one's neighbor are *ipso facto* offenses toward God.

One could no doubt stop here. It could be concluded a bit hastily that Judaism values social morality above ritual practices. But the order could also be reversed. The fact that forgiveness for ritual offenses depends only on penitence—and consequently only on us—may project a new light on the meaning of ritual practices. Not to depend on the other to be forgiven is certainly, in one sense, to be sure of the outcome of one's case. But does calling these ritual transgressions "transgressions against God" diminish the gravity of the illness that the Soul has contracted as a result of these transgressions? Perhaps the ills that must heal inside the Soul without the help of others are precisely the most profound ills, and that even where our social faults are concerned, once our neighbor has been appeased, the most difficult part remains to be done. In doing wrong toward God, have we not undermined the moral conscience as moral conscience? The ritual transgression that I want to erase without resorting to the help of others would be precisely the one that demands all my personality; it is the work of *Teshuvah*, of Return, for which no one can take my place.

To be before God would be equivalent then to this total mobilization of oneself. Ritual transgression—and that which is an offense against God in the offense against my neighbor—would destroy me more utterly than the offense against others. But taken by itself and separated from the impiety it contains, the ritual transgression is the source of my cruelty, my harmfulness, my self-indulgences. That an evil requires a healing of the self by the self measures the depth of the injury. The effort the moral conscience makes to reestablish itself as moral conscience, *Teshuvah*, or Return, is simultaneously the relation with God and an absolutely internal event.

There would thus not be a deeper interiorization of the notion of God than that found in the Mishna stating that my faults toward the Eternal are forgiven me by the Day of Atonement. In my most severe isolation, I obtain forgiveness. But now we can understand why *Yom Kippur* is needed in order to obtain this forgiveness. How do you expect a moral conscience affected to its marrow to find in itself the necessary support to begin this progress toward its own interiority and toward solitude? One must rely on the objective order of the community to obtain this intimacy of deliverance. A set day in the calendar and all the ceremonial of solemnity of *Yom Kippur* are needed for the "damaged" moral conscience to reach its intimacy and reconquer the integrity that no one can reconquer for it. This is the work that is equivalent to God's pardon. This dialectic of the collective and the intimate seems very important to us. The Gemara even preserves an extreme opinion, that of Rabbi Judah Hanassi, who attributes to the day of *Yom Kippur* itself—without *Teshuvah*—the power to purify guilty souls, so important within Jewish thought is the communal basis of inner rebirth. Perhaps this gives us a general clue as to the meaning of the Jewish ritual and of the ritual aspect of social morality itself. Originating communally, in collective law and commandment, ritual is not at all external to conscience. It conditions it and permits it to enter into itself and to stay awake. It preserves it, prepares its healing. Are we to think that the sense of justice dwelling in the Jewish conscience—that wonder of wonders—is due to the fact that for centuries Jews fasted on *Yom Kippur*, observed the Sabbath and the food prohibitions, waited for the Messiah, and understood the love of one's neighbor as a duty of piety?

Should one go so far as to think that contempt for the *mitzvah* compromises the mysterious Jewish sense of justice in us? If we Jews, without ritual life and without piety, are still borne by a previously acquired momentum toward unconditional justice, what guarantees do we have that we will be so moved for long?

I turn now to the Gemara. The idea that no one can obtain forgiveness from God for a fault committed toward another person without having first appeased the offending party is in contradiction with a biblical verse. Let us mention in passing that Talmudic discussions sometimes present themselves as a search for agreement between an idea and a text, while behind this search, which is a bit scholastic and likely to discourage frivolous minds that are nonetheless quick to criticize, much bolder undertakings are concealed. In any case, Rabbi Joseph bar Helbe puts the following objection to Rabbi Abbahu (who no doubt thought the way our Mishna did):

> How can one hold that faults committed by a man against another are not forgiven him by the Day of Atonement when it is written (1 Samuel 2): "If a man offends another man, Elohim will reconcile."

This is in express opposition to our Mishna! Here the offense committed toward another person is rectified, according to the biblical verse, by the good grace of Elohim, of God, without any prior reconciliation with the offended man.

To this the interlocutor replies: What does Elohim mean? Are you sure that Elohim is equivalent to God? Elohim is translated as judge! The answer is not without foundation. Elohim in a general sense means authority, power, and consequently, very often, judge. Now everything is in accordance with the Mishna. If a man commits a fault toward another man, God does not intervene. An earthly tribunal is necessary to create justice among men! Even more than a reconciliation between the offender and the offended is needed—justice and a judge are necessary. And sanctions. The drama of forgiveness involves not two players but three.

Rabbi Joseph bar Helbe nevertheless does not feel he has been defeated. If Elohim translates as judge and if the word of the verse just translated as "will reconcile" is to mean "will bring justice," if instead of "God will reconcile" one must read "the judge will bring justice," how is one to come to terms with the end of the verse? The end of the verse, as translated by the French rabbinate, states: "If it is God himself that he [man] offends, who will intercede for him?" In this latter part of the verse, God is no longer designated by the term Elohim but by the Tetragrammaton which does designate God himself and not only the judge. The term earlier translated as "will bring justice" becomes "will intercede." If we want to read this end in accordance with the beginning, we would come to understand it thus: "But if the Eternal himself is offended, who will bring justice?" An absurd translation, the commentator tells us: As if the Eternal did not have enough servants capable of enacting his justice!

Rabbi Joseph bar Helbe, to maintain the same meaning for all the terms throughout the verse, keeps to his position, which consists in attributing to God the role of the one who erases the fault of the man who has offended another man.

But the Gemara decidedly rejects this view. This is the version it proposes:

> If a man commits a fault toward another man and *appeases him,* God will forgive; but if the fault concerns God, who will be able to intercede for him, *if not repentance and good deeds.*

The solution consists in inserting the italicized words into the biblical verse in order to bend it toward the spirit of the Mishna. One cannot be less attached to the letter and more enamored of the spirit! It is thus a very serious matter to offend another man. Forgiveness depends on him. One finds oneself in his hands. There can be no forgiveness that the guilty party has not sought! The guilty party must recognize his fault. The offended party must want to receive the entreaties of the offending party. Further, no person can forgive if forgiveness has not been asked him by the offender, if the guilty party has not tried to appease the offended.

But does Rabbi Joseph bar Helbe, who is so expert in exegesis, uphold the literal meaning of the verses? Doesn't he also have an idea in the back of his head? "If a man offends another man, Elohim forgives or Elohim straightens out or Elohim reconciles. . . . " Is it possible that Rabbi Joseph bar Helbe thinks that incidents between individuals do not shake the equilibrium of creation? Will you interrupt the session if someone leaves the room offended? What is it all in the face of Eternity? On the superior plane, the plane of Elohim, within the absolute, on the level of universal history, everything will work itself out. In a hundred years, no one will think about our sorrows, our little worries and offenses!

Rabbi Joseph bar Helbe thus opposes the thesis of the Mishna with a thesis that will seduce many a modern person. The doctrine which wants to be severe toward the subjective and the individual, toward little private happenings, and which exalts the exclusive value of the universal, awakens an echo in our soul, which is enamored of greatness. The tears and laughter of mortals do not count for much; what matters is the order of things in the absolute. You must see Rabbi Joseph bar Helbe's exegesis to the end: The irreparable offense is that done to God. What is serious is the attack of a principle. Rabbi Joseph bar Helbe is skeptical regarding the individual. He believes in the Universal. An individual against an individual has no importance at all; but when a principle is undermined, there you have catastrophe. If man offends God, who could set the disorder straight? There is no history which passes above history. There is no Idea capable of reconciling man in conflict with reason itself.

The text of the Gemara rises against this virile, overly virile, proposition, in which we can anachronistically perceive a few echoes of Hegel; it is against this proposition, which puts the universal order above the interindividual order, that the text of the Gemara rises. No, the offended individual must always be appeased, approached, and consoled individually. God's forgiveness—or the forgiveness of history—cannot be given if the individual has not been honored. God is perhaps nothing but this permanent refusal of a history which would come to terms with our private tears. Peace does not dwell in a world without consolations. On the other hand, the harmony with God, with the Universal, with the Principle, can only take place in the privacy of my interiority, and in a certain sense, it is in my power.

So much for the first half of my text. Is it without immediate relation to the question of forgiveness posed by German guilt? I am not so sure of that.

The following paragraph justifies the seriousness of a verbal offense.

> Rabbi Isaac has said: Whoever hurts his neighbor, even through words, must appease him (to be forgiven), for it has been said (Proverbs 6:1–3): "My son, if you have vouched for your neighbor, if you have pledged your word on behalf of a stranger, you are trapped by your promises; you have become the prisoner of your word. Do the following, then, my son, to regain your freedom, since you have fallen into the other's power: go, insist energetically and mount an assault upon your neighbor (or neighbors)." And the Gemara adds its interpretation of the last sentence: If you have money, open a generous hand to him, if not assail him with friends.

"To insist energetically" would mean "to open one's purse." "To mount an assault upon one's neighbor" would mean to send to the offended party friends as intercessors. Strange interpretation! We are, it would seem, in complete incoherence. Indeed, the Talmud wants to show the seriousness of a verbal insult. If you have said one word too many to your neighbor, you are as guilty as if you had caused a material injury. No forgiveness is possible without having obtained the appeasement of the offended! And in order to prove this, a passage from the Book of Proverbs is quoted in which the issue is not insults but money. John lends money to Paul and you have guaranteed the repayment of the loan. You are certainly henceforth prisoner of the word you pledged. But in what respect does this principle of commercial law have anything to do with hurtful words?

Could the lesson here be about the identity of injury and "monetary loss"?[3] Or is it that what we are being taught here concerns the essence of speech? How could speech cause harm if it were only *flatus vocis*, empty speech, "mere word"? This recourse to a quotation which seems totally unrelated to the topic, and to which only a seemingly forced reading brings us back from afar, teaches us that speech, in its original essence, is a commitment to a third party on behalf of our neighbor: the act *par excellence*, the institution of society. The original function of speech consists not in designating an object in order to communicate with the other in a game with no consequences but in assuming toward someone a responsibility on behalf of someone else. To speak is to engage the interests of men. Responsibility would be the essence of language.

We can now understand the "misreadings" of the Talmudic interpretation. "Insist energetically and mount an assault upon your neighbor" means, to be sure, in the first place, insisting to the debtor to whom you have given your guarantee that he fulfil his obligation. But what does insistence mean if not the intention to pay from one's own pocket? That the extent of the commitment is measured in cash, that the sacrifice of money is, in a way, the one which costs the most is a Talmudic constant. Far from expressing some sordid materialism, it denounces the hypocrisy hidden in the ethereal spiritualism of possessors. The "insisting to the debtor" and the "mounting an assault upon one's neighbor" of which the Book of Proverbs speaks are necessary to redress the wrong done to the creditor if this redress is not to be gratuitous or spiritual. Verbal injury demands no less. Without the hard work of reconciling numerous wills, without material sacrifice, the demand for forgiveness and even the moral humiliation it involves can make room for cowardice and laziness. The effort inherent in action begins when one strips oneself of one's goods and when one mobilizes wills.

Let us draw a general lesson from our commentary. While the sages of the Talmud seem to be doing battle with each other by means of biblical verses, and to be splitting hairs, they are far from such scholastic exercises. The reference to a biblical verse does not aim at appealing to authority—as some thinkers drawn to rapid conclusions might imagine. Rather, the aim is to refer to a context which allows the level of the discussion to be raised and to make one notice the true import of the data from which the discussion derives its meaning. The transfer of an idea to another climate—which is its original climate—wrests new possibilities from it. Ideas do not become fixed by a process of conceptualization which would extinguish many of the sparks dancing beneath the gaze riveted upon the Real. I have already had occasion here to speak of another process which consists in respecting these possibilities and which I have called the paradigmatic method. Ideas are never separated from the example which both suggests and delimits them.

Let us apply this methodological lesson to what follows. "To offend through speech"—we have just learned the real weight of speech. We are going to be told the ultimate meaning of every affront. The text we are about to read teaches us the following: One must seek the forgiveness of the offended party but one is freed with respect to him if he refuses it three times.

Rab Jose bar Hanina has said: Whoever asks of his neighbor to release him should not solicit this of him more than three times, for it has been said (when, after the death of Jacob, Joseph's brothers beg for forgiveness): "Oh, for mercy's sake, forgive the injury of thy brothers and their fault and the evil they did you. Therefore forgive now the servants of the God of your father their wrongs" (Genesis 50:17).

There would be three entreaties, or a ternary rhythm, in this passage, which would prove the thesis of Rab Jose bar Hanina. The commentators discuss its cogency. What does it matter? I would like to spend some time on the choice of biblical verse. What example of an offense was sought in the Bible for the occasion? It is the story of the brothers who sold their brother into slavery. The exploitation of man by man would therefore be the prototypical offense, imitated by all offenses (even verbal).

We can apply this same method to the passage already commented upon in the beginning, about the transgressions against man and against God. "If a man offends another man, Elohim reconciles . . . but if the transgression is against God. . . . " The sentence is said by the great priest Eli admonishing his sons. Unworthy priests, they seduced the women who came to the Tabernacle and took an undue share of the offerings of the faithful. "My children, stop doing this," Eli said to them, "if a man does wrong to another man, God will forgive, but if the fault is toward God, who will intercede?" But the fault of Eli's sons seems to be toward men. The injury done to God, then, is the abuse of power that the very person put in charge of safeguarding the principle slides into. Who will be able to intercede? Who can intervene? In the name of what Law? Those who are given the responsibility of applying the Law reject the Law and turn the scale of values upside down.

The last part of the text to be commented on is in a way anecdotal. I have shortened it and have kept two of the four anecdotes found on p. 87a, so as not to go beyond the time allotted me. The stories show the dialectic of forgiveness unfolding according to the principles just established.

"Rab once had an altercation with a slaughterer of livestock." The text does not tell us who was right or who was wrong. The commentators unanimously agree that Rab was in the right. But the butcher did not come on *Yom Kippur* eve to ask forgiveness of Rab. Rab therefore felt it was his duty to bring forth this demand for forgiveness, for the sake of the offender, and decided to appear before the person who insulted him. Here we have a reversal of obligation. It is the offended party who worries about the forgiveness that the offender does not concern himself with. (In a passage I have left out, the offended party walks back and forth in front of the offender to give him an opportunity to ask for forgiveness.) Rab goes out of his way to provoke a crisis of conscience in the slaughterer of livestock. The task is not easy! Rab's disciple, whom he meets on the way, is aware of this. This disciple, Rav Huna, asks: "Where is the master going?" "To reconcile with so and so." To which Rab Huna replies, without illusions: "Abba (familiar name of Rab) is going to commit a murder." Rab Huna is convinced that the slaughterer will not be moved by Rab's gesture, which will only aggravate the fault of the slaughterer. Excessive moral sensitivity will become the cause of death. We are far from the forgiveness generously and sovereignly granted *urbi et orbi*. The game of offense and forgiveness is a dangerous one. But Rab ignores the advice of his pupil. He finds the slaughterer at his professional occupation. He is seated and hammering an ox head. He nevertheless raises his eyes to insult once again the person coming humbly toward him. "Go away, Abba. I have nothing in common with you." The expression is marvelously precise and underlines one of the essential aspects of the situation. Mankind is spread out on different levels. It is made up of multiple worlds that are closed to one another because of their unequal heights. Men do not yet form one humanity. As the slaughterer keeps strictly to his level, he keeps on hammering the head; suddenly a bone breaks loose from it and kills him. It is certainly not of a miracle that the story wants to tell us but of this death within the systems in which humanity closes itself off. It also wants to speak to us of the purity which can kill, in a mankind as yet unequally evolved, and of the enormity of the responsibility which Rab took upon himself in his premature confidence in the humanity of the Other.

We are coming to the second story: "Rab (the man just referred to, so sensitive and so dangerous) was commenting on a text before Rabbi (before the famous Rabbi, the editor of the Mishna) in Rabbi's school. When Rab Hiyya came in (he was Rab's uncle) he started his reading from the beginning again. Bar Kappara came in—he began again; Rab Simeon, the son of Rabbi (the director's son!) came in, and Rab again went back to the beginning." (It was already a slightly parochial conference: For the first half of the session, people gather; the middle of the session is the point at which people begin to leave!)

> Then Rab Hanina bar Hama came in and Rab said: How many times am I to repeat myself? He did not go back to the beginning. Rav Hanina was wounded by it. For thirteen years, on *Yom Kippur* eve, Rab went to seek forgiveness, and Rav Hanina refused to be appeased.

He never forgave. This is the end of the story.

Would an offense between intellectuals be the most irreparable? This may be one of the meanings of the text. There are levels on which an offense would be unforgivable, which means above all that there are levels which require of us the greatest circumspection. Rab the just could be refused a pardon. It is better then—and this is in opposition to the easy terms promised by free grace—not to offend than to seek to set matters straight after the fact. Next to the famous Talmudic text promising those who repent places to which no just man is admitted, there is another text, no less worthy of credence: No repentant sinner can have access to the place of the just, who have never sinned. It is better not to sin than to be granted forgiveness. This is the first and necessary truth, without which the door is opened to every perversion.

One can nevertheless ask some questions, and the Talmud asks them. We have just learned that whoever asks his neighbor to release him from the wrong done to him should not ask more than three times. Why did Rab entreat thirteen times? Answer: Rab, that is altogether different. He is an exceptional being, or, if you wish, the situation is exceptional. He has offended his master. The injury done to the master differs from all other injuries. But isn't the other man always to some degree your master? You can behave like Rab. For has anyone, in any case, ever finished asking for forgiveness? Our wrongs appear to us as we humble ourselves. The seeking for forgiveness never comes to an end. Nothing is ever completed.

But how could Rav Hanina have been so harsh as to refuse thirteen times to grant the forgiveness that was humbly sought of him? He refused thirteen times, for on the fourteenth *Yom Kippur*, Rab, unforgiven, left to teach in Babylon. Rav Hanina's attitude is even less understandable, given the teaching of Raba: "One forgives all sins to whoever cedes his right." Whoever cedes his right behaves, in fact, as if he had only obligations and as if well-ordered charity began and ended not with oneself but with the other. Didn't Rab Hanina's intransigence put Rab in the position of the one to whom all sins will be forgiven?

The Gemara's explanation of Rab Hanina's behavior makes me ill at ease. Rab Hanina had a dream in which Rab appeared, hanging from a palm tree. Whoever appears thus in a dream is destined to sovereignty. Rab Hanina could foresee the future sovereignty of Rab, that is to say, his becoming head of the academy. (Is there another sovereignty for a Jew?) Thus, Rab Hanina, having guessed that Rab would succeed him, preferred to make him leave. A petty story!

This makes no sense. Our text must be understood in another way. I worked hard at it. I told my troubles to my friends. For the Talmud requires discourse and companionship. Woe to the self-taught! Of course one must have good luck and find intelligent interlocutors. I thus spoke of my disappointment to a young Jewish poet, Mrs. Atlan. Here is the solution she suggests: Whenever we have dreams, we are in the realm of psychoanalysis and the unconscious, of a psychoanalysis before the letter, to be sure. The Talmud—the spirit wrestling with the letter—would not have been able to keep up its struggle if it were not all the wisdom of the world before the letter. Now, in the story that is troubling us, what is at stake? Rab recognizes his fault and asks Hanina for forgiveness. The offended party can grant forgiveness when the offender has become conscious of the wrong he has done. First difficulty: the good will of the offended party. We are sure of it, given the personality of Rab Hanina. Why then is he so unbending? Because there is another difficulty: Is the offender capable of measuring the extent of his wrongdoing? Do we know the limits of our ill will? And do we therefore truly have the capacity to ask for forgiveness? No doubt Rab thought he had been a bit brusque in refusing to begin his reading of the text again when Rab Hanina bar Hama, his master, came into the school. But Rab Hanina finds out through a dream more about Rab than Rab knew about himself. The dream revealed Rab's secret ambitions, beyond the inoffensive gesture at the origin of the incident. Rab, without knowing it, wished to take his master's place. Given this, Rab Hanina could not forgive. How is one to forgive if the offender, unaware of his deeper thoughts, cannot ask for forgiveness? As soon as you have taken the path of offenses, you may have taken a path with no way out. There are two conditions for forgiveness: the good will of the offended party and the full awareness of the offender. But the offender is in essence unaware. The aggressiveness of the offender is perhaps his very unconsciousness. Aggression is the lack of attention *par excellence*. In essence, forgiveness would be impossible. I am indebted to my young Diotima for having guided me so well (even if the revelatory dream in the story was not dreamed by the patient).

But perhaps there is something altogether different in all this. One can, if pressed to the limit, forgive the one who has spoken unconsciously. But it is very difficult to forgive Rab, who was fully aware and destined for a great fate, which was prophetically revealed to his master. One can forgive many Germans, but there are some Germans it is difficult to forgive. It is difficult to forgive Heidegger. If Hanina could not forgive the just and humane Rab because he was also the brilliant Rab, it is even less possible to forgive Heidegger. Here I am brought back to the present, to the new attempts to clear Heidegger, to take away his responsibility—unceasing attempts which, it must be admitted, are at the origin of this colloquium.

So much for the page from the tractate *Yoma*. Since you still grant me a few minutes, I will compare this page, in which the issue was not murders but verbal offenses, to a more-tragic situation, in which forgiveness is obtained at a greater price, if it is still possible to obtain it.

The program of this year's colloquium does not include, to my keen regret, the usual Bible commentary by André Neher. I know that in this final section of my presentation, devoted to the Bible, I will not fill the gap but only make it more obvious. But at least in this way I will link my commentary to the principal theme of this meeting: the problems confronting us regarding our relations with the Germans and Germany.

Chapter 21 of 2 Samuel reports that there were three years of famine in the time of King David. The king asked the Eternal about it and found out that "this was because of Saul and that city of blood and because he put the Gibeonites to death"; this verse is as mysterious as an oracle. The Gibeonites were a Canaanite tribe mentioned in the Book of Joshua. Their lives were spared because they presented themselves to the conquerors of the Promised Land under false trappings, as originating from a distant, non-Canaanite land. By means of this trick, they obtained an oath of alliance. Once their ruse was discovered, they were reduced to the status of water carriers and woodcutters. This was the way the oath was honored, but the ancient biblical text does not speak of any violence they might have been subjected to on Saul's part. Our text mysteriously states: "Saul sought to strike at them in his zeal for Israel." To be sure, a thousand years later, the Talmud will explain Saul's wrongs. But without waiting so long, David sends for the Gibeonites in order to hear their grievances. They complain that King Saul had made their presence on the land of Israel impossible, that he had persecuted them and had tried to destroy them. They want neither gold nor silver. No compensations! They have no hatred toward the children of Israel but they want seven of Saul's descendants to be handed over to them. They will put them to death by nailing them to the rock on the Mountain of Saul. And David answers: I shall give them.

The book of Samuel then goes on to tell that David went and took from Rizpah, daughter of Aiah, Saul's concubine, two of her sons, that he also took five sons from Michal, daughter of Saul. (She had been David's own wife but Saul had her marry someone else during David's disgrace and exile. The difficulty lies in trying to figure out how she could have five sons, but the main point is that she had them.) David took pity on Mephibosheth, son of Jonathan. The seven unfortunate princes, given over to the Gibeonites, were nailed to the surfaces of a rock. But Rizpah, daughter of Aiah, stayed with the corpses from the season of the first fruits of barley (from the day after Passover) until the first rains (the time of Succoth). Each evening she covered the bodies of the tortured with bags, protecting them from the birds of the air and the beasts of the fields.

Do admire the savage greatness of this text, whose extreme tension my summary poorly conveys. Its theme is clear. It is about the necessity of talion, which the shedding of blood brings about whether one wants it or not. And probably all the greatness of what is called the Old Testament consists in remaining sensitive to spilled blood, in being incapable of refusing this justice to whoever cries for vengeance, in feeling horror for the pardon granted by proxy when the right to forgive belongs only to the victim. But here is what the Talmud has to say about it (tractate *Yebamot*, pp. 58b–59a):

David would not have waited three years to search for the causes of the famine which hit his country. He had first thought that the cause of the disaster lay in the corruption of men. Was the famine punishing idolatry?

No foreign cult was found in Israel. Debauchery? Not a single loose woman in all the land. It was next assumed—and this seems to be as serious although more secret than either idolatry or debauchery—that there were people in Israel who promise without keeping their promise, that there were beautiful speeches without actions, that there were welcoming committees without welcome. Such welcoming committees must not have been found in Israel.

Then David said to himself: The disaster is not a result of the way of life. There must be a political wrong here, an injustice which is not caused by private individuals. The king asks God and gets a double answer. The mysterious verse about Saul's fault would reveal two as yet unredressed injustices: a wrong done toward the Gibeonites, who were destroyed by Saul; a wrong committed toward Saul, to whom a royal burial had not been granted. His remains were not buried with the honors due to royal rank.

But the Talmud also knows the fault of Saul toward the Gibeonites, for which we cannot find a trace in the Bible. It would have been an indirect one. In executing the priests of the city of Nov, Saul left the Gibeonites who served them without a means of subsistence. The Midrash affirms that the crime of extermination begins before murders take place, that oppression and economic uprooting already indicate its beginnings, that the laws of Nuremberg already contain the seeds of the horrors of the extermination camps and the "final solution." But the Midrash also affirms that there is no fault which takes away the merit: there is simultaneously a complaint against Saul and the recalling of his rights. Merits and faults do not enter into an anonymous bookkeeping, either to annul each other or to increase one another. They exist individually. That is, they are incommensurable, and each requires its own settlement.

How could David have spared Mephibosheth? Doesn't pity lead to the exception, to the arbitrary, to injustice? The Talmud reassures us. David was not being partial at the moment of the selection of the victims. It is the Holy Ark which separated the guilty from the innocent sons among Saul's descendants. It is an objective principle. But then what happens to David's pity, which the biblical text nonetheless mentions? It is a prayer to save Mephibosheth. Let us take a general principle out of this pious text: To recognize the priority of the objective does not exclude the role of individuals; there is no heart without reason and no reason without a heart.

Second question: does one have the right to punish children for the faults of their parents? Answer: it is better that a letter of the Torah be damaged than that the name of the Eternal be profaned.

To punish children for the faults of their parents is less dreadful than to tolerate impunity when the stranger is injured. Let passersby know this: in Israel, princes die a horrible death because strangers were injured by the sovereign. The respect for the stranger and the sanctification of the name of the Eternal are strangely equivalent. And all the rest is a dead letter. All the rest is literature. The search for the spirit beyond the letter, that is Judaism itself. We did not wait until the Gospels to know that.

Last question: How were people able, in opposition to the strict prohibition of the Torah, to leave human corpses exposed for so many months and to profane the image of God they bear? Same answer: "It is better that a letter of the Torah be damaged than that the name of God be profaned." The image of God is better honored in the right given to the stranger than in symbols. Universalism has a greater weight than the particularist letter of the text; or, to be more precise, it bursts the letter apart, for it lay, like an explosive, within the letter.

We have here then a biblical text which the Midrash spiritualizes and interiorizes but which it preserves in its unusual power and harsh truth. David is not able to oppose a victim who cries out for justice, even if this justice is cruel. To the one who demands "a life for a life," David answers, "I shall give." And yet the Gemara teaches more. A verse of the text (1 Samuel 21:2) indicates to us, seemingly as a simple piece of historical information: "The Gibeonites were not part of the children of Israel but of the rest of the Amoreans. . . . " To this preliminary verse, the Gemara attaches the meaning of a verdict. It is David who would have excluded the Gibeonites from the community of Israel and relegated them to the Amoreans. To belong to Israel, one must be humble (place something or someone higher than oneself), one must know pity and be capable of disinterested acts. The Gibeonites excluded themselves from Israel.

What difference is there between pity and generous action? Doesn't one presuppose the other? That is not certain. There are people whose hearts do not open before their neighbor runs a mortal risk, just as there are people whose generosity turns away from men fallen to the level of hunted animals. Under the Occupation we learned these distinctions, just as we also knew souls full of humility, pity, and generosity—souls of Israel beyond Israel. The Gibeonites who lacked pity put themselves outside Israel.

One can understand even more precisely the three signs by which Israel is recognized. To humility are added the sense of justice and the impulse of disinterested goodness. But strict justice, even if flanked by disinterested goodness and humility, is not sufficient to make a Jew. Justice itself must already be mixed with goodness. It is this mixture that is indicated by the word *Rahamim*, which we have badly translated as "pity." It is that special form of pity which goes out to the one who is experiencing the harshness of the Law. It is no doubt this pity which the Gibeonites lacked!

I have the impression that I have come back to the theme evoked by Mr. Jankélévitch when he opened this colloquium, even though no one in this hall has asked that the descendants of our torturers be nailed to the rocks. The Talmud teaches that one cannot force men who demand retaliatory justice to grant forgiveness. It teaches us that Israel does not deny this imprescriptible right to others. But it teaches us above all that if Israel recognizes this right, it does not ask it for itself and that to be Israel is to not claim it.

And what remains as well, after this somber vision of the human condition and of Justice itself, what rises above the cruelty inherent in rational order (and perhaps simply in Order), is the image of this woman, this mother, this Rizpah Bat Aiah, who, for six months watches over the corpses of her sons, together with the corpses that are not her sons, to keep from the birds of the air and the beasts of the fields, the victims of the implacable justice of men and of God. What remains after so much blood and tears shed in the name of immortal principles is individual sacrifice, which, amidst the dialectical rebounds of justice and all its contradictory about-faces, without any hesitation, finds a straight and sure way.

NOTES

1. For a description of this organization, see my introduction, pp. xi–xii. (Trans.)
2. See note 1 to Levinas's Introduction. (Trans.)
3. Levinas uses an idiomatic expression here, *plaie d'argent*, which means not only monetary loss but also a loss or wound which is not fatal or, for that matter, even serious. There is an irony in the expression and thus in the sentence that was difficult to reproduce. (Trans.)

THE TEMPTATION OF
TEMPTATION

■ From the Tractate *Shabbath,* pp. 88*a* and 88*b* ■

And they stopped at the foot of the mountain . . .

—Exodus 19:17

*Rav Abdimi bar Hama bar Hasa has said: This teaches us that
the Holy One, Blessed be He, inclined the mountain over
them like a tilted tub and that He said: If you accept the Torah, all is well, if not here will be your grave.*

*Rav Aha bar Jacob said: That is a great warning concerning
the Torah. Raba said: They nonetheless accepted it in the time
of Ahasuerus for it is written (Esther 9:27): "The Jews acknowledged and accepted. They acknowledged what they accepted."*

*Hezekiah said: It is written (Psalm 76:9): "From the heav-
ens thou didst utter judgment: the earth feared and stood
still (calm)." If it was frightened, why did it stay calm? If it
remained calm, why did it get frightened? Answer: First it
was frightened and toward the end it became calm.*

*And why did the earth become afraid? The answer is pro-
vided by the doctrine of Resh Lakish. For Resh Lakish taught:
What does the verse (Genesis 1:31) mean: "Evening came,
then morning, it was the sixth day?" The definite article is
not necessary. Answer: God had established a covenant with
the works of the Beginning: If Israel accepts the Torah, you
will continue to exist; if not, I will bring you back to chaos.*

*Rav Simai has taught: When the Israelites committed
themselves to doing before hearing, 600,000 angels came
down and attached two crowns to each Israelite, one for the
doing, the other for the hearing. As soon as Israel sinned,*

This reading was given in the context of a colloquium consecrated to "The Temptations of
Judaism," held in December 1964. The proceedings were published in *Tentations et actions de
la conscience juive: Données et débats* (Paris: P.U.F., 1971). Levinas's commentary is on pp.
163–182 and the discussion following it on pp. 182–188.

1,200,000 destroying angels came down and took away the crowns, for it is said (Exodus 33:6): "The children of Israel gave up their ornaments from the time of Mount Horeb."

Rav Hama bar Hanina said: At Horeb they adorned themselves, as was just said (ornaments to be dated from the time of Mount Horeb) and at Horeb they gave them up, according to our verse: "They renounced from the time of Mount Horeb."

Rabbi Johanan said: Moses deserved to keep them all, for it is said just afterward (Exodus 33:7): "Now Moses would take the tent. . . ."

Resh Lakish said: The Holy One, Blessed be He, will give us back the crowns in the future, for it is written (Isaiah 35:10): "Those redeemed by the Eternal One will come back thus and will reenter Zion singing, an eternal joy upon their head. . . ." Eternal joy—the joy from of old.

Rabbi Eleazar has said: When the Israelites committed to doing before hearing, a voice from heaven cried out: Who has revealed to my children this secret the angels make use of, for it is written (Psalm 103:20): "Bless the Lord, Oh, His angels, you mighty ones, who do His word, hearkening to the voice of His word."

Rav Hama bar Hanina has said (Song of Songs 2:3): "Like an apple tree amidst the trees of the forest is my beloved amidst young men." Why is Israel compared to an apple tree? Answer: to teach you that just as on an apple tree fruits precede leaves, Israel committed itself to doing before hearing.

A Sadducee saw Raba buried in study, holding his fingers beneath his foot so tightly that blood spurted from it. He said to him: People in a hurry, for whom the mouth passes before the ears, you always find yourselves in a state of headlong haste. You should have listened in order to know whether you were able to accept, and if you were not able to accept, you should not have accepted. Raba answered him: It is written about us who walk in integrity: "The integrity of the upright guides them"; about those who walk upon tortuous paths, it is written: "The crookedness of the treacherous destroys them" (Proverbs 11:3).

I will be as brief as possible. This afternoon, there will be three presentations instead of the two originally scheduled. I absolutely want you to be able to hear everyone.

My text is drawn from the tractate *Shabbath*, pages 88*a* and 88*b*. My conscience is not at ease. In choosing as the title of my commentary, "The Temptation of Temptation," haven't I given in to the temptation of putting exponents onto words, as though they were numbers? Other scruples beset me. During this morning's session, there was a call to action: It is high time for interpretations to come to an end so that the world can finally undergo some changes! I was going to give up my commentary. But I regained some confidence when I thought of the impossibility of escaping all discourse, even at the moment when the world is in the process of changing. Will it not be necessary to put some questions to the comrades who are changing the world? And how is one to escape the horizons opened up by this questioning speech?

Finally, I am a bit embarrassed that I always comment on the aggadic texts of the Talmud and never venture forth into the Halakhah. But what can I do? The Halakhah demands an intellectual muscle which is not given to everyone. I cannot lay claim to it. My modest effort will consist in seeking for the unity and progression of thought in the text, which, as you can already see, is made up of a series of apparently unconnected observations.

For those who are listening to me for the first time, I want to emphasize that my commentary does not intend to decode a supposedly ciphered language. I do not assume that the masters whose discussion I am spelling out had a tacit understanding regarding the symbolic value of the terms used. I do not possess a key with which to decipher magical formulae. In any case, our text bears no resemblance to them.

Finally, in my commentary, the word "God" will occur rarely. It expresses a notion religiously of utmost clarity but philosophically most obscure. This notion could become clearer for philosophers on the basis of the human ethical situations the Talmudic texts describe. The reverse procedure would no doubt be more edifying and more pious but it would no longer be philosophical at all. Theosophy is the very negation of philosophy. We have no right to start from a pretentious familiarity with the "psychology" of God and with his "behavior" in order to understand these texts, in which we see traces of the difficult paths which lead to the comprehension of the Divine, coming to light only at the crossroads of human journeyings, if one can express it thus. It is these human journeyings which call to or announce the Divine.

The temptation of temptation may well describe the condition of Western man. In the first place it describes his moral attitudes. He is for an open life, eager to try everything, to experience everything, "in a hurry to live. Impatient to feel."[1] In this respect, we Jews all try to be Westerners, just as Gaston Bachelard tried to be a rationalist. Ulysses' life, despite its misfortunes, seems to us marvelous, and that of Don Juan enviable, despite its tragic end. One must be rich and a spendthrift and multiple before being essential and one. With what conviction did Mr. Amar utter the words "to enter history" this morning! Oh, above all, we cannot close ourselves off to any possibility. We cannot let life pass us by! We must enter history with all the traps it sets for the pure, supreme duty without which no feat has any value. There would be no glory in triumphing in innocence, a concept defined purely negatively as a lack, associated with naivete and childhood, marking it as a provisional state. But is it forbidden to seek another antithesis to the temptation of temptation? This commentary will venture forth in that direction.

In *The Republic*, after having drawn the ideal of a just but austere State, Plato is made to change his plan. A just and reasonable City is needed. But it must have everything. New needs must arise and proliferate in it. All temptations must be possible. In the Midrash about Noah, the Talmudists, with irony, add *shedim*—demons, spirits without bodies—to the beings who take refuge in the Ark. These are the tempters of postdiluvian civilizations without which, no doubt, the mankind of the future could not be, despite its regeneration, a true mankind.

Christianity too is tempted by temptation, and in this it is profoundly Western. It proclaims a dramatic life and a struggle with the tempter, but also an affinity with this intimate enemy. After having heard yesterday's talks, I think that the person of Christ still remains remote for us. Jews, or at least the vast majority of Jews, remain particularly indifferent to Jesus. This Jewish unresponsiveness to the person who is the most moving to Christians is undoubtedly a great scandal for them. But, on the other hand, all Western Jews are particularly drawn by the dramatic life, the life of temptations which the Christian life is. Christianity tempts us by the temptations, even if overcome, which fill the days and nights even of its saints. We are often repelled by the "flat calm" which reigns in the Judaism regulated by the Law and by ritual.

Westerners, opposed to a limited and overly well defined existence, want to taste everything themselves, want to travel the universe. But there is no universe without the circles of Hell! In the whole as a totality, evil is added to good. To traverse the whole, to touch the depth of being, is to awaken the ambiguity coiled inside it. But temptation makes nothing irreparable. The evil which completes the whole threatens to destroy everything, but the tempted ego is still outside. It can listen to the song of the sirens without compromising the return to its island. It can brush past evil, know it without succumbing to it, experience it without experiencing it, try it without living it, take risks in security. What is tempting is this purity in the midst of total compromise or this compromise which leaves you pure. Or, if you wish, the temptation of temptation is the temptation of knowledge.

The temptation of temptation is not the attractive pull exerted by this or that pleasure, to which the tempted one risks giving himself over body and soul. What tempts the one tempted by temptation is not pleasure but the ambiguity of a situation in which pleasure is still possible but in respect to which the Ego keeps its liberty, has not yet given up its security, has kept its distance. What is tempting here is the situation in which the ego remains independent but where this independence does not exclude it from what must consume it, either to exalt it or to destroy it. What is tempting is to be simultaneously outside everything and participating in everything.

The temptation of temptation is thus the temptation of knowledge. The repetition once begun no longer comes to a stop. It is infinite. The temptation of temptation is also the temptation of temptation of temptation, etc. The temptation of temptation is philosophy, in contrast to a wisdom which knows everything without experiencing it. Its starting point is an ego which, in the midst of engagement, assures itself a continual disengagement. The ego is perhaps nothing but this. An ego simply and purely engaged is naive. It is a temporary situation, an illusory ideal. But the ego and its separation from its engaged self so that it can return to its noncompromised self may not constitute the ultimate condition of man. Overcoming the temptation of temptation would then mean going within oneself further than one's self. Cannot the pages upon which we are about to comment show us the way?

One can perceive a certain conception of knowledge, occupying a privileged position in Western civilization, behind or, as a background to, the set of values ruling our morality, or at least in agreement with the feelings animating it.

To join evil to good, to venture into the ambiguous corners of being without sinking into evil and to remain beyond good and evil in order to accomplish this, is to know. One must experience everything through one's own self but experience it without having experienced it yet, before engaging oneself in the world. For experiencing itself is already committing oneself, choosing, living, limiting oneself. To know is to experience without experiencing, before living. We want to know before we do. But we want only a knowledge completely tested through our own evidence. We do not want to undertake anything without knowing everything, and nothing can become known to us unless we have gone and seen for ourselves, regardless of the misadventures of the exploration. We want to live dangerously, but in security, in the world of truths. Seen in this manner, the temptation of temptation is, as we have already said, philosophy itself. It is a noble temptation, hardly a temptation anymore, more in the nature of courage, courage within security, the solid basis of our old Europe.

But opinion, recognized as the sole enemy because it takes advantage of credulity and ignorance, legitmates, if one can put it this way, this all-encompassing curiosity, this unlimited and anticipatory indiscretion which constitutes knowledge, seat of the *a priori* and of the fact. It makes us forget the unsavory joy of knowledge, its immodesty, the abdications and incapacities peculiar to it. It makes us forget all that could, in times of great dangers and catastrophes, have reminded us of the Luciferian origins of this nobility and of the temptation to which this indiscretion responds. Certainly knowledge is worth infinitely more than opinion. But perhaps we are not facing an alternative. Perhaps the demand for truth which legitimates this temptation of curiosity can find purer paths. That, at any rate, is the hypothesis which guides this commentary.

Philosophy, in any case, can be defined as the subordination of any act to the knowledge that one may have of that act, knowledge being precisely this merciless demand to bypass nothing, to surmount the congenital narrowness of the pure act, making up in this manner for its dangerous generosity. The priority of knowledge is the temptation of temptation. The act, in its naivete, is made to lose its innocence. Now it will arise only after calculation, after a careful weighing of the pros and cons. It will no longer be either free or generous or dangerous. It will no longer leave the other in its otherness but will always include it in the whole, approaching it, as they say today, in a historical perspective, at the horizon of the All. From this stems the inability to recognize the other person as other person, as outside all calculation, as neighbor, as first come.

It is not just the legitimate need to find a meaning for action and to act consciously which is satisfied in the total lucidity of the knowledge preliminary to the act. There is also a gesture of refusal toward naive spontaneity, the condition—but is it true?—of the generosity of the movement done without calculation. The goal of knowledge is to bring this naivete—understood as the antithesis of generosity[2]—to take everything upon itself, both good and evil, so that it can be shown everything, be tempted and conjure this danger of the unknown in the midst of the danger of temptation. The temptation of temptation is the life of Western man becoming philosophy. Is it philosophy?

Any act not preceded by knowledge is considered in an unfavorable light: it is naive. Only philosophy takes away naivete. Nothing else seems to take philosophy's place here. Can one oppose to it the spontaneity whose innocence it is called upon to remove?

Isn't an act done apart from knowledge, isn't the generosity of pure spontaneity, leaving aside for the moment all cultural influence, in itself dangerous? Besides, isn't naive generosity in its essence a provisional situation which can only preserve from temptations artificially? Can one oppose the naivete of faith to the temptation of temptation when it reveals its philosophical and scientific aspect, as certain as this faith may seem of the divine message to which it adheres? Can childhood answer the Tempter with confidence in the long run? An affirmative answer to this question is sometimes given by Christianity. But spontaneous engagement, in contrast to a theoretical exploration which should, in principle, precede it, is either impossible and dangerous, or provisional.

It may be possible, however, to oppose to knowledge preceding engagement something other than innocent doing, childlike and beautiful
like generosity itself, something other than doing in the sense of pure
praxis. For the latter cuts through Gordian knots instead of untying them
and is contemptuous of the information with which the European
tempted by temptation, simultaneously an adventurer and a man living in
supreme security, wants to surround himself. This European is certain at
least of his retreat as subject into his extraterritorial subjectivity, certain
of his separation with respect to any other, and thus assured of a kind of
irresponsibility toward the All. It may be, however, that the notion of
action, instead of indicating *praxis* as opposed to contemplation, a move
in the dark, leads us to an order in which the opposition of engagement
and disengagement is no longer decisive and which precedes, even conditions, these notions.

The Revelation which is at stake in the following text will permit us to
discover this order prior to the one in which a thought tempted by temptation is to be found.

In the logic of Western thought, Revelation, unless it wants to appear
useless, must comprise elements which no reason could discover. Consequently, these elements must rest on an island of fideism or in a blind confidence in the transmitter of these elements. They must make those who
accept them run the risk of having been duped by the Devil. If, on the other
hand, these elements are accepted because they already recommend themselves to the discernment of the one who accepts them, then they are in the
domain of philosophy. They would already be in its domain even if reason
were to decide only upon the authority of the messenger. For here, too, it is
the·inner certainty of the faithful which would control what Revelation
conveys. The paradox is that Revelation nonetheless claims to overcome the
apparently insurmountable waverings and doubts of Reason.

The text on Revelation on which we are commenting bears precisely on
this relation between the message of truth and the reception of this message. For the recipient of the message cannot yet benefit from the discernment which this message is to bring him. The text, then, will shed light on
whether it is possible to escape the temptation of temptation without either
reverting to childhood or always violently restraining it. Perhaps the text
suggests a way of avoiding both the alternative of an infinitely cautious old
age and of an inevitably rash childhood by establishing the relation between
being and knowing in another way. It may set to work a notion which takes
away the value that the temptation of temptation has acquired for us.

I have cut up the text into small paragraphs. It is, in any case, something
that happens of itself. The difficulty lies more in the building and sewing
back together. That is what we shall try to do. And, according to our cus-

tom, we will comment on the text point by point instead of simply passing quickly over the whole.

> And they stopped at the foot of the mountain . . . Rav Abdimi bar Hama bar Hasa has said: This teaches us that the Holy One, Blessed be He, inclined the mountain over them like a tilted tub and that He said: If you accept the Torah, all is well, if not here will be your grave.

The words of Rav Abdimi bar Hama refer to Exodus 19:17, which is about a rather important event in the life of Israel: the giving of the Torah. "At the foot of the mountain"? The text, in fact, expresses itself differently: "below the mountain," *betashtit hahar.* The commentator is quibbling over a Hebrew expression. Is he sticking to the letter? Does he not know Hebrew? Is he so uncultivated as to lend an absolute meaning to prepositions without taking into account the meaning that derives from context? Or is Rav Abdimi pretending to be doing all this in order to convey a teaching? Israel is placed *below* the mountain, if we translate the text literally. The mountain is thus changed into an upside-down bucket. It threatens to crush the tribes of Israel if they refuse the gift of the Law. What wonderful circumstances in which to exercise one's free will—a sword of Damocles! The Israelites coming out of Egypt are about to receive the Torah. The negative freedom of those set free is about to transform itself into the freedom of the Law, engraved in stone, into a freedom of responsibilities. Is one already responsible when one chooses responsibility? This is the problem suggested by Rav Abdimi. Does he think, then, that the choice for responsibility is made under threat and that the Torah would not have been chosen freely?

The choice of the Jewish way of being, of the difficult freedom of being Jewish, would have been a choice between this way and death. Already *eyn berera!*[3] "the Torah or death," "the truth or death," would not be a dilemma that man gives himself. This dilemma would be imposed by force or by the logic of things. The teaching, which the Torah is, cannot come to the human being as a result of a choice. That which must be received in order to make freedom of choice possible cannot have been chosen, unless after the fact. In the beginning was violence. But we may be dealing here with a consent other than the one given after inspection. Perhaps death threatens a betrayal. Reason would rest either on violence or on a mode of consent that cannot be reduced to the alternative liberty-violence and whose betrayal would be threatened by violence. Wouldn't Revelation be precisely a reminder of this consent prior to freedom and non-freedom? Therefore it would not simply be a source of knowledge parallel to those which come from natural insight. Adherence to it would not coexist *side by side* with the internal adherence which works through evidence. The first, Revelation, would condition the second, Reason. The Torah, received without violence, as it is commonly understood, would be precisely that which precedes freedom of thought. Thus, the Torah would play a role of the first importance in the theory of knowledge itself. The content of the received Torah would be able to be expressed in its inner coherence, just as all the philosophies inspired by it or denying it. But this coherence of a system must not be taken for the *prior* experience of the Torah itself.

Would the choice between truth and death be a reference to education, the process by which the mind receives training under the master's rod in order to rise toward comprehension? That the mind needs training suggests the very mystery of violence's anteriority to freedom, suggests the possibility of an adherence prior to free examination and prior to temptation. This adherence cannot be considered naive, for naivete is an unawareness of reason in a world dominated by reason. It lags behind. It does not condition. Of course I could also ask myself whether "Torah or death" means that outside the Torah Judaism sees nothing but desolation and, that, in this sense, the choice for the Torah was rational and free. But it would once again affirm that no hesitation was possible, that the free choice of the Torah was made without any possibility of temptation.

Let us put aside momentarily the possibility of a prior consent, as distinct from reason as it is from violence; let us put aside the analysis of a notion of consent pointing to a third way, which cannot be identified with unreasonableness. It is equally clear that this way cannot be identified with the philosophical notion of reason. Henceforth, the following objection is understandable.

Rav Aha bar Jacob said: That is a great warning concerning the Torah.

"Great warning" is the commentators' attempt to translate an obscure expression, the meaning of which would be, they claim, to be put on one's guard. We are indeed well warned: If the Torah is accepted under threat of death, we are not accountable in case of transgression. Let us allow ourselves to be tempted then. Everything is allowed! To accept without examining or because of violence, refusing to be tempted in this manner—isn't that giving oneself over to the infinite and irresistible temptations of irresponsibility? If reason is to emerge from a choice made without reason, how is one to keep oneself from making unreasonable choices? Or, to come back to our way of formulating the problem: If temptation defines the philosophical reason of the West, does this definition exhaust the notion of reason? The answer: the refusal of temptation, the trust granted from the start, should not be defined negatively. The order thus founded extends, after the fact, to the act of foundation. Reason, *once it comes into being,* includes its pre-history.

Raba said: they nonetheless accepted it in the time of Ahasuerus, for it is written (Esther 9:27): "The Jews acknowledged and accepted. They acknowledged what they accepted."

Let us first take these lines in their literal sense. If, at the foot of Mt. Sinai, the Torah was imposed through violence, it was "assumed,"[4] as they say today, later, after Jewish history had been lived. A charming story! Esther, but also Haman; dangers and miracles. What a good thing it is to be Jewish! Unless such incidents would inspire one to pull out. From now on, one would rather live without triumphs and without Haman, without miracles and without disasters.

But to justify the Torah by choosing in the course of Jewish history the day after a dangerous adventure, experienced because of unfaithfulness to this Torah (for that is how the unexpected events of the Megillah are to be explained for the Talmud), is perhaps to insinuate that the link between the giving of the Torah and the threat of death has a meaning different from that of a truth imposed through violence. The Torah itself is exposed to danger because being in itself is nothing but violence, and nothing can be more exposed to violence than the Torah, which says *no* to it. The Law essentially dwells in the fragile human conscience, which protects it badly and where it runs every risk. Those who accept this Law also go from one danger to the next. The story of Haman irritated by Mordecai attests to this danger. But the irresistible weight of being can be shaken only by this incautious conscience. Being receives a challenge from the Torah, which jeopardizes its pretention of keeping itself above or beyond good and evil. In challenging the absurd "that's the way it is" claimed by the Power of the powerful, the man of the Torah transforms being into human history. Meaningful movement jolts the Real. If you do not accept the Torah, you will not leave this place of desolation and death, this desert which lays to waste all the splendors of the earth. You will not be able to begin history, to break the block of being stupidly sufficient unto itself, like Haman drinking with King Ahasuerus. You will not be able to exorcise fatality, the coherence of determined events. Only the Torah, a seemingly utopian knowledge, assures man of a place.

The Talmudic text on which I have just commented certainly has not taken the biblical text of the Book of Esther literally. I wish to underscore this permanent dissonance between what the Talmud draws from the biblical text and what is found in that text literally. Similarly, I wish to underscore our attempt to translate Talmudic discourse into modern language. It means that we draw from an allusive and enigmatic mode of speaking, a bearer of multiple meanings, a few schematic representations. I wish to emphasize this so that our friend Rabi, when he reviews this colloquium in the newspapers, does not repeat his objection to the preceding one: "I went back to the indicated biblical texts and nothing of what the Talmud is made to say on their subject is to be found there. . . . " I have insisted more than once that the Talmudic spirit goes radically beyond the letter of Scriptures. Its spirit was nonetheless formed in the very letters it goes beyond, so as to reestablish, despite apparent violences, the permanent meaning within these letters.

The biblical text to which ours refers is about Esther, who institutes a festival involving gifts to the poor, a feast, and readings of the Megillah in order to commemorate the deliverance of Purim. The Israelites "acknowledged and accepted" all this. But the word for "acknowledged," *kymu*, can also mean "they fulfilled it." To receive the gift of the Torah—a Law—is to fulfil it before consciously accepting it. Ten centuries after Mount Sinai, what had been a forced acceptance would be freely accepted. But, here, when we look more closely, we see that this free acceptance amounts to practicing before adhering. Not only does acceptance precede examination but practice precedes adherence. It is as if the alternatives liberty-coercion were not the final ones, as if it were possible to go beyond the notions of coercion and adherence due to coercion by formulating a "practice" prior to voluntary adherence. Consequently, it is as if the adherence given under constraint revealed a beyond-freedom-and-constraint, a commitment leaving no room for what we normally call adherence. In the very last part of our text, would it be this that is called *Temimut?*

Let us summarize the result reached up to this point: Freedom begins in what has all the appearance of a constraint due to threat. The text might be teaching us this pedagogy of liberation. But is it a pedagogy? Is it a method for children? Without being less pure than the freedom that would arise from freedom (in the non-engagement of the one who is tempted and who tries his luck), the freedom taught by the Jewish text starts in a non-freedom which, far from being slavery or childhood, is a beyond-freedom.

This introduces what follows, in which the theme broadens. The following passage in fact shows us that this anteriority of acceptance in relation to freedom does not merely express a human possibility but that the essence of the Real depends on it. In this anteriority lies hidden the ultimate meaning of creation:

Hezekiah said: It is written (Psalm 76:9): "From the heavens thou didst utter judgment: the earth feared and stood still."

The universe in which the power of the Eternal is manifested is scared by his word. The word *veshakta*, which we have translated as "was still," means, of course, the stillness of peace and consequently literally expresses calm. This explains the ensuing question: How could the earth have experienced two contrary feelings simultaneously, that of fear and that of calm?

Did our Talmudists not read Corneille and did they not hear of a "obscure clarté qui tombe des étoiles"?[5] Insensitive to literary effects, they must also be wary of dialectics for Hezekiah to be able to ask the following question:

If it was frightened, why did it stay calm? If it remained calm, why did it get frightened? Answer: First it was frightened and toward the end it became calm.

Hezekiah is not only ignorant of Corneille and wishes to ignore the reconciliation of opposites but also seems certain that Psalm 76 has to do with the gift of the Torah. On this point, let us restrain our irony. Don't great thoughts become clear through great experiences? Don't we moderns say: Here are the circumstances that finally made me understand such and such a saying in Pascal or Montaigne? Aren't the great texts great precisely because of their capacity to interact with the events and experiences that shed light on them and which they guide? In the end, doesn't one have the right to ask, when reading Psalm 76, which concrete situation justifies this lyricism, which, after all, is not a mere rhetorical flourish?

But let us return to our text. We now know how the contradiction of verse 9 and of Psalm 76 resolves itself. But here is a new question:

> And why did the earth become afraid? The answer is provided by the doctrine of Resh Lakish: For Resh Lakish taught: What does the verse (Genesis 1:31) mean: "Evening came, then morning, it was *the* sixth day"? The definite article is not necessary. Answer: God had established a covenant with the works of the Beginning (with the Real called to come forth): If Israel accepts the Torah, you will continue to exist; if not I will bring you back to chaos.

(The sixth day of Creation alludes to a definite day: the sixth day of the month of Sivan, the day of the giving of the Torah.)

The mountain turned upside down like a tub above the Israelites thus threatened the universe. God, therefore, did not create without concerning himself with the meaning of creation. Being has a meaning. The meaning of being, the meaning of creation, is to realize the Torah. The world is here so that the ethical order has the possibility of being fulfilled. The act by which the Israelites accept the Torah is the act which gives meaning to reality. To refuse the Torah is to bring being back to nothingness. One can now see how verse 9 of Psalm 76, which earlier seemed to undergo a forced reading [*qui, tout à l'heure, semblait sollicité*], extends the meaning of the situation we have examined above to the entirety of Being. The unfortunate universe also had to accept its subordination to the ethical order, and Mount Sinai was for it the moment in which its "to be" or "not to be" was being decided. The refusal of the Israelites would have been the signal for the annihilation of the entire universe. How does being realize its being? The question of ontology will thus find its answer in the description of the way Israel receives the Torah. This way consists—such is the thesis we are upholding—in overcoming the temptation of evil by avoiding the temptation of temptation.

We are coming to the third part, which is essential for our presentation. It will bring out the unique nature of an event such as the giving of the

Torah: one accepts the Torah before one knows it. This shocks logic and can pass for blind faith or the naivete of childish trust, yet it is what underlies any inspired act, even artistic, for the act only brings out the form in which it only now recognizes its model, never glimpsed before. But we must ask ourselves whether every inspired action does not derive from the unique and original situation of the giving of the Torah. Doesn't the meaning of inspiration itself emerge from this situation? More precisely, doesn't the reversal of the normal chronology of accepting and knowing indicate a going beyond knowledge—a going beyond the temptation of temptation—but a going beyond different from that which would consist in a return to childish naivete. The latter, in fact, is still on this side of all temptation, does not protect against it, and, essentially provisional, itself asks to be protected. To go beyond the temptation of temptation could not be the deed of an underdeveloped human nature. It is a perfectly adult effort.

> Rav Simai has taught: When the Israelites committed themselves *to doing* before *hearing*, 600,000 angels came down and attached two crowns to each Israelite, one for the *doing*, the other for the *hearing*.

"We will do and we will hear." Rav Simai emphasizes the extraordinary nature of this biblical statement. Six hundred thousand angels came down—the number is not random. Each Israelite had his angel. The gift of the angels will remain of a personal nature, and the angels attach two crowns to each Israelite, one for the "doing" and the other for the "hearing." Jewish tradition has taken pleasure, we know, in this inversion of the normal order, where hearing precedes doing. The tradition has not exhausted all the resources of this error in logic and all the merit which consists in acting before understanding.

Is it certain, though, that the Israelites spoke against all logic and against all reasonable reason? Maybe they expressed their trust. Through trust in him who speaks, we promise to obey and now we will listen to what he tells us. Nothing is less paradoxical, except the very origin of trust prior to all examination. The Talmudic text will nonetheless call the paradox of this inversion an "angel's mystery" several sentences later and consequently seems very conscious of the problem. Martin Buber, in his translation of the Bible, finds an ingenious interpretation. He takes the letter *vav* of the text as a subordinate conjunction, which is a perfectly legitimate usage. "We will do *and* we will understand" becomes "We will do *in order* to understand."

We think we must look further. The question is not to transform action into a mode of understanding but to praise a mode of knowing which reveals the deep structure of subjectivity, with which our text ends, *Temimut*. Thus, the concern to show, in the first place, that the apparently upside-down order is, on the contrary, fundamental. Indeed, the commentators ask themselves why only two crowns rewarded the "we shall do and we shall hear." Wasn't a third crown needed to reward the reversal of the sequence?

But is it certain that the crowns were rewards? Weren't they the very splendor that doing and hearing take on when they follow each other in the inverse order to that of logic? Wouldn't hearing and doing in this reversal cease being a misunderstanding and a partial doing? The angels' crowns consecrated the splendor that these notions take on in the new order. In it, they become sovereign. We will try to explain this paradox. Let us simply emphasize that the inverted order is opposed to the one in which the temptation of temptation functions.

> As soon as Israel sinned, 1,200,000 destroying angels came down and took away the crowns, for it is said (Exodus 33:6): "The children of Israel gave up their ornaments from the time of Mount Horeb."
>
> Rav Hama bar Hanina said: At Horeb they adorned themselves as was just stated (ornaments to be dated from the time of Mount Horeb) and at Horeb they gave them up, according to our verse: "They renounced from the time of Mount Horeb."

Mount Horeb at times indicates the time and place of renouncing and at other times that of the ornaments. But the Talmudist's reading consists above all in connecting the exaltation of Sinai (Horeb) to the fall. They are nearly simultaneous. The Jew is at Horeb to be adorned, and already he is stripped: We are simultaneously armed against all accommodation with the situation of someone who is tempted by evil and already falling. The excellent choice that makes doing go before hearing does not prevent a fall. It arms not against temptation but against the temptation of temptation. Sin in itself does not destroy *Temimut*, the integrity which expresses itself in the "We will do" preceding the "We will hear." The sin here responds to temptation but is not tempted by temptation: it does not question the certainty of good and evil. It remains an unadorned sin, ignorant of the triumph attained by faults liberated from scruples and remorse. Thus a path back is available to the sinner. The adherence to the good of those who said "We will do and we will hear" is not the result of a choice between good and evil. It comes before it. Evil can undermine this unconditional adherence to the good without destroying it. This adherence is incompatible with any position beyond or above the good, whether it be the immoralism of esthetes or politicians or the supra-moralism of the religious, all that moral extraterritoriality opened up by the temptation of temptation. This undoubtedly indicates that the doing which is at stake here is not simply *praxis* as opposed to theory but a way of *actualizing without beginning with the possible*, of knowing without examining, of placing oneself beyond violence without this being the privilege of a free choice. A pact with good would exist, preceding the alternative of good and evil.

Unadorned sin. The Israelites feel sorry after their so rapid, so easy fall. "The children of Israel gave up their ornaments." Certainly, this text refers to sadness, but it also refers to its cause. The Torah is not about to tell us a paltry story about jewels, even if it involves the unusual event of women who no longer adorn themselves. In a sacred text, we could only be dealing with essential jewels, with celestial crowns lost because of those who wanted to become like other people, to examine before accepting, without fearing the temptation of temptation. They could not but feel their original connection with the good, which had made them say: "We will do and we will hear."

Why 600,000 angels to bring the crowns and double that number to take them away? These crowns were beautiful and heavy, each requiring the efforts of an angel. But the generous act of human rising goes halfway to meet the glory which crowns it. It could also be, however, that the fall of living men, no longer equal to the culture they bear, immediately bequeaths this culture, become deadweight, to the philologists, who, with difficulty, raise it to the level of their theories. There you have Judaism, without Jews, handed over to the historians!

But the celestial crowns were not lost for everyone.

> Rabbi Johanan said: Moses deserved to keep them all, for it is said just afterward (Exodus 33:7): "Now Moses would take the tent. . . . "

Whatever the reference to Exodus might be, Moses did keep his two crowns. Our childlike trust in Moses is confirmed and flattered. But isn't there more in this text? Perhaps the text wishes to speak to us of those moments of Jewish history in which Judaism remains nearly without Jews, as did Mr. André Amar and the young student who took part in yesterday's discussion. He asked whether Judaism had become a mere abstraction, so greatly does reality clash with the mythical model in the books. The text may be speaking to us of those times in which Judaism is practiced or studied only by a tiny minority, perhaps by only one man, when it seems to be completely contained in treatises, immobilized between book bindings, and when living Jews have lost all influence as Jews. The text affirms, without, alas, proving it, that even in those conditions, Judaism has not lost all its luster. Moses, even if he loses his kingdom, remains a crowned king. The young student who spoke yesterday, anxious that in order to rediscover his Judaism he always addressed himself to Jews who had themselves lost it, can put his mind at rest. The masters of the Talmud foresaw the situation. They find it serious but not desperate. Judaism has not lost its radiance because, for a time, it happens to live only in a few consciences or to have gone back into the books that transmit it, like Moses' mind withdrawn to his tent. Here Resh Lakish speaks again:

> Resh Lakish said: The Holy One, Blessed be He, will give us back the crowns in the future, for it is written (Isaiah 35:10): "Those redeemed by the Eternal

One will come back thus and will reenter Zion singing, an eternal joy upon their head. . . . " Eternal joy—the joy from of old.

Moses will therefore not remain the only one crowned. Judaism will come out of the books which contain it and come out of the narrow circles which practice it. The messianic promise is not possible unless the original perfection is given back to each person individually, unless each person finds his own crown again. I do not lay further stress on this, as the text seems to say it directly without waiting for the commentator.

Our text now comes back to the paradoxical order of "We shall do and we shall hear." The Talmudists keep on being astonished by it. The two paragraphs which follow forcefully underline the importance of this sequence and also show how concerned the Talmudists were to distinguish the inversion of order from the expression of the simplicity of childlike souls.

> Rabbi Eleazar has said: When the Israelites committed to doing before hearing, a voice from heaven cried out: Who has revealed to my children this secret the angels make use of, for it is written (Psalm 103:20): "Bless the Lord, Oh, His angels, you mighty ones, who do His word, hearkening to the voice of His word."

They do before hearing. It is a secret of angels which is in question here, not the consciousness of children. Israel would thus have been another Prometheus. It would have seized upon the secret of pure, unmixed intelligences. "We will do and we will hear," which seemed to us contrary to logic, is the order of angelic existence.

And here is the second passage emphasizing the same idea. The new order is not simply natural and spontaneous.

> Rav Hama bar Hanina has said (Song of Songs 2:3): "Like an apple tree amidst the trees of the forest is my beloved amidst young men." Why is Israel compared to an apple tree? Answer: to teach you that just as on an apple tree fruits precede leaves, Israel committed itself to doing before hearing.

But where has anyone ever seen apple trees bearing fruit before leaves?

Rav Hama says it is so: such apple trees exist! The Tosafists[6] ask the same question. Nothing proves, they say, that the Hebrew text is speaking of apple trees and apples. It is citron trees that are being discussed here. Citrons stay on the tree for two years and can thus seem to be waiting for leaves. The image is beautiful. Here we are, in a marvelous orchard, where the fruits come before the leaves. Marvel of marvels: a history whose conclusion precedes its development. All is there from the beginning. The fruit which negates the seed is the image *par excellence* of the negativity of history and dialectics. The fruit is there from all eternity. History does not grow but extends. The final order awaits the leaves among which other fruits will appear.[7]

For our question, that of the temptation of temptation, the idea of a fruit preceding leaves (and flowers) is obviously essential. The Torah is received outside any exploratory foray, outside any gradual development. The truth of the Torah is given without any precursor, without first announcing itself in its idea (like Malebranche's God), without announcing itself in its "essay," in its rough draft. It is the ripe fruit which is given and thus taken and not that which can be offered to the childish hand, groping and exploring. The true which offers itself in such a fashion is the good, not allowing the one who receives it time to look around and explore. Its urgency is not a limit imposed on freedom but attests, more than freedom, more than the isolated subject that freedom establishes, to an undeniable responsibility, beyond commitments made, for in them the absolutely separated self can put itself into question, claiming to hold the ultimate secret of subjectivity.

But here is the final section. This priority of doing over hearing, this inversion of the logical sequence—the secret of angels—gives rise to an exchange of ideas between two interlocutors, a Sadducee and a sage of Israel. We have a debate within a debate. Is he the same Sadducee of whom we spoke this morning? The editors of the Talmud sometimes write "Sadducee," sometimes "Min," sometimes even "philosopher." An anti-Jewish Christian? In any case, it is someone who does not recognize the Jewish way of being in the truth, someone who cannot accept the particularism of the Jewish attitude in regard to truth: the Sadducee is a European.

A Sadducee saw Raba buried in study. . . .

Buried in study! How amazing! These people who want to act before hearing are not ignoramuses. One sees them always studying,

holding his fingers beneath his foot and rubbing it so hard that blood spurted from it.

The sight is not edifying enough. One might have expected to see Raba meditating dreamily, while caressing his beard or rubbing his hands. Raba's gesture is odd: he rubs his foot so hard that blood spurts out. That was the degree to which he forgot himself in study!

As if by chance, to rub in such a way that blood spurts out is perhaps the way one must "rub" the text to arrive at the life it conceals. Many of you are undoubtedly thinking, with good reason, that at this very moment, I am in the process of rubbing the text to make it spurt blood—I rise to the challenge! Has anyone ever seen a reading that was something besides this effort carried out on a text? To the degree that it rests on the trust granted the author, it can only consist in this violence done to words to tear from them the secret that time and conventions have covered over with their sedimentations, a process begun as soon as these words appear in the open air of history. One must, by rubbing, remove this layer which corrodes them. I think you would find this way of proceeding natural. Raba, in rubbing his foot, was giving plastic expression to the intellectual work he was involved in. Thus, he was deep in thought when the Sadducee began to insult him:

> People in a hurry for whom the mouth passes before the ears (You speak before hearing, you give your agreement before examining), you are always in a state of headlong haste. You should have listened in order to know whether you were able to accept, and if you were not able to accept, you should not have accepted.

The objection is clear: headlong haste appears as the greatest error in judgment. You go too quickly, you accomplish before hearing, you do not take your distance, you are not lucid. And Raba—to place the relation of man to Revelation outside the order in which "good sense" functions—refers to Scriptures. The Sadducee, or the Min, accepts Scriptures. The verse should be able to convince him.

> It is written about us who walk in integrity: "The integrity of the upright guides them"; about those who walk upon tortuous paths, it is written: "The crookedness of the treacherous destroys them." [Proverbs 11:3]

The quotation cannot be reduced to a simple appeal to authority. Neither is it necessary to take it as a "moralizing" text, promising security to the obedient and threatening the rebel with ruin. Don't integrity and perversity have to do here with the logical structure of the subject? Wouldn't integrity here be a norm of knowledge rather than a norm of conduct? The subjectivity completely made for the true would be the one which would enter into an alliance with it prior to any manifestation of this truth in an idea.

But here is where the logical integrity of subjectivity leads: the direct relation with the true, excluding the prior examination of its terms, its idea—that is, the reception of Revelation—can only be the relation with a person, with another. The Torah is given in the Light of a face. The epiphany of the other person is *ipso facto* my responsibility toward him: seeing the other is already an obligation toward him. A direct optics—without the mediation of any idea—can only be accomplished as ethics. Integral knowledge or Revelation (the receiving of the Torah) is ethical behavior.

Such a knowledge does not need to interrupt its course to ask itself what road to follow, oriented as it is from the beginning. "We will do and we will hear" does not express the purity of a trusting soul but the structure of a subjectivity clinging to the absolute: the knowledge which takes its distance, the knowledge without faith, is *logically* tortuous; examining prior to adherence—excluding adherence, indulging in temptation—is, above all a degeneration of reason, and only as a result of this, the corruption of morality.

The yes of "we will do" cannot be an engagement of a doing for doing's sake, of an I know not what wonderful *praxis*, prior to thought, whose blindness, even if it be that of trust, would lead to catastrophe. Rather, the yes is a lucidity as forewarned as skepticism but engaged as *doing* is engaged. It is an angel's knowledge, of which all subsequent knowledge will be the commentary; it is a lucidity without tentativeness, not preceded by a hypothesis-knowledge, or by an idea, or by a trial-knowledge. But such a knowledge is one in which its messenger is simultaneously the very message.

To hear a voice speaking to you is *ipso facto* to accept obligation toward the one speaking. Intelligibility does not begin in self-certainty, in the coincidence with oneself from which one can give oneself time and a provisional morality, try everything, and let oneself be tempted by everything. Intelligibility is a fidelity to the true; it is incorruptible and prior to any human enterprise; it protects this enterprise like the cloud which, according to the Talmud, covered the Israelites in the desert. Consciousness is the urgency of a destination leading to the other person and not an eternal return to self. But the "we will do" does not exclude the "we will hear." Prior fidelity is not a naivete—everything in it can and must become speech and book calling forth discussions. The innocence of which Mr. Jankélévitch spoke—I admire his gift of being able to fathom texts he thinks closed to him because of language skills—is an innocence without naivete, an uprightness without stupidity, an absolute uprightness which is also absolute self-criticism, read in the eyes of the one who is the goal of my uprightness and whose look calls me into question. It is a movement toward the other which does not come back to its point of origin the way diversion comes back, incapable as it is of transcendence—a movement beyond anxiety and stronger than death.

This uprightness is called *Temimut*, the essence of Jacob. Integrity, taken in its logical meaning and not as a characteristic of a childlike disposition, indicates, if it is thought through to the end, an ethical configuration. But Jacob, the man of integrity, the most upright of men, *Ish Tam*, is also the man aware of evil, crafty and industrious.

Allow me to add a few philosophical considerations, either inspired by this commentary or which inspired the commentary in the first place.

Have we, under the label of integrity, exalted the antiscientific attitude? Have we thus relegated Judaism, among the doctrines of obedience without thinking, to the conservatism of opinion and reaction? Have we been rash in affirming that the first word, the one which makes all the others possible, including the *no* of negativity and the "in-between-the-two" which is "the temptation of temptation," is an unconditional *yes?*

Unconditional, certainly, but not naive. We have underscored sufficiently that a naive *yes* would remain defenseless against the *no* and against the temptations which would arise in its heart to devour the very heart which has brought these temptations into being. In question here is a *yes* older than that of naive spontaneity. We think, like our text, that consciousness and seeking, taken as their own preconditions, are, like naivete, the temptation of temptation, a tortuous path leading to ruin. The *bogdim* are the unfaithful, breaking a fundamental covenant. To them are opposed the *yesharim*, the upright. Uprightness, an original fidelity to an indissoluble alliance, a belonging with, consists in confirming this alliance and not in engaging oneself headfirst for the sake of engaging oneself.

Will it be said that this prior alliance was not freely chosen? But one reasons as though the ego had witnessed the creation of the world and as though the world had emerged out of its free will. This is the presumptuousness of the philosopher. Scripture makes Job a reproach of it.

Is the distinction between free and non-free ultimate? The Torah is an order to which the ego adheres, without having had to enter it, an order beyond being and choice. The ego's exit from being occurs before the ego-which-decides. This exit is not accomplished through a game without consequences played in some corner of being in which the ontological warp is loose. It happens through the weight exerted on one point of being by the rest of its substance. This weight is called responsibility. Responsibility for the creature—a being of which the ego was not the author—which establishes the ego. To be a self is to be responsible beyond what one has oneself done. *Temimut* consists in substituting oneself for others. This does not indicate any servileness, for the distinction between master and slave already presupposes an established ego.

To say that the person begins in freedom, that freedom is the first causality and that the first cause is nobody, is to close one's eyes to that secret of the ego, to that relation with the past which amounts neither to placing oneself at the beginning to accept this past consciously nor to being merely the result of the past. The personal form of being, its ego-ness, is a destruction of the crust of being. All the suffering of the world weighs upon the point where a separation is occurring, a reversal of the essence of being. A point substitutes itself for the whole. More precisely, this suffering, this impossibility of escaping, brings about the very separation. Would one wish to reverse the terms? Would the world put all the weight of its suffering on the ego because the latter would be free to sympathize or not to sympathize? Would only the free being be aware of the weight of the world he has thus taken upon himself?

It will at least be admitted that this freedom does not have any leisure time in which to assume this burden and that, as a result, it is from the start as if compressed or un-done by suffering. This condition (or uncondition) of hostage is an essential modality of freedom—its primary modality—and not an empirical accident of a freedom always remaining above it all. In this impossibility of running away from the imperious cry of the creature, the assumption (of responsibility) in no way goes beyond passivity.

Certainly, my responsibility for everyone can also manifest itself by limiting itself: the ego may be called in the name of this unlimited responsibility to concern itself about itself as well. The fact that every other, my neighbor, is also a "third party" in relation to another neighbor, invites me to justice, to weighing matters, and to thought. And the unlimited responsibility, which justifies this concern for justice and for self and for philosophy can be forgotten. In this forgetfulness egoism is born. But egoism is neither first nor ultimate. The impossibility of escaping from God—which in this at least is not a value among others—is the "mystery of angels," the "We will do and we will hear." It lies in the depths of the ego as ego, which is not only for a being the possibility of death, "the possibility of impossibility," but already the possibility of sacrifice, birth of a meaning in the obtuseness of being, of a subordination of a "being able to die" to a "knowing how to sacrifice oneself."

NOTES

1. Viazemsky, cited by Pushkin as an epigraph to the first Canto of *Eugene Onegin*. [Prince Peter Viazemsky (1792–1878) was a poet and one of Pushkin's best friends. (Trans.)]

2. The French reads *comprise comme antithèse de la generosité*. Throughout this section naivete has been associated with generosity, not its antithesis. It is difficult to interpret Levinas's meaning here. (Trans.)

3. *Eyn berera*: Hebrew expression meaning "no choice." (Trans.)

4. "Assumed" here means to accept consciously one's condition; the term figures prominently in the vocabulary of existentialist philosophy. (Trans.)

5. "An obscure light falling from the stars" (*Le Cid*, act 4, scene 3). (Trans.)

6. See note 3 of Levinas's Introduction. (Trans.)

7. The identification of the fruits which appear in the Bible has become a matter of linguistic habits. Why not take the liberty of translating as "citron" that which the tradition translates as "apple"? By what right, for instance, is the forbidden fruit, the cause of original sin, identified with an apple? The Rabbis of the Talmud maintain that the forbidden fruit, the eating of which led to the knowledge of good and evil, was wheat. They link the fall of mankind to its basic food. At least, we understand that botany is not at issue in all this.

PROMISED LAND OR PERMITTED LAND

■ From the Tractate *Sotah,* pp. 34*b*–35*a* ■

That they may explore the land for us.
—Deuteronomy 1:22

Rav Hiyya bar Abba said: The explorers sought only the shame of the land, for about this it has been said, "That they may explore (veyashperu) the land." And elsewhere it has been said (Isaiah 24:23): "The moon will be ashamed (veshapra) and the sun will be confounded. . . ."

"Here are their names: for the tribe of Reuben, Shammua, son of Zaccur" (Numbers 13:4). Rav Isaac said: We have a tradition according to which the explorers are named after their actions, but we only know how to interpret one name, that of Sethur, son of Michael. Sethur because he has given the lie to (sathar) the words of the Holy One, Blessed be He. Michael, because he has weakened him (mak). Rav Johanan has said: We can explain yet another name: Nahbi, son of Vophsi, because he hid (hihbi) the words of the Holy One. Son of Vophsi, because he jumped over (pasa) the attributes of the Holy One, Blessed be He.

"They went toward the South and he came to Hebron" (Numbers 13:22). The text should have been: and "they came." Raba answered: This teaches us that Caleb, separated himself from the "plot of the explorers," prostrated himself on the graves of the patriarchs and implored: My fathers, ask for mercy so that I may be preserved from the "plot of the explorers." For Joshua, Moses had already granted mercy, for it is written (Numbers 13:16): "And Moses gave the name of Joshua to Hoshea, son of Nun." May Yah (God) preserve you

This reading was given in the context of a colloquium consecrated to Israel, held in November 1965. The proceedings were published in *Israël dans la conscience juive: Données et débats* (Paris: P.U.F., 1971). Levinas's commentary appears on pp. 151–166 and the discussion that follows on pp. 187–193.

from the "plot of the explorers." That is why it is written
(Numbers 14:24): "As to my servant Caleb, since he was animated by a different spirit. . . ."

"There lived Ahiman, Sheshai, and Talmai . . . (Numbers
13:22). Ahiman, because he was the strongest amongst his
brothers (Ah-Yamin); Sheshai, because he covered the earth
with pits; Talmai, because he dug furrows in the earth. (Another explanation: Ahiman built Anath, Sheshai built Alash,
and Talmai built Telbesh.)

Descendants of Anak: they surpassed (maanikim) the sun
in size (or they wore the sun on a necklace around their
neck).

"Hebron was founded seven years before Zoan" (Numbers
13:22). What does "was founded" mean? If "to found" is taken
literally, how is one to accept that a father establish his
younger son before his elder one? But is it not written (Genesis 10:6): "The descendants of Ham: Cush, Mizraim, Put and
Canaan?" "Founded" can then only mean this: Hebron was
seven times more cultivated than Zoan. And yet in all the
land of Israel, there is no place with more rocks than Hebron; that is why the dead are buried there. Among all countries there is none more fertile than Egypt, for it is written
(Genesis 13:10): "Like the garden of the Lord, like the land of
Egypt." And in the whole of Egypt, there is no place more
fertile than Zoan, for it is written (Isaiah 30:4): "For his
princes were at Zoan." And, despite this, Hebron was seven
times more cultivated than Zoan.

Is Hebron full of rocks? Is it not written (2 Samuel 15:7):
"After a period of forty years had gone by, Absalom said to
the King, let me go to Hebron. . . ." And did not Rab Iwya
(and according to others, Rabbah ben Hanan) say: He went to
find sheep in Hebron. And is it not taught: the rams of
Moab, the sheep of Hebron?—That is not an objection: it is
because the soil there is barren that Hebron had pastures and
that livestock grew fat there.

"They returned from exploring the land and went and
came back" (Numbers 13:25–26). Rabbi Johanan said in the
name of R. Simeon bar Yohai: the going is compared to the
return. The return happened with "bad intentions"; the going was already with these "bad intentions."

They told him and said: "We went further" (Numbers
13:27) "but the people is strong" (Numbers 13:28). Rav
Johanan said in the name of Rabbi Meir: Slander which does
not have some basis in truth does not last long.

"Caleb calmed the people about Moses" (Numbers 13:30).
Rabbah said: he seduced with words. When Joshua began to
address them, they cried out: that lopped-off head seeks to
speak! Then Caleb thought: If I admonish them, they will
answer me in the same way and will reduce me to silence.
So he said: Has the son of Amram done nothing but this?
They then thought he was going to attack Moses and became quiet. He then continued: He brought us out of Egypt,
split the sea for us and fed us manna. Shouldn't we listen to
him, even if he were to tell us to build ladders and ascend to
heaven! "We shall go up and gain possession of it" (Numbers
13:30).

"But the men who had gone with him said: 'We will not
be able to . . . ' " (Numbers 13:31).

Rav Hanina bar Papa said: the explorers uttered a great
thing at that moment: "He is stronger than we are" (Numbers 13:31). Do not read "than we are." Read "than Him."
Even the Boss, so to speak, cannot remove his tools from
there.

"It is a land which uses up its inhabitants" (Numbers
13:32). Raba taught: The Holy One, Blessed be He, said: I had
a good intention but they interpreted it for the worst. My intention was good: wherever they went the leading citizens
died so that, in the confusion, they could not be noticed.
Some say: It is Job who died and all the inhabitants were in
mourning. But they interpreted it in a bad sense: it is a land
which uses up its inhabitants.

"And we were in our own sight as grasshoppers, and so
we were in their sight" (Numbers 13:33).

Rav Mershasheya said: The explorers were lying. They
could be grasshoppers in their own eyes; but how could they
know that they were so in the eyes of others! That is not an
objection, the latter—the inhabitants—were eating their fu-
neral meal under the cedars. When the former—the Israelite
spies—saw them, they climbed the trees; they sat in them.
They would then hear the ones below exclaim: we see men
like grasshoppers in the trees.

"Then the whole community broke into loud cries and
the people wept" (Numbers 14:1). Raba said in the name of
Rabbi Johanan: It was the ninth of Av and the Holy One,
Blessed be He, said: They cried without cause; I will change
this day into a permanent day of lamentation.

"And the whole community thought to stone them," and
immediately afterward: "And the Glory of God appeared in

*the Tent of the Meeting" (Numbers 14:10). Rav Hiyya bar
Abba said: This teaches us that they took rocks and threw
them against Him who is above.*

*"Those who spread such calumnies about the earth died
of the plague" (Numbers 14:37). Rav Simeon bar Lakish said:
They died an unnatural death. Rav Hanina bar Papa said:
Rav Shila of Kefar Temarthah taught: This meant that their
tongue was elongated and reached down to their navel and
that worms issued from the navel to the tongue and from
the tongue to the navel. Rav Nahman bar Isaac said: They
died of diphtheria.*

The text I have chosen in the Talmud is about the crisis which occurred
at the end of the first year of the Israelites' journey in the desert and which
explains why this journey lengthened by thirty-nine years, to become a
forty-year journey. It is not by accident that this journey, meant to be very
short, became a long wandering.

Numbers, chapter 13, tells the following story: The Eternal One advises
Moses to send some men to explore the land of Canaan, which was promised to the children of Israel. These explorers are chosen. The Bible tells us
their names; among the twelve are Joshua and Caleb; the explorers, upon
returning, declare that the land promised to Israel is one that Israel will not
be able to enter or to live in. It is fertile, to be sure, but it is also a land that
kills or devours its inhabitants, a land that wears them down; moreover, it
is a land settled and guarded by men too powerful for such as the Israelites.
The community of Israel despairs. The ten explorers (only Caleb and
Joshua had testified in favor of the Promised Land) then die stricken with a
strange disease (strange according to the Midrash).

That is the biblical story, which is not for me to comment on. My task is
to comment on the two pages of commentary that the Babylonian Talmud,
in its tractate *Sotah*, devotes to this narrative. What seems so simple in the
biblical text, the fear which seizes the children of Israel when they are just
about to reach their goal, will become problematic in the Talmudic text we
are reading. In the great fear of the explorers, we may discover anxieties
more familiar to us, which were discussed here this very morning. You will
see—I may be promising you too much and my lack of caution makes me
nervous—that in the course of history, Jewish thought, like Jewish conscience, has known every scruple, every remorse, even when it came to the
most sacred rights of the people troubled by this thought.

I will give my commentary based on the translation you have before
you. It is a translation done in great haste, amidst a thousand other preoc-
cupations. Do not be too demanding as far as its style is concerned: I am

nonetheless rather pleased that the somewhat dry nature of this unadorned text pierces through, even in translation. One would have to—but am I up to the task?—draw some water from this desert text.

I hope that our dear friend Rabi, who has always been sympathetic to my efforts despite the disappointment caused him by the obscurity of my method and its results, will allow me to dispense with methodological considerations, which perhaps will come into focus through the application I will once again make of this hermeneutic.

In the sentences immediately preceding the ones I have translated, we learn—let this not shock those used to the literal meaning of the Bible— that the sending of the explorers had not at all been commanded by God. The text in Numbers says the exact opposite, to be sure. But by combining this text with the one in Deuteronomy, the Talmudic commentators attribute the sending of the explorers to a decision made by men. To explore this Promised Land, which is so near, not to go toward it with all of one's might, but to try first to determine what is going on there, would be—and the Talmud shows its complete sovereign freedom here, its capacity to impart to the narratives and images of the Bible their profound, that is, their real meaning—a human thought. Consequently, the crisis which this story relates is also a human crisis.

Let us now look at the first paragraph of the text:

> "That they may explore the land for us" (Deuteronomy 1:22).
> Rav Hiyya bar Abba said: The explorers sought only the shame of the land, for about this it has been said, "That they may explore (*veyashperu*) the land" (Deuteronomy 1:22). And elsewhere it has been said (Isaiah 24:23): "The moon will be ashamed (*veshapra*) and the sun will be confounded. . . . "

Veyashperu does indeed mean "may they explore," but *veshapra* means "will be ashamed"; and "the moon will be ashamed and the sun will be confounded." The second meaning colors the first; those who will explore the land will cover it with shame. The explorers' intention was thus not honest. Instead of becoming acquainted with the land they were about to enter, the explorers would have decided in advance to put it to shame. What an odd method of exegesis! A forced reading [*sollicitation*] of the text, if ever there was one. But also an attempt to animate the text through correspondences and echoes. It will manifest its arbitrariness more and more as it goes along.

However, when the Talmudist, commenting on a biblical text, refers to another biblical text—even if the reference is arbitrary—one must read carefully the context of the quoted passage. What matters is not the explanation of a word. At issue here is the association of one biblical "landscape" with another, in order to extract, through this pairing, the secret scent of the first. In Isaiah, the prophet foretells of an anguished earth, but one delivered by the triumph of the Eternal One. When the Eternal One triumphs, "the moon is ashamed and the sun is confounded." The commentators of the text of Isaiah do not ignore the fact that this passage is about a cosmic event, but they note that the confounding of the moon and the sun can indicate the confounding of their worshippers. The worshippers of the sun and the moon will be ashamed when the pure truth of God manifests itself. Let us bring all this together: the explorers go toward this land so that this land will be shamed, so that the worshippers of this land—for example, the Zionists of that time—will be shamed. They have decided, in the name of truth, to confound the Zionists.

Please excuse these anachronisms, these excesses of language. We are among ourselves, we are among intellectuals, that is, among people to whom one tells the whole truth. The intellectual has been defined as the one who always misses the mark but who, at least, aims very far. Rabi has said that he is the one who refuses reasons of State, that is, who tells the truth. Here is a third definition: the man with whom one does not use euphemisms, to whom one tells the truth. Let us be fearless then. In the passage on which we are commenting, we are informed of the intention of a few men to put to shame all those who want and hope for the Promised Land. The Promised Land would not be allowed.

There is, then, a worship of the earth and a shame attached to this worship, and I am sorry that Domenach is not here, for he would have seen that there are Jews who, exactly like Christians, want land, but sense some shame in this desire, in this covetousness.

Let us read the second paragraph. There is obviously no text less in need of commentary than a list of names.

> "Here are their names: for the tribe of Reuben, Shammua, son of Zaccur" (Numbers 13:4). Rav Isaac said: We have a tradition according to which the explorers are named after their actions, but we only know how to interpret one name, that of Sethur, son of Michael.

There are, in fact, twelve names in the biblical text: the first is Shammua ben Zaccur, and at the very end there is Sethur ben Michael. We are told, here at any rate, that these names are not without meaning, that these people bore predestined names, or that they were named as a result of their conduct. As if by chance, it is no longer known how these predestined names or surnames should be interpreted—the tradition would have been lost. Only one name is understood: Sethur ben Michael. Do admire the etymologies; they force [sollicitent] the text, they are far-fetched. Sethur comes from the verb form sathar, which means "he has given the lie to": he has given the lie to the acts of the Holy One. "Sethur because he has given the lie to (sathar) the words of the Holy One, Blessed be He. Michael, because he has weakened him (*mak*)." Not only would the name of Sethur be pre-destined but even also that of his father.

The first concern of the explorers would therefore have consisted in giving the lie to the legend about the acts accomplished by the Holy One, by contesting, demystifying, sacred history; all that was done, the coming out of Egypt and the miracles and the promises, all that is not true. Or at least it is possible not to talk about it. Sacred history can be passed over in silence. Sacred history can be perfectly explained by history itself, by political, economic, social history. Jewish history is like any other history. Michael may well mean in good Hebrew "Who is like God." (Do you know of a more beautiful name? A prayer made into a name!) Come on now! Michael comes from the word *mak*, which means "weak." Michael means "weak God." The Holy One is not only a God who has never done anything; He is a God who can do nothing. He will never be able to conquer the Promised Land. He is a soft God. It is insane to follow him!

> Rav Johanan has said: We can explain yet another name: Nahbi, son of Vophsi, because he hid (*hihbi*) the words of the Holy One.

Rav Johanan is thus more learned than Rav Isaac. The piece of information he provides is valuable.

The explorers undermined the legend of sacred history; they said that God would not be able to fulfil his promises; but now, in addition, they are contesting that He has ever promised anything at all. He promised nothing. When one wants to criticize at any cost, one even uses arguments that contradict each other. He has done nothing, He has promised nothing, He is weak.

> Son of Vophsi, because he jumped over (*pasa*) the attributes of the Holy One, Blessed be He.

He jumped over His attributes, and it is again very serious. The essential attribute of God is to reward virtue and to punish vice; they jumped over even His attributes. They were perfect atheists. God can do nothing, He has never done anything, He has promised nothing and does not care at all if virtue is rewarded and vice punished.

This then is the meaning of the revolt of these men: a crisis of atheism, a crisis much more serious than the crisis of the Golden Calf. The Golden Calf, that was still religious: one switched gods. Here, nothing is left, one contests the very attributes of divinity.

What makes this crisis yet more acute (or more interesting) is the dishonesty (or the irony) of those who tell about it. One must be suspicious of their references. When these references are convincing—but are they ever?—they are not interesting. One must notice the way this apparent dishonesty is winking at us. They would have lost the tradition pertaining to the meaning of the other names of the explorers! Read these names. Does one need a tradition to understand the virtues registered in these names? One need only think about the roots of these words and show less imagination than that which drew from Vophsi he-who-jumped-over! Shammua ben Zaccur: he who listens, son of he who remembers; Shaphat ben Hori: he who judges, son of he who is free; Igal ben Joseph: the redeemer, son of Joseph; Palti ben Rafu: he who spares, son of he who was healed. I cannot indulge in this etymological game on all twelve names, but I understand why those who upheld that our explorers were corrupt from birth preferred to forget the tradition! What a lucky amnesia! They found *mak* in Michael but forgot that Michael means "Who is like God." For Gaddiel ben Sodi, they forgot that he is the son of the Mystery. All the noble meanings of the names of the guilty were miraculously lost! Don't we have here an effort to remove the suspicion that this whole hateful conspiracy was a plot of the righteous? Let us not in the least imagine that the denial of God's power, of sacred history, of divine promises and divine justice, occurred in the midst of people who were as pure as the intellectuals of the Left. You see then that with its "dishonesty" the Talmud has singularly deepened the literal meaning of the biblical text.

Now we can understand the third paragraph.

"They went toward the South and he came to Hebron" (Numbers 13:22).

Isn't there a mistake in agreement in this sentence? "They went" and "he came"; the first half of the verse is in the plural and the second half is in the singular—something which purists can obviously not forgive. Who has ever seen an error of syntax in the Bible? Have the Talmudists ever allowed themselves poetic license? In any case, here they cannot let the error go by: the text should have been "and they came," in the plural. If it is "he came" and not "they came," that is because they were numerous when they left but only one went all the way to the end.

Raba answered: This teaches us that Caleb separated himself from the "plot of the explorers," prostrated himself on the graves of the patriarchs and implored (listen to Caleb's prayer): My fathers, ask for mercy so that I may be preserved from the plot of the explorers.

Caleb resisted but there had been temptation, such an irresistible temptation, that upon the graves of the patriarchs no wish seemed to him more urgent than this one: "God, preserve me from my friends. . . . Make it so that I will not be tempted to follow the plan of the explorers."

But a second righteous man figured among the twelve: Joshua. Was he safe from the temptation that Caleb overcame? It was spared him in another way. Moses had taken his precautions (they had therefore been necessary). It is written (Numbers 13:16):

"And Moses gave the name of Joshua to Hoshea, son of Nun."

He placed the letter *yod* before his name, which joined to the *he* of Hoshea, becomes *Yah*, which means God: "May God preserve you from the plot of the explorers."

Here are indicated two ways of escaping temptation (I want to acknowledge those who have allowed me to penetrate into my text more deeply, in the study sessions and classes in which we "turned it every which way," and I want to cite not only my friend Dr. Nerson, for the whole interpretation, but also on this particular point my friend Theo Dreyfus): Caleb's way of resisting the seduction of the explorers (who, perhaps, sin only through an excess of justice) consists in staying within the ancestral tradition, in integrating himself within the rigorously national history of Israel, within its transmitted customs, in entrusting himself to this land in which his ancestors are buried, out of which good came into the world and from which no evil can emerge: Caleb prostrates himself on the grave of Abraham, Isaac, and Jacob at Hebron. Joshua's way is different. Through the first two letters of his name, the idea of God was inserted into his nature. Did he not accede to this honor through the teaching he received by serving Moses? No doubt this teaching received directly from the master was needed to preserve him from the temptation of the explorers. Caleb is preserved by his loyalty to an ancestral tradition, by his loyalty to the past. But here our conjecture is again confirmed: the explorers had what it takes to tempt the righteous.

The next paragraph seems to interrupt the narrative flow. It will tell us for the first time what this promised and explored land is like; it will let us know what the inhabitants of this land are like:

"There lived Ahiman, Sheshai, and Talmai . . . " (Numbers 13:22).

And the text continues:

Descendants of Anak. . . .

Using these proper names as a pretext, the Talmud will take complete license to inform us about the state of this land before the coming of the Israelites. These etymologies can certainly not convince anyone, but they only serve as pretexts.

First, Ahiman. It is broken down into two words: *Ah,* "brother," and *Yamin,* "straight" or "strong." A brother stronger than the two others. No equality between the three brothers; there was organization and hierarchy, which is the condition natural for society; but force counted in this hierarchy.

Next is Sheshai. Here matters are even less clear. The etymological reasoning follows obscure paths but the conclusion is clear. Sheshai, when walking, covered the earth with pits. Wherever he set his foot, a hole was dug. He undoubtedly did not have the sensitivity to inquire whether he was crushing someone or something while he was walking. He was a force of nature *[une force qui va].* The third one was called Talmai. Here the etymology is easier. Talmai evokes furrows. The third dug furrows wherever he went: constructor, builder, farmer.

Another explanation—but some commentators feel that it completes the first one, and that is why the text which conveys it is put in parentheses:

Ahiman built Anath, Sheshai built Alash and Talmai built Telbesh.

These three cities do not appear on any map. As for the dictionaries, they refer us to our very text. Let us draw the main point from it. The inhabitants of Canaan—farmers as spontaneous as the forces of nature and yet capable of organization—are also builders of cities. To build, to dwell, to be—a Heideggerian order.

This then was what awaited the children of Israel there. We have not yet commented upon the words "descendants of Anak." *Anak*—"giants." These three men were giants. They were enormous, "they surpassed the sun in size." Other commentary: "They wore the sun like a medallion attached to a necklace." They were magnificent beings, very big, blond, I suppose, since they eclipsed or equaled the sun. I think of Sergei Essenin's poem: "I carry the sun in my arms, like a bundle of oats."[1] Magnificent children of the Earth, who live side by side with visible celestial realities—that whole pagan communion of the earth and the sky—that is what the indigenous inhabitants of the country which was to become the land of Israel suggested to "twelve lowly Jews." We can now understand the anxiety of our men better.

Here then is the first and most banal hypothesis (first because in Talmudic texts multiple meanings coexist; it is a way of thinking in which the example is not the mere particularization of a concept but in which the example holds together a multiplicity of meanings): the strength of the inhabitants of Canaan frightened these puny Jews, just out of the Egyptian ghettos. How to oppose them in the name of a God who, heaven knows, never shows Himself, who does not speak, who did indeed speak on Mount Sinai, but about whom it was never known if He spoke at great length, if He said all that is attributed to Him, if He did not limit Himself to the first sentence, to the first word or even to the first letter of the Decalogue, which, as if by chance, is the unpronounceable *aleph!* Of what worth are all the attributes and promises attributed to so enigmatic a God? Of what worth are all the abstractions and subtleties of Revelation before the splendid appearance of the children of the Earth who wear the sun as a medallion?

One can also suppose, and later this will become clearer, that the explorers, confronted by the inhabitants of Palestine, had misgivings—about what Vigée said yesterday and what many others have said when they speak of Israeli children. Perhaps the explorers caught a glimpse of *sabras.* Fear seized them; they said to themselves: this is what awaits us there; these are the future children of Israel, those people who make holes wherever they set foot, who dig furrows, build cities, and wear the sun around their necks. But that is the end of the Jewish people!

One must not share these fears, but only understand them. Let us not forget the end of the story the Torah tells us: the explorers were severely punished for their doubts and—perhaps, as we shall see—for their scruples. Everything we are saying here and our entire endeavor to guess the interior crisis of these explorers should not make us forget the end of the story and the condemnation it teaches.

But the fear of the explorers can be interpreted yet another way. We will try to extract this third possibility, already suggested, from the rest of the text. Let us formulate it now: perhaps the explorers had moral qualms. They may have asked themselves whether they had the right to conquer what had been so magnificently built by others. How to dissipate so understandable an anxiety? But let us first take a look at the text:

"Hebron was founded seven years before Zoan" (Numbers 13:22).

The verses on which we are about to comment seem at first glance rather insignificant. They no doubt mention evocative names and places. These have for a Jew, a reader of the Bible, a poetic power similar to that contained in words such as "daughter of Minos and Pasiphae" for a reader of Racine. Caleb went as far as Hebron. There Ahiman, Sheshai, and Talmai dwelled, and Hebron was founded seven years before Zoan. But now let us take part in the playful discussion of the Talmudists. Let us, for the moment, wed ourselves to the apparently futile problems which seem to preoccupy them. They ask themselves: "What does 'was founded' mean?" Don't they know the word "to found"? Certainly. But if the word "to found" were to be taken in its literal sense, then it would have to be admitted that a father established his younger son before his older one. But it is written (Genesis 10:6): "The descendants of Ham: Cush, Mizraim, Put and Canaan." Canaan was therefore younger than Mizraim, Egypt. How is one to

accept that Ham established his younger son Canaan in his city seven years
before building Zoan, the Egyptian city, for Mizraim, his older son? Ah,
Ham, the venerable patriarch—what irony in this text!—imagine Ham having become a patriarch and establishing his children. The conflicts he had
had with his father in his youth are forgotten. Now he is a venerable old
man, just and respectful of the birthrights of his children. Not to acknowledge this right without which no tradition is possible, to steal this right
from one's brother, is good only for a Jew like Jacob. Ham, on the other
hand, rigorously respects the right of the elder son. He first founded cities
for Mizraim, who is the elder, and only afterward for Canaan, the younger.
How can it be then that a city intended for the elder is more recent by seven
years than the city of the younger? What, in fact, is being discussed? Is the
priority of the land in which Israel settles chronological? From the Canaanite perspective, this land can certainly not compete with the ancient civilizations. The Talmudists know very well that the priority of Palestine does not
come to it from its pre-Israelite past. Hebron was not really founded seven
years before Zoan, seven years before Egypt, but it received culture according to a different order. In the land of Israel, founding must have a new
meaning:

> Hebron was seven times more cultivated than Zoan. And yet in all the land of
> Israel, there is no place with more rocks than Hebron; that is why the dead are
> buried there. Among all countries there is none more fertile than Egypt, for it is
> written (Genesis 13:10): "Like the garden of the Lord, like the land of Egypt."
> And in the whole land of Egypt, there is no place more fertile than Zoan, for it
> is written (Isaiah 30:4): "For his princes were at Zoan." And, despite this, He-
> bron was seven times more cultivated than Zoan.

Its superiority is not of the same order as that of the great Eastern civilizations. Hebron was not founded before Zoan but it was seven times more
cultivated. Consequently, the poorest, the rockiest, the most wretched area
of Israel's land, reserved for graves (and, as if by chance, Abraham, Isaac,
and Jacob are buried there), is the most cultivated, the richest in spiritual
potentials, richer than the land which had greater real antiquity and greater
visible splendor. We have here a first answer to the question which troubles
the explorers. When I give answers instead of deepening the questions, I
take away from my text, but, after all, one also has to remember that here,
in Europe, we like results. The first answer to the explorers' question, or,
more precisely, to the third interpretation we have given to this question, is
the following: The children of Israel will go into an already inhabited country; but in this country, the tombs of the ancestors Abraham, Isaac, and
Jacob are to be found. Despite the rocks, despite the vast quantity of sand,
this country holds more possibilities than Zoan, which is located in the
midst of Egypt, in the midst of civilization; it calls upon those who are

capable of realizing these potentials. Aren't some rights conferred through moral superiority? It must certainly be explained in what this superiority consists. But one can also doubt that moral superiority, of whatever kind, permits an expropriation. I think that Mr. Domenach doubts it. And I can calm him: the Talmudists who relate the entire story on which I am commenting also doubt it: the invocation of rights due to the moral superiority of Israel is improper.

In the first place, is this superiority evident? Does Hebron evoke only the moral grandeur of Israel? Is Abraham the only memory we have of Hebron? Is sacred history a history of holiness only? That is the awful question concealed in the banal discussion which follows, an awful question quite foreign to the notorious complacency associated with the conscience of the Pharisees. In our text, someone asks: Is Hebron really so poor? Isn't it written (2 Samuel 15:7): "After a period of forty years had gone by, Absalom said to the king, let me go to Hebron. . . . "? When Absalom plots against King David, he goes to Hebron to unite everyone against his father. "He went to Hebron." Why did he go to Hebron? He said to his father: "I will go to Hebron to offer sacrifices there." Did he need to go to Hebron for that? No. Then what did he go in search of there? He went to find sheep for his sacrifice. There were sheep then in Hebron? Hebron was therefore a rich country. And is it not taught elsewhere: the "rams of Moab, the sheep of Hebron"? Thus, the rams come from Moab and the sheep from Hebron. There is no contradiction! In rocky regions and not very fertile soils, pastures abound. Consequently, the text alluded to confirms that Hebron is the poorest city of Israel but more valuable than Zoan; because the soil there is barren, Hebron has pastures and livestock.

We have just summarized a discussion which does not change the situation one bit: Hebron was indeed the poorest region. Why this discussion then? Because it destroys the argumentation of a moment ago. Earlier we had said: We, the Israelites, have a right to this land because we have the Bible. The objection consists in reminding us of the very teaching of this Bible and of the deeds it relates. People of the Book? Nothing but sons who honor their fathers? Children who obey all the moral principles? What about Absalom? The example is wonderfully well chosen. Bad lots are not lacking in the Bible; but isn't Absalom in a certain sense the counterpart of Ham, the founder of the land of Canaan? Remember what Ham did. He made fun of his father's nakedness. And Absalom? Here a euphemism is in order, even in the presence of intellectuals: he cohabited with all his father's concubines on the roof of the royal palace. So much for the superiority of Judaism! Which obviously gives it the right to conquer a country! One can understand the explorers; one can understand the revolt of the pure. They asked themselves, dear Rabi: By what right are we going into this land? What moral advantage do we have over the inhabitants settled in this country? You see that the Talmud has thought of everything and that—much as we may be sure, Mr. Neher, of our right attested to by the Bible—we will not be able to exercise our sovereignty, as President Goldman deplored yesterday, over the whole of the Diaspora, where all the books have been read.

Let us now go back to the text. It shows us that the plot of the explorers did not come about solely as the result of the exploration itself and that it was, like all questions of conscience, an *a priori* problem.

"They returned from exploring the land and went and came back" (Numbers 13:25–26).

The Hebrew text is redundant.

Rabbi Johanan said in the name of R. Simeon bar Yochai: the going is compared to the return. The return happened with "bad intentions"; the going was already with these "bad intentions."

Bad intentions which were good intentions: those of an overly pure conscience. It begins to doubt God because God's command asks us either what is above our strength or what is beneath our conscience. The Promised Land is not permitted land.

They told him and said: "We went further" (Numbers 13:27) "but the people is strong" (Numbers 13:28). Rav Johanan said in the name of Rabbi Meir: Slander which does not have some basis in truth does not last long.

We are being given a lesson in rhetoric, a lesson the Devil has learned well: to lie efficiently, start by telling the truth in order to give credibility to your lie. But it may be that Rav Johanan finds some truth in the words of the explorers regarding the moral problem they raise, independent of the details of the report. Our passage in its entirety can have no other meaning than to suggest that this is a blameworthy moral sensitivity and a morally twisted one. But the plot could never have corrupted so many consciences if none of the reasons governing the actions of the explorers and none of the arguments they put forward were justifiable.

Then "Caleb calmed the people about Moses" (Numbers 13:20). This is badly translated, for the word *el* in Hebrew indicates a direction, toward something or someone, and Caleb calmed the people *toward* Moses; his speech was directed first toward Moses, and that is how he got the people's attention; he won them over. He began to speak as if he too were an enemy of Moses. By starting to speak against Moses, he won the trust of the rebels. Another lesson in rhetoric. Indispensable in the struggle against the beguilements of the Devil: one must use the Devil's own tools. Here, there is an important detail: What about Joshua? Did he keep a prudent silence all the time? "When Joshua began to address them, they cried out: 'that lopped-off head seeks to speak?' " This is what had happened: The first protest against the report of the explorers and the call to carry out the great and noble deeds for which Israel was made came from Joshua. But he was reduced to silence by the crowd and insulted. An impaired man! A man without children, say the commentators. A man alone. A man who has nothing to lose in the enterprise he is urging forward. A pure cleric who has no earthly attachments and is by this very fact incapable of sacrifice. His renunciation proves nothing. In an enterprise one must be able to risk values acquired or established with difficulty—a patrimony, a family, a work, an institution. One should not be like the person who can say *omnia mea,* etc. Joshua would be a Zionist for others, a Zionist who cannot (or does not want to) engage his children—in either case, a bad Zionist. He has only the right to keep silent. That is why Caleb thought that a ruse was needed in order to make the impertinent people who managed to reduce Joshua to silence listen. That is why he pretends to attack Moses:

> Has the son of Amram done nothing but this? They then thought he was going to attack Moses and became quiet.

Did he not call him the son of Amram? Has he done nothing but this?

> He brought us out of Egypt, split the sea for us and fed us manna. Should we not listen to him, even if he were to tell us to build ladders and ascend to heaven?

Where does the idea of a ladder and of heaven, which are missing in the biblical text, come from? Doesn't the text say: "We shall go up and gain possession of it" (Numbers 13:20)? It is this "We shall go up" which the Midrash uses as a pretext to introduce the idea of a "ladder to ascend to heaven."

I apologize for completely neglecting rhetoric in constructing this commentary: I am yielding the secret to you without waiting until the end. What meaning do Caleb's words have? Is he simply following the cult of personality, defending Moses' policies, come what may? Or is he aware of the disproportion that exists between messianic politics and all other politics? Is our history an ordinary history then? Moses brought us out of Egypt; our history begins with an act of liberation. He split the sea for us; he conquered the forces of nature. He fed us manna. Miraculous food: the real miracle is not that the manna falls from heaven but that it corresponds exactly to our needs. To be nourished on manna: not to need to stock up; messianic times. One need no longer think about tomorrow, and in this sense too we are at the end of time. If Moses brought us out of Egypt, split the sea, and fed us manna, do you think, then, that under his leadership we are going to conquer a country the way one conquers a colony? Do you think that our act of conquest can be an imperialistic act? Do you think that we will appropriate a plot of land for ourselves so that we can use and abuse it? We are going—and here the text is extraordinarily explicit—we are going toward this land in order to experience celestial life.

"We are going into this land to ascend to heaven." We will not possess the land as it is usually possessed; we will found a just community in this land. I am telling you this in a very flat way, but that is what it means to sacralize the earth. I very much liked Professor Baruk's comment yesterday: "To sacralize the earth is to found a just community on it."

You will say that everyone can imagine that he is founding a just society and that he is sacralizing the earth, and will that encourage conquerors and colonialists? But here one must answer: to accept the Torah is to accept the norms of a universal justice. The first teaching of Judaism is the following: a moral teaching exists and certain things are more just than others. A society in which man is not exploited, a society in which men are equal, a society such as the first founders of kibbutzes wanted it—because they too built ladders to ascend to heaven despite the repugnance most of them felt for heaven—is the very contestation of moral relativism. What we call the Torah provides norms for human justice. And it is in the name of this universal justice and not in the name of some national justice or other that the Israelites lay claim to the land of Israel.

> "But the men who had gone with him said: 'We will not be able to . . .'" (Numbers 13:31).
> Rav Hanina bar Papa said: the explorers uttered a great thing at that moment: "He is stronger than we are" (Numbers 13:31). Do not read "than we are." Read "than Him."

In Hebrew, the word *mimenu,* meaning "than we are," is punctuated and vocalized the same way as *mimenu,* meaning "than him." (In Aramaic, there apparently is a difference between the two vocalizations.) The explorers would have said: the inhabitant of this land is stronger than He. Stronger than God. And the Talmud adds:

Even the Boss, so to speak, cannot remove his tools from there.

A totally mysterious statement. And all this would be a "great thing"!

One can see rather well the meaning of the first reflection: the native inhabitant of Canaan is stronger than God. At least two interpretations are possible: against the strength of this indigenous population, nothing moral can hold its own. He is moral reality; they are historical reality. According to this first lesson, the great thing expressed by the explorers would be human despair before the failure of ideas, which are always crushed by history, the universal vanquished by the local.

But this text can be read differently, and the explorers will reveal themselves to be yet purer than we imagine: he is stronger than He. The right of the native population to live is stronger than the moral right of the universal God. Even the Boss cannot retrieve the tools entrusted to them; as long as the tools correspond to their needs, there would be no right on earth that could deprive them of them; one cannot take away from them the land on which they live, even if they are immoral, violent, and unworthy and even if this land were meant for a better destiny.

Earlier we put into question the morality of Israel, which was capable of producing an Absalom. Here the thought is more radical: even an absolutely moral people would have no right to conquest.

This is how far the second interpretation goes: it always accompanies the first and will accompany it to the end. This is how far the purity of the explorers, the purity of their atheism, would go: even the Boss cannot remove his tools from this land.

"It is a land which uses up its inhabitants" (Numbers 13:32). Raba taught: The Holy One, Blessed be He, said: I had a good intention but they interpreted it for the worst. My intention was good: wherever they went the leading citizens died so that, in the confusion, they could not be noticed. Some say: It is Job who died and all the inhabitants were in mourning. But they interpreted it in a bad sense: it is a land which uses up its inhabitants.

The Talmud takes, or pretends to take, the expression "this land uses up its inhabitants" for a lived experience. It is a land where one gets used up easily. Heart attacks are frequent there. People work too hard and die early. The proof? There were only funerals around us during the exploration! The explorers want to frighten. In the desert, obviously, one lives much better! The bad faith of these people is beyond doubt. Oh, sublime plan of the Eternal One, which they misjudged! The God of Justice would have caused some people from there to die (especially renowned ones, which is not very serious for the population) so that rich funerals would take the attention of the inhabitants away from our ever so ungrateful explorers! And yet again we understand these people, oh beautiful incorruptible consciences. What, then, does the Talmud want?

Does it want to attribute such great Machiavellianism to the Eternal One or to say that the great designs of history must sometimes occur without the knowledge of individuals? Does evil not need to be put to sleep at times? Must freedom be granted to those who want to kill freedom? The explorers, in the purity of their egalitarian conscience, denounced as antidemocratic the wisdom which excluded from freedom the murderers of freedom, which reduced thoughts too oriented toward politics to their private concerns. Let us remind our listeners that in all this we are not dealing with a problem of history. Were the Canaanites actually so mean? This is the hypothesis or the initial given within which we must place ourselves. Without it, everything we have just said is perfectly meaningless!

> "And we were in our own sight as grasshoppers, and so we were in their sight" (Numbers 13:33).
> Rav Mershasheya said: The explorers were lying.

Here, we catch them in the very act of lying.

> They could be grasshoppers in their own eyes; but how could they know that they were so in the eyes of others?

That is, indeed, not possible; but there is a semblance of an answer, and it is very odd that the Talmudic text, which wants to attack the explorers, this time takes their defense.

> That is not an objection, the latter—the inhabitants—were eating their funeral meal under the cedars. When the former—the Israelite spies—saw them, they climbed the trees; they sat in them. They would then hear the ones below exclaim: we see men like grasshoppers in the trees.

And that is how they knew they had been taken for grasshoppers by the Canaanites. It is a situation as strange as it is natural. Didn't someone say recently: "We are one hundred million strong to crush you." When Israel arms itself against its neighbors, pacifists ask: How do you know that your neighbors do not want to make peace with you? Did they say so? Yes, they did say so; they told us we were like grasshoppers. It is a remarkably contemporary passage. That way of taking human faces for grasshoppers! Or that way of taking the historical act of Return for a movement of grasshoppers. Oh, the forewarned intelligence of realists! Always, at the beginning, there is a dance of grasshoppers. On this point, the explorers tell the truth. They knew that the inhabitants took them for grasshoppers.

> "Then the whole community broke into loud cries and the people wept" (Numbers 14:1). Raba said in the name of Rabbi Johanan: It was the ninth of Av and the Holy One, Blessed be He, said: They cried without cause; I will change this day into a permanent day of lamentation.

These were then useless scruples. They cried for no reason. The tears of beautiful souls are dangerous when they are without cause. They provoke real misfortunes which resemble the imaginary ones. Moreover, those who are about to conquer a country the way heaven is conquered, those who ascend, are already beyond such delicate tears. They not only commit themselves to justice but also apply it rigorously to themselves. Already, they are potentially exiled. The date of their exile is fixed before that of their conquest. They do not know that their crisis is the source of their right, for there is no right that cannot be revoked. They assume a responsibility without indulgence and are summoned to pay for their own injustice with their exile. Only those who are always ready to accept the consequences of their actions and to accept exile when they are no longer worthy of a homeland have the right to enter this homeland.—You see, this country is extraordinary. It is like heaven. It is a country which vomits up its inhabitants when they are not just. There is no other country like it; the resolution to accept a country under such conditions confers a right to that country.

And here is the last word.

"Those who spread such calumnies about the earth died of the plague" (Numbers 14:37). Rav Simeon bar Lakish said: They died an unnatural death.

Just as their protests were unnatural.

Rav Hanina bar Papa said: Rav Shila of Kefar Temarthah taught: This meant that their tongue was elongated and reached down to their navel and that worms issued from the navel to the tongue and from the tongue to the navel. Rav Nahman bar Isaac said: They died of diphtheria.

One death is less harsh than the other. Which one? That is not important. What matters is the idea of two punishments. The fault itself is thus open to two interpretations. This was our assumption throughout the whole of our commentary. Did the crime of the explorers consist of being too pure and of having thought that they did not even have rights to this land? Or did these people back off from a project which seemed to them utopian, unrealizable? Did they think their right lacked might or that they had no rights, that the Promised Land was not permitted to them?

In both cases, the explorers were wrong, but the two hypotheses formulated about the punishment which befell them indicate the difference between the two possible reasons for their guilt.

NOTE

1. Sergei Esenin (1895–1925), one of the great Russian poets of the twentieth century. This quotation is from his poem "Oktoif" (1917). (Trans.)

"AS OLD AS THE WORLD?"

■ From the Tractate *Sanhedrin*, pp. 36b–37a ■

Mishna   *The Sanhedrin formed a semi-circle so that its members could see each other.*

Two clerks of the court stood before the judges, one to the right and one to the left, and they recorded the arguments of those who would acquit and those who would condemn.

Rabbi Judah said: There were three court clerks, one recording the arguments for acquittal, the second the arguments for conviction, and a third both the ones for acquittal and the ones for conviction. Three rows of students of the Law were seated before the judges. Each knew his place; if it became necessary to invest someone, the one appointed was from the first row; in such a case, a student from the second row moved up to the first and a student from the third row to the second. The most competent person in the assembled public was chosen and was placed in the third row. And the last to come did not sit in the place of the first (in the row, who had gone up to the other row) but in the place which was suitable for him.

Gemara   *From which text does this come? Rav Aha bar Hanina said: We learn from verse 3, chapter 7 (of the Song of Songs): "Your navel is like a round goblet full of fragrant wine; your belly like a heap of wheat hedged about with roses."*

"Your navel": that is the Sanhedrin. Why the navel? For the Sanhedrin is in session at the navel of the universe.

"A goblet" (in Hebrew, aggan) because it protects (in Hebrew, meggin) the entire universe.

"Round" (in Hebrew, sahar, crescent of the moon), for it resembles the crescent of the moon.

"Full of drink" (in the text: not lacking in liquid): for if

This reading was given in the context of the colloquium "Is Judaism Necessary to the World?" held in October 1966. The proceedings were published in *Tentations et actions de la conscience juive: Données et débats* (Paris: P.U.F., 1971). Levinas's commentary appears on pp. 275–291 and the discussion that follows on pp. 305–321.

one of its members has to absent himself, it is ensured that twenty-three remain (in session), corresponding to the small Sanhedrin. Otherwise, he cannot leave.

"Your belly is like a heap of wheat": everyone profits from wheat; everyone finds to his taste the reasons adduced for the verdicts of the Sanhedrin.

"Hedged with roses": even if the separation is only a hedge of roses, they will make no breach in it.

About this, a "Min" said to Rav Kahana: You claim that during her time of impurity a woman forbidden to her husband nevertheless has the right to be alone with him. Do you think there can be fire in flax without its burning? Rav Kahana answered: The Torah has testified for us through a hedge of roses; for even if the separation is only a hedge of roses, they will make no breach in it.

Resh Lakish said: It can be answered on the basis of the following text (Song of Songs 4:3) "Your brow (rakkathek) is like a pomegranate." Even those established as good-for-nothings among you are full of mitzvot, as a pomegranate is full of seeds.

Rav Zera said: That is to be deduced from the following text: "Ah, the smell of my son's clothes is like the smell of a field watered by the Lord" (Genesis 27:27). One should not read begadav (his clothes) but bogedav (his rebels.)

About this it is told: some good-for-nothings lived in the neighborhood of Rav Zera. He brought them close to himself so that they could do Teshuvah (the return to the good). This irritated the sages. When Rav Zera died, the good-for-nothings said: Until now, the little-man-with-the-burned-thighs prayed for us. Who is going to pray for us now? They thought about it and did Teshuvah.

"Three rows of students . . . " Abaye said: It follows from this that when one moved, they all moved. And when one said: up until now I was in first place and now I am in last place, he was answered, according to Abaye: Be last among lions and do not be first among foxes.

You have before you the text to be commented on. As in all previous years—and this is not merely a formal excuse—I feel inadequate to the task entrusted to me. The public, responding to these commentaries so favorably as to intimidate me, has in its midst many people who know the Talmud infinitely better than I do. I feel heartened, in any event, by the presence of my dear friend Dr. Henri Nerson, to whom I am greatly indebted, even for the little that I might say. Because he has studied with an incomparable master, he knows that, in comparison to real science, our approximations can only court the rewards bestowed on good intentions.

I will comment on the text I have chosen from the beginning to the end and not only on the least difficult passages, which can give rise to moments of brilliance. I will try, with my feeble means but with all my might, to look everywhere. The difficulty does not lie in the absence of treasures but in the inadequacy of the tools at my disposal for the dig.

At first reading, the articulations of the passage selected seem rather clear. It does not resemble a document written in code or even a text hiding its implications. It deals with the organization of the supreme court, the Sanhedrin. In what way is it connected to the theme of our colloquium, on the need that the world may have of Judaism? I will try to show this. I need not have given it any thought: a Talmudic text, even when it does not try to prove it, always proves that Judaism and the Jews are necessary to the world.

The Sanhedrin is described to us. I take the Sanhedrin to be what it is claimed to be in the text, leaving out of consideration the historical side completely. It may never have existed as it is described here. The word *sanhedrin* is Greek. The institution may be the product of diverse influences external to Judaism. But the text is to be taken as it is given: it is through it that for at least eighteen centuries, Jewish tradition has thought about the supreme institution of justice.

Our Mishna, the oldest part of our text—what follows it is more recent and is supposed to provide the commentary on it—teaches us that the Sanhedrin formed a semi-circle "so that its members could see each other." Thus it was shaped like an amphitheatre. The special feature about it was that no one ever saw anybody else's back, only full faces or profiles. Never was the interpersonal relationship suspended in this assembly. People saw each other face-to-face. The "dialogue," as they say today, was thus never interrupted, nor did it get lost in an impersonal dialectic. It was an assembly of faces and not a joint stock company.

It is, however, a semi-, or open, circle. Because the point is precisely that the judges who sit on the court remain open to the outside world when they discuss the cases submitted to their jurisdiction or when they give their verdict. In the open space of the semi-circle, according to the commentators, appeared the litigants and the witnesses. There too stood the clerks of the court. Open circle: the judges who are at the heart of Judaism, who are its "navel" and who are even—as you will soon see—at the navel of the world, are open to the world or live in an open world. It is not yet a closed synagogue. It is open. It is in any case not a synagogue but a court.

Here, then, is a first answer to the questions raised by the theme of our colloquium, a first answer coming from a somewhat unexpected angle: I still do not know if the world needs the Jew. But the Jew needs the world; that is certain.

> Two clerks of the court stood before the judges, one to the right and one to the left, and they recorded the arguments of those who would acquit and those who would condemn.

Another version exists on this point: the court clerks were not two but three, "one recording the arguments for acquittal, the second the arguments for conviction, and a third both the ones for acquittal and the ones for conviction."

In the first version, there are two recordings for every argument. The recording of arguments is thus not a mechanical process. It is not a tape-recorder but people who record. The era has something to do with it, no doubt, but the symbol goes beyond this: two people record each argument because two witnesses are needed for a fact to be established. The recording is thus testimony. Every truth must be attested. The truth of a fact refers to the veracity of the people who testify to it. That is why, in the hypothesis of two court clerks, both must note down all the arguments. But in the hypothesis of the second version, in which the court clerks are three, they can become specialized: one records the arguments for, the other the arguments against, but the third records both so that each notation is attested to twice. The type of specialization introduced in the second version respects the principle which consists in likening notation to testimony.

Now for something novel, never seen in a court of law: in front of the judges sit "students of the Law," those who study the Torah but are not yet invested as judges. The court is indeed not a synagogue; it is a little bit of a school. Study of the Law and jurisdiction, theory and practice, rigor and mercy—in Judaism, all the polarizations of the spirit belong to the duality of the house of study and the court.

Some technical information now: There are two kinds of Sanhedrin. The full Sanhedrin, which has supreme jurisdiction, comprises seventy-one judges, but in Jerusalem, where our text places us, there are two other Sanhedrins of twenty-three judges each. Only a court of at least twenty-three members can judge in cases involving the death penalty. An ordinary court of three people is not competent in that situation. What was said earlier of the disposition of the judges in a semi-circle applies to every Sanhedrin. What follows now concerns the Sanhedrin of twenty-three judges. In particular, we are told that in the Sanhedrin of twenty-three people there are more than twenty-three people: three rows of students are seated before the judges.

> Three rows of students of the Law were seated before the judges. Each knew his place.

Each knew his place: it is an order excluding contingency. One did not sit just anywhere; the classification was rigorous. There were twenty-three students in each row. Why this number? Three times twenty-three makes sixty-nine. For this is what could happen.

Imagine that the court of twenty-three judges is discussing a case on which the life of a man depends. Twelve vote for the death of the accused, and eleven vote to spare his life. Jewish law does not permit a death sentence on the basis of a majority of only one vote. The judges in a semi-circle are seated on the benches each in his place; the "students of the Law" are seated on the floor before them, each according to his rank. Two among them are asked to come up—the first ones in the first row, to increase the court by two judges. Before the twenty-five judges, the case is argued again. And this time too the majority carries by only one vote: thirteen against twelve. Again, two students are made judges: the first ones in the first row. This can go on until there are seventy-one judges, the number of the great Sanhedrin. Thus, it is necessary to keep a large reserve present at court, allowing it to reach seventy-one members, if need be, the number which cannot be surpassed. What happens if the vote of the seventy-one is split, with the majority again winning by only one vote? The judges will reopen the discussion to try to win the needed vote, for one sentence or the other. If those who are in favor of the supreme sanction are not thirty-seven, the accused is released. Among Jews, one does not condemn to death by a majority of only one vote.

> Three rows of students of the Law were seated before the judges. Each knew his place; if it became necessary to invest someone, the one appointed was from the first row; in such a case, a student from the second row moved up to the first, and a student from the third row to the second.

Because the three rows always had to be full, in order to fill the empty places created at the very end of the last row,

> The most competent person in the assembled public was chosen. . . . And the last to come did not sit in the place of the first but in the place which was suitable for him.

Everyone thus moved up one notch. The one from the public who acceded to the rank of student took the last place. The hierarchical order remained intact. The text confirms it again: each went to the place which was suitable for him. A rigorous hierarchy in itself, objectively; but it was also respected and known by all, a subjectively recognized hierarchy: "Each knew his place." An absolute order.

I have just finished commenting on the Mishna. What does the Gemara say?

It will introduce new perspectives into the description of the order which governs the Sanhedrin.

It all begins with a question. It is a commonly asked question. In fact, when a *Tanaite*, a master of the Mishna, states a Mishna, the *Amoraim*, the masters of the Gemara, can either accept the teaching because it comes from an indisputable authority (it is, in any case, always disputed but remains indisputable) or they can seek the scriptural source from which the teacher drew his teaching. What is the basis, then, for the structure of the Sanhedrin which was just taught to us?

Here, our friend Rabi—my friend, for he always (legitimately) verifies what I say—here, Rabi will ask himself, once again, whether it is possible to draw from the biblical text what the Rabbis of the Talmud strive to draw from it. And his usual skepticism in this area will apparently have an easy victory today. To the questions "From where do we get this?" "From where do we know it?" "From which verse does this derive?" a strange answer will be given. The foundation for the institution of the Sanhedrin that we have just described and commented on in accordance with the Mishna will be sought in such a way as to attest to a seemingly narrow, dishonest, or bizarre mind. An allusion which would justify the institution will be found in a piece of ancient Hebrew literature by seemingly clinging to the letter of the text. In this particular case, this is especially inopportune: Doesn't the Sanhedrin, as its name indicates, in all likelihood refer to foreign traditions, notably to Greek civilization? What a thorough ignorance of history is attested to when a Hebrew origin is sought for a cultural form borrowed from Greece!

But perhaps we can attribute less naive views to the Talmudists: Whatever the historical causality and the antecedents of ideas and institutions might be—they always conceal their origin—what matters is the discovery of the convergence of the spiritual efforts of mankind or, and this is even more likely but does not contradict the first interpretation, what matters is to know *in what spirit something is borrowed.* Given this, in seeking a foundation for borrowing in the letter of a past which is not its own, the borrower links what he is borrowing to a tradition and formulates, beyond the similarities of structure, the meaning he is giving to what he is borrowing. Whatever the channel of history through which the Sanhedrin was established in Israel, whatever the forms of its historical existence in pre-exilic society, it is interesting to know what meaning Jewish thought and sensibility attributed to it. For it is around this institution that, for twenty centuries, the notion of justice and of truth have been reflected upon and experienced.

But even if one accepts our interpretation of the maneuver which consists in going back to a Hebrew text so as to understand the basis for an institution suspected of Hellenic origin, the nature of the text chosen for this purpose will still astonish us. The Sanhedrin, with its magnificent semi-circle, making human faces show themselves to each other, with a perfect hierarchy, attesting to an objective and subjective absolute order, will find its basis in an erotic poem, in a verse of the Song of Songs.

Of course, the Song of Songs permits of a mystical interpretation, but for those who are forewarned—or, without prior assumptions, for the mysticism of the Song of Songs is not a mystification—it is an erotic text. The verse to which the Gemara refers can leave no doubt on the subject. As I understand it, this is the essential point of my entire Talmudic reading today. Let us enjoy this paradox! One may grant, in exceptional cases, that an erotic text can deepen to the point of reaching a mystical meaning. We are in the presence of a stranger enterprise: an erotic text founding a court of law and a system of justice:

> Rav Aha bar Hanina said: we learn (what was said about the Sanhedrin) from verse 3, chapter 7 (of the Song of Songs): "Your navel is like a round goblet full of fragrant wine; your belly like a heap of wheat hedged about with roses."

Chapter 7:3 of the Song of Songs would then be proclaiming the Sanhedrin. How? It is certainly not a matter of establishing a direct connection between justice and love. That would be a bit facile and a bit insipid: justice would be founded on love and love on the erotic. I leave this path to others! Should I prematurely reveal my conclusions? But this is what will guide my reading. Perhaps justice is founded on the mastery of passion. The justice through which the world subsists is founded on the most equivocal order, but on the domination exerted at every moment over this order, or this disorder. This order, equivocal *par excellence*, is precisely the order of the erotic, the realm of the sexual. Justice would be possible only if it triumphs over this equivocalness, all grace and all charm and always very close to vice. The danger preying upon justice is not the temptation of injustice, flattering the instinct of possession, domination, and aggression. The danger which lurks is vice, which, in our Western world, belongs to the private sphere, which is "no one's business" and does not compromise the generosity and valor of those who struggle "for progress and justice," if we are to trust the opinion of the intellectual elites.

The teaching which the reference to the Song of Songs suggests to me has certainly had illustrious defenders since then. Think of Tolstoi's *Resurrection*, in which it is highly important to know what the judges and the members of the jury have done and thought in the private sphere to be able to decide according to their conscience in court. Like our text, Tolstoi wanted there to be a harmony between the order of love—susceptible to every vice—and the order of absolute spirit. And it is really the order of absolute and universal spirit—but where people show their faces to each other—and the absolute hierarchy within this order that the Sanhedrin represents.

How then can we justify putting the Sanhedrin and the erotic verse from the Song of Songs side-by-side? How is an erotic verse to take on an austere meaning, even if the austerity "preserves" the danger it is overcoming? Here the special way of the Talmud comes in. We must enter into its game, which is concerned with the spirit beyond the letter, yet it extricates this spirit on the basis of the letter, and is, for this very reason, wonderful.

"Your navel is like a round goblet," says the text. It would be obvious that the navel refers to the Sanhedrin, for the Sanhedrin is in session at the navel of the universe. This is a way of indicating the centrality of the absolute justice that the Sanhedrin, by definition, metes out, the justice of the Torah. It is a way of indicating the ontological nature of these acts of justice. By speaking of justice in erotic terms, the eroticism of the terms has been overcome, all the while preserving in the meaning of the terms a fundamental link to the realm that has been overcome.

For a very long time, I have mused about this text. When one is not a specialist in the Talmud, one can have musings where others have ideas. I said to myself: How beautiful is this image of the navel of the universe! The creature has been cut off from its source of nourishment but the place where justice is pronounced is in the trace of creation; the coming about of justice recalls this heavenly food. I was pleased with this musing. I sometimes still ask myself whether it was only a musing. A friend brought me back to ordinary reality and to generally held notions. He reminded me that the image of the navel of the world is Greek and that, in Aeschylus' *The Eumenides*, Delphi is called the navel of the world.

That made me reread *The Eumenides*. I was very moved by it, even saddened: in this work which one reads in one's youth, a witness to a world that did not know the Scriptures, I found a greatness which proved to me that everything must have been thought from time immemorial. After reading *The Eumenides* one can legitimately ask oneself if there is anything else left to read. A struggle opposes Zeus' justice to the justice of the Eumenides, the justice with forgiveness to the justice of unrelenting vengeance. Zeus is already the "god of the suppliants and the persecuted," and his eyes see all! Without a doubt, I am getting closer to the question we are debating.

Is Judaism necessary to the world? Isn't Aeschylus enough? All the essential problems are broached there. The Eumenides are not expelled; vengeance-justice is not simply dismissed once and for all. The Eumenides express themselves in wonderful tones when they get indignant about those young gods, generous and "open," forgetful of strict justice, who already resemble all those jovial fellows of our day who have nothing but charity and prescription on their lips—love, indulgence, forgiveness. In her great wisdom, Athena keeps the Eumenides and finds a function for them in her city. Only the vote of men determines whether it will be the ancient gods or the new gods, but the result is established through each voice having equal weight. No one can simply reject once and for all the goddesses of vengeance, and only men—mortal and potential victims of evil—are qualified to express their views here. And Delphi is called the navel of the world, for it is there that pure and just gods dwell, who know how to interpret the will of Zeus, of a god who, in this tragedy, is an extremely decent god.

Our Jewish contribution to the world is therefore in this world as old as the world itself. "As old as the world," the title I gave this little commentary is thus an exclamation, a cry of despondency. There would be nothing new in our wisdom! The text of *The Eumenides* is at least five centuries older than the Mishna with which my text opens. *The Eumenides* is nonetheless three centuries later than the prophets of the Bible. And that was my first consolation.

But aside from the question of priority, an essential question remains. Is there nothing besides the lofty lesson of Hellenistic humanism in what is called—improperly perhaps—the message of monotheism? The Sanhedrin believes itself to be at the navel of the world, but every nation believes it is at the center of the world! The very idea of nation arises each time that a human group thinks it dwells at the navel of the world. It is precisely because of this that it wants sovereignty and claims every responsibility. Where, then, is the difference between Delphi and Jerusalem? Let us be on our guard against facile and rhetorical antitheses: we are justice, they are charity; we love God, they love the world. From authentic spiritualities, no spiritual adventure is withheld. And Hellenism is probably a somewhat authentic spirituality. It is in the nuances of the formulations, in the inflections of the speaking voice, as strange as this may appear, that the abysses which separate the two messages open. I did not come here, after all, to interpret Aeschylus. But, in returning to our text, and in examining it a bit more carefully—and with a bit less mistrust—we may perhaps have occasion to discover in the Sanhedrin an aspect slightly different from the one which emerges when one reflects upon the other navels of the world.

What does the text say?

"Your navel," that is the Sanhedrin. Then, "a goblet." The Hebrew word used for goblet by the Song of Songs is *aggan*. The Talmudist will read into *[va solliciter]* this word. He will read *meggin* in *aggan*. *Meggin* means "protects." This therefore confirms that the navel indicates the Sanhedrin. Is it not true that the Sanhedrin protects the entire universe? A questionable etymology, perhaps, but a certainty as to the gist of the matter, the universal meaning of the court: it protects the universe. The universe subsists only because of the justice made in the Sanhedrin. The role of Judaism, of which the Sanhedrin is the center, is a universal role, a deaconry in the service of the totality of being.

A "round goblet." The Hebrew word *sahar* means "crescent of the moon." The Sanhedrin resembles the crescent of the moon, an allusion, if you wish, to the semi-circular shape of the court. It is thus through the word "round" that the arrangement of the seats of the members of the Sanhedrin finds confirmation. That is what had to be demonstrated.

The rest of the verse follows: "full of drink." The Hebrew text states: *al yehassar hamezeg*, "not lacking in liquid." This is another allusion to the Sanhedrin, for the Talmud says: "If one of the members has to absent himself, it is ensured that twenty-three remain (in session), corresponding to the small Sanhedrin. Otherwise he cannot leave." The drink that fills the round goblet expresses the inner regulation of the Assembly. This is what it prescribes in the great Sanhedrin of seventy-one members: It must be ensured that twenty-three are always present. Thus the members can absent themselves in order to attend to their private business, but "drink must never be lacking"; no one can dispose of his person until public service is guaranteed. This is the regulation of civil servants. The obligations to the service of all do not result from individual obligations and rights but are prior to them. We have here healthy principles, to be sure, that civil servants can sometimes forget. But the precociousness of this teaching aside, it does not seem to be exclusive to Israel.

Let us go back to the text. Always with the concern to prove that the Sanhedrin is the fulfilment of a biblical verse, the end of it is commented on: "Your belly is like a heap of wheat":

> Everyone profits from wheat; everyone finds to his taste the reasons adduced for the verdicts of the Sanhedrin.

One can certainly legitimately doubt—according to Western principles of exegesis—that the analogy between the body of the beloved and the Sanhedrin is perfect or convincing. That is not the issue. How characteristic of the Jewish spirit—even the popular one—is this comparison of the logical reasons for a conclusion to the taste of a hearty meal! When you find a new reading of the text for one of those habitués of the old books—and the life of a Talmudist is nothing but the permanent renewal of the letter through the intelligence—he will tell you that it tastes good. Reason eats ideas. The rational premises motivating a verdict are good wheat. The intellect is a life.

The last phrase of the verse remains: "hedged with roses." What could be more poetic than this "hedged with roses"? The Talmudic text interprets in prose:

> Even if the separation is only a hedge of roses, they will make no breach in it.

This does not make it any clearer. What are the commentators saying? They are saying the following: these members of the Sanhedrin who hold the fate of the universe in their hands, what do they do with their own transgressions, their own vices? Are they not exposed to all temptations, just like the men they are called upon to judge? No. To be a judge in Israel, one must be an exceptional man: even if only a hedge of roses separates judges from sin, they will make no breach in it. They master their instincts completely. That the man judging over men has to be better than men is a requirement for which no half-measure can be substituted—even if the requirement is utopian: perhaps a civilization which does not delight in temptations, which does not like the temptation of temptation, sometimes succeeds in conquering temptation itself. We will come back soon to the strategy accounting for this victory. In any case, one must take it or leave it: the Sanhedrin, navel of the universe, is possible only with such a human breed. Otherwise, justice is a mockery.

A hedge of roses is a very thin enclosure. To separate the judges from vice, one need not build a stone wall; it is sufficient to plant a hedge of roses. The enclosure of roses is tempting in itself: the hand spontaneously goes toward the flower. In what separates us from evil resides an equivocal seduction. This enclosure is less than an absence of enclosure. When there is nothing between you and evil, it is possible not to bridge the distance, but when there are roses—all the literature of evil, the flowers of evil—how is one to resist it? But that is how the members of the Sanhedrin are separated from evil. Must I insist on it? This last trait explains the entire meaning of the text I have commented on until now. There is no justice if the judges do not have virtue in the flatly moral sense of the term. There cannot be a separation between the private life and the public life of the judge. It is in the most intimate area of his private life, in the secret garden—or hell—of his soul that his universal life either blossoms or fades. Soul and mind do not constitute two separate realms.

At this point—and one expected it—an objection is raised:

About this, a "Min" said to Rav Kahana . . .

and you will certainly admire this Min, who was probably already a Parisian and whose objection has some punch and whose formulations are already well-coined.

You claim that during her time of impurity

(Excuse me for the preciseness but the Talmud says all things with purity.)

a woman forbidden to her husband nevertheless has the right to be alone with him. Do you think there can be fire in flax without its burning?

Let me explain this objection. The Book of Leviticus at a certain point enumerates the kin with whom sexual relations are forbidden, as they are considered incestuous. According to rabbinic law, it is even forbidden for men and women to be alone with the people who are prohibited to them—even if their motives are altogether honorable. But the woman forbidden to her husband during her times of impurity can continue to live alone with him. She is not made to move out. Thus the Min's objection.

Who is this Min? I said, because of the roguishness of his expression, that he was Parisian. The term—it is technical—designates the Sadducee, that is, the Israelite who keeps only to the letter of the texts and refuses rabbinic exegesis. One understands the sting of his objection, directed against the rabbinic reading of Leviticus. But the name Min can indicate, in a general way, anyone who, while accepting the Bible, refuses rabbinic exegesis, aside from the Sadducean refusal: the Christian refusal, shaking off the yoke of the Law and the quibbling of the Pharisees. Wouldn't our Min represent the Christian position? He would have said to Rav Kahana: "Strange people! The woman forbidden by the Law to her husband you allow to remain alone with him. You have not properly weighed the ardors of concupiscence. In the matter of sinning, there exists only the alternative between the monk's asceticism of complete isolation and a life in which everything is allowed."

What does Rav Kahana answer?

The Torah has testified for us through a hedge of roses; for even if the separation is only a hedge of roses, they will make no breach in it.

The text testifies for us. It is your own text—you Sadducees or you Christians—which evokes the hedge of roses. A hedge, which is the thinnest of thin obstacles, which, as I said earlier, in *separating* you from sin, invites you to cross through it: the Torah has identified for us a relation with evil symbolized by a hedge of roses. Or, if you wish a less theological language, Judaism conceives the humanity of man as capable of a culture which preserves him from evil by separating him from it by a simple barrier of roses.

But what is new in the lines I am commenting on now, in relation to what preceded them, is considerable. What was said before of the judge is now said of the entire Jewish people. Rav Kahana is no longer speaking of the court. He is speaking of the Jewish people: the excellence demanded earlier of the members of the Sanhedrin is extended to the Jewish people in its entirety. Mr. Arnold Mandel was saying this morning: There is no notion of the masses in the idea the Jewish people has of itself. All belong—or must belong—to the elite. Our Talmudic passage agrees with Mr. Mandel. But Judaism does not affirm any national or racial pride by this: it teaches what, in its opinion, is possible for man. And, it is through this teaching, perhaps, that the world needs Judaism. That, after all, is more interesting than the monotheistic theology that the world has, in many respects, assimilated! We will see that our text goes yet further. There is still half a page to comment on. Matters will deepen.

But before proceeding let us emphasize one more important thing: morality begins in us and not in institutions which are not always able to protect it. It demands that human honor know how to exist without a flag.

The Jew is perhaps the one who—because of the inhuman history he has undergone—understands the suprahuman demand of morality, the necessity of finding within oneself the source of one's moral certainties. He knows that only a hedge of roses separates him from his own fall. He always suspects thorns beneath those roses: One had to find within oneself the certainty that this barrier was a real obstacle.

This, then, manifestly, is what Rav Kahana's answer means: "This hedge of roses testifies for us." In the Jew, a new man is heralded. He brings to the Min's so-called realism, so-called lucidity, something that the Min does not understand. Nothing utopian, please believe me. In the Jewish communities of the villages Hitler exterminated in eastern Europe, some men and women were so radically separated from evil that a hedge of roses was enough to guarantee their purity or, if you prefer, could do nothing against it.

Does the text contain a hint of an apology? Why not? I wonder whether there has ever been a discourse in the world that was not apologetic, whether the *logos* in itself is not apology, whether our first awareness of our existence is an awareness of rights, whether it is not from the beginning an awareness of responsibilities, whether, rather than comfortably entering into the world as if into our home, without excusing ourselves, we are not, from the beginning, accused. I think it is a little like that that one tries to be Jewish, that it is like that that one merits being called a human being.

Our text conveys yet another important idea: what matters for the human being is to realize, not to invent, the ideal. Take the text of *The Eumenides.* If I have read it wrongly, let the humanists in this room correct me. It is about saving man from despair. It is less concerned about improving him. In our text, the main point is to realize a human being that a simple hedge of roses protects against temptation. Let us note, in coming back to the idea of the hedge of roses, the meaning conferred on it by the commentator Maharsha,[1] to whom I have already referred. The enclosure is in itself seduction. Hence one can understand its way of protecting as the following: everything in the world that is charming, tempting, seductive, invites us to be vigilant. Let us be twice as careful. No indulgence. Be prepared. Rigorism.

This morning it was deplored that we have lost contact with the natural world. But the entire Jewish tradition has wanted to put a time for reflection between natural spontaneity and nature. Ah, that Jewish intellectualism! The fence of roses is the trifling partition of ritual—which stops us.

The text can be read in yet another way. Many readings are possible as long as they are not in poor taste. What stops us is not at all the unbearable yoke of the Law, which frightened St. Paul, but a hedge of roses. The obligation to follow the commandments—the *mitzvot*—is not a curse for us. It brings us the first scents of paradise. I would like to allude again to André Spire[2] and his poem about the Jew who is bored in "the places of pleasure." The yoke of the Law is merely an enclosure of roses. Spire found this simply through the testimony of his conscience, without the texts. But where does this conscience come from? As a result of texts formulated and realized for generations, such a conscience arises and, for a while, endures beyond its origins. But this brings me to the following paragraph:

> Resh Lakish said [Rav Kahana had answered the question of the Min earlier. Resh Lakish has another answer:] It can be answered on the basis of the following text: . . .

And once again it is a reference to the Song of Songs (4:3), and once again it is a verse from an erotic poem:

> "Your brow [*rakkathek*] is like a pomegranate.

I cannot evaluate the poetic worth of this metaphor. But here is its exegetical worth, thanks to a word play on *rakkathek* (your brow) and *rekanin* (good-for-nothings).

> Even those established as good-for-nothings among you are full of *mitzvot* (of fulfilled commandments) as a pomegranate is full of seeds.

Resh Lakish gives you an answer to the question which arose in your minds as you listened to the praise of those men who are protected from temptation by a hedge of roses. How do such men become reality? By means of *mitzvot*. The originality of Judaism consists in confining itself to the manner of being, of which Léon Askenazi will speak much better than I: in the least practical endeavor, a pause between us and nature through the fulfilment of a *mitzvah*, a commandment. The total interiorization of the Law is nothing but its abolition.

Resh Lakish's expression has no other meaning. Unless one wants to believe in some racial excellence or other of Judaism or in a merit granted by pure grace, one must say with Resh Lakish and with the Jewish tradition: for there to be justice, there must be judges resisting temptation. There must be a community which carries out the *mitzvot* right here and now. The delayed effect of *mitzvot* carried out in the past cannot last forever.

That the mere fact of race is not a guarantee against evil, the Talmud saw and said better than anyone and with nearly unbearable force: the Jew without *mitzvot* is a threat to the world. In the tractate *Betsa*, p. 25b, we are taught that the Torah was given to the toughest people there is and that, if it had not been given to it—or if the Jewish people were to lose it—no people on earth could resist it. An antisemitic outlook in the Talmud, that has some spice to it! The Jew as invader, against defenseless peoples. The only obstacle to this ascent without defeat: the Torah. This text is, no doubt, admirably lucid as to the inescapable ambiguity of the human condition in general and may echo a passage in Cicero (*Tusculanes* IV:37) in which Socrates, whose face seemed to Zopyrus to testify to every vice, admitted—despite the astonishment of all—having come into the world with every vice reflected in his face but having freed himself from them through reason. But it is also a text without illusions as to the quality of Jewish chromosomes. "The Jew among men like a dog among beasts," not like a lion! "Like a rooster among winged creatures," not like an eagle! If one compares him to trees, he is like the tree which knows how to cling to the rocks! What vitality! What proliferation! That is why the Torah was given to him. A Torah of fire, the only one capable of tiring this encroaching vitality. And when the Talmudic passage I am interpreting today has the nerve to affirm that "the worst good-for-nothings among them are nevertheless as full of mitzvot as the pomegranate is full of seeds," that is because the power of these mitzvot is presupposed—their power to penetrate the soul. Also presupposed is the history that has made Israel submit to them, and, above all, the force of will which at Mount Sinai could decide for the mitzvot—which are stronger than all the forces of evil and vulgarity that Jews and the rest of mankind undoubtedly have in common as long as one keeps to the "purely natural" plane. The Talmud, after all, does not think that the Jews are more dog or rooster than others, even if it is spontaneously led, like Socrates, to judge its own nature severely (the Jew is less self-assured than one imagines). The privilege of Israel resides not in its race but in the mitzvot which educate it. The effect of the mitzvot lasts beyond their practice, that is true. But, as I have already said, not indefinitely.

What Judaism brings to the world, therefore, is not the easy generosity of the heart, or new and immense metaphysical visions, but a mode of existence guided by the practice of the mitzvot. That, at any rate, is the answer of Resh Lakish.

But there is a third answer to the question asked by the Min, which—as you can see—three sages of the Talmud answer in different time periods. Each one seeks a text attesting to the excellence of Israel which would explain its ability to resist temptations.

Rav Zera said: That is to be deduced from the following text:

And here we have the first Rabbi who abandons the Song of Songs in order to bring us back to the famous text of Genesis in which Jacob, wearing his brother's clothes, comes to seize through ruse the blessing destined for Esau. The blind Isaac smells the smell of his son Esau's clothes, which Jacob is wearing, and exclaims:

"Ah, the smell of my son's clothes is like the smell of a field watered by the Lord." (Genesis 27:27).

And the commentators add: It is not the smell of Esau's clothes which brought the scent of Paradise but Jacob's coming into the room. As for the clothes, all one needs to do is read the word *begadav*, "his clothes," as *bogedav*, "his rebels." Jacob bore within himself all those who, in future generations, would rebel against the Law—but this was nonetheless incense to Isaac's nostrils. It seems we are going back to the idea of a little while ago: The least worthy among the Israelites are full of merit, as the pomegranate is replete with seeds.

I think, however, that the theme of the disguised is crucial here, and that Rav Zera's answer opens up a new perspective on the excellence of Israel for us, on the human excellence able to preserve from sin, from vice, from temptation. Doesn't Jacob, in putting on the violent Esau's clothes, take on his brother's responsibilities? How to preserve oneself from evil? By each taking upon himself the responsibility of the others. Men are not only and in their ultimate essence "for self" but "for others," and this "for others" must be probed deeply. I will say a couple of words about that for the several philosophers present in this room, that is, for everyone. Nothing is more foreign to me than the other; nothing is more intimate to me than myself. Israel would teach that the greatest intimacy of me to myself consists in being at every moment responsible for the others, the hostage of others. *I can be responsible for that which I did not do and take upon myself a distress which is not mine.*

The Talmudist says it through word play: his clothes, *begedav*, his rebels, *bogedav.* Isaac had a premonition of all the rebels that would come out of Jacob. But Jacob already bore the weight of all that rebellion. The scent of Paradise is Jacob bearing the weight of all that he will not do and that others will do. For the human world to be possible—justice, the Sanhedrin—at each moment there must be someone who can be responsible for the others. Responsible! The famous finite liberty of the philosophers is responsibility for that which I have not done. Condition of the creature. Responsibility that Job, searching in his own impeccable past, could not find. "Where were you when I created the World?" the Holy One asks him. You are a self, certainly. Beginning, freedom, certainly. But even if you are free, you are not the absolute beginning. You come after many things and many people. You are not just free; you are also bound to others beyond your freedom. You are responsible for all. Your liberty is also fraternity.

Responsibility for the sins you did not commit, responsibility for the others. The story about Rav Zera that our text will now dwell on—and which looks like an edifying tale but is wonderful in our context—confirms the reading we have just given of Rav Zera's answer:

> About this, it is told: some good-for-nothings lived in the neighborhood of Rav Zera.

They were his neighbors.

He brought them close to himself so that they could do *Teshuvah*. This irritated the sages.

They undoubtedly felt that the dignity of a scholar of the Torah forbade such associations, as they risked compromising the dignity of the Torah in the public eye. Or perhaps they thought that Rav Zera's enterprise was hopeless. But Rav Zera continued to associate with these good-for-nothings. He undoubtedly felt responsible for these people, must have considered it his duty to act upon the indeclinable and separate liberties of others. And, undoubtedly, an indeclinable liberty yields, in mysterious ways, to an indeclinable liberty, which wants absolutely and unto death to substitute itself for the other—for his sin and his distress:

When Rav Zera died, the good-for-nothings said: Until now, the little-man-with-the-burned-thighs prayed for us. Who is going to pray for us now? They thought about it and did *Teshuvah*.

It must indeed be explained why Rav Zera was a little-man-with-burned-thighs. This digression will not take us away from the theme preoccupying us. The Talmud (*Baba Metsia*, p. 85a) tells us that Rav Zera, who had been educated in the Babylonian Talmudic academies, was struck when he came to the Holy Land by the very different style of study which prevailed there. The Babylonians were used to discussion; they attacked, asked questions, and put their masters and their interlocutors on the spot. In the Holy Land, the word of the master, like the university lecture, flowed of itself. All the students did was take notes. Rav Zera had needed to fast one hundred days to obtain the grace of forgetting the Babylonian method and to get used to the method of the Holy Land.

Was he right? It is unlikely, although Rav Zera bothered no one by this desire to conform and although he sinned against the mind and not against souls. There had been another fast: Rav Eliezer, head of the community, who was responsible for all the questions relating to communal life, was on the verge of death; and Rav Zera knew that this administrative life would fall upon him in case Rav Eliezer died. He thus fasted another hundred days so that Rav Eliezer would not die and so that administrative charges would not interfere with his own, Rav Zera's, studies. I think that such intellectual selfishness, such a refusal of the philosopher to take upon himself the obligation to be king, merits as much of a sanction in the Talmudic city as it does in the Platonic city, even if it were to draw Rav Eliezer from the jaws of death. But the sanction, perhaps extending to the first two fasts as well, was inflicted upon him after the third fast. For there had been a third fast of one hundred days—this time for a chimerical project that would never have occurred to the Eumenides.

Rav Zera wished that the fire of hell no longer have a hold on him.

Already very close to success, he would sit by a burning stove without being affected by the flames. Except on the day the sages of the Talmud, his colleagues, looked at him. The moment their gazes were directed at him, the fire regained its power over Rav Zera and burned his thighs. I think that, when the eyes of our colleagues are upon us, the fire of hell always regains its rights over us. I think also that the sages of the Talmud opposed practices which encroached upon the rights of hell: for whatever the rights of charity may be, a place had to be foreseen and kept warm for all eternity for Hitler and his followers. Without a hell for evil, nothing in the world would make sense any longer. I think, above all, that personal perfection and personal salvation are, despite their nobility, still selfishness, and that the purity of man which the hedge of roses protects is not an end in itself. But Rav Zera, in the text commented on here, tries to save others from hell—and by a means other than fasting—other men who are probably not followers of Hitler. They can find the way back if someone takes their distress and their fault upon himself. In the world, we are not free in the presence of others and simply their witnesses. We are their hostages. A notion through which, beyond freedom, the self is defined. Rav Zera is responsible for all those who are not Hitler. That may be something that we would not find in Aeschylus.

The man who is hostage to all others is needed by men, for without him morality would have no place to start. The little bit of generosity that occurs in the world requires no less. The Jewish tradition has taught this. Its exposure to persecution is perhaps only a fulfilment of this teaching—a mysterious fulfilment, for it happens unbeknownst to those who fulfil it.

By way of conclusion, there remains only the end of our text. The condition which guarantees the meaning of everything that has just been said is the existence of order and the subjective certainty of this existence.

"Three rows of students . . . ": Abaye said: It follows from this that when one moved, they all moved.

All. We understood it from the start. When someone from the row of students goes up to take his place among the judges, the first place in the row is now empty and everyone moves up one place. Number one in the second row will thus become the last one in the first row. So, what's the big deal? He was first in his village. Now he is last in Rome. The Latins do not hesitate: It is better to be first in one's village. And we understand them very well: What does one look for in our world if not the recognition of our peers, who in their turn are also seeking ours? Each affirms himself in relation to the others. A contingent distribution! A classification in which no one has a real place. In the Sanhedrin the order is not relative. The one who is last in the first row is reminded that it is better to be last in a procession of lions than at the head of a pack of foxes. Men find their place in the world in relation to the absolute place, in relation to the *Makom*.

NOTES

1. Maharsha-Samuel Eliezer Edels (1551–1631): eastern European rabbi and Talmudic commentator. Since 1680, his "notes" to the Talmud (Hiddushin) have been included in most editions of the Talmud as Hiddushe Maharsha. (Trans.)

2. André Spire (1868–1966): French poet and Zionist leader, best remembered as the leader of the Jewish revival movement in twentieth-century French literature and as a literary theorist and innovator. The line Levinas quotes may come from Spire's poem "L'Ancienne Loi" (The ancient law), in which the following verse occurs: "Tu auras beau faire, dit-elle, jamais tu n'aimeras vraiment leurs théâtres, leurs musées, leurs palais, leur amusettes." [You can try all you want, she said, but never will you really like their theatres, their museums, their palaces, their entertainments.] *Poèmes juifs* (Paris: Albin Michel, 1959), p. 29. (Trans.).

From the Sacred to the Holy

FIVE NEW TALMUDIC READINGS

PREFACE

The talks gathered in this volume were delivered between 1969 and 1975 at
the Colloquia of French-speaking Jewish Intellectuals, organized by the
French section of the World Jewish Congress. We have retained the rhythm
of their original oral version in their current written form and have included as well a few reminders of the circumstances in which they were
spoken. We did this also for the earlier talks, which appeared under the title
Four Talmudic Readings in 1968.

This form seems suited to the presentation of passages from the Talmud,
which is an oral teaching. Even in its transformation into tractates, the Talmud preserved the openness and the challenge of living speech. It cannot be
summarized by the term "dialogue," which is so abused today. This discourse does not resemble any other literary genre: Talmudic speech is no
doubt its model and its proper, privileged place. Besides, are we dealing with
a question of literature in this speech which wishes not to be written? It is a
speech whose elevation adapts to—or makes use of—a certain barrenness
of words, a certain conciseness of form, as if it were still gesture, delighting
in allusion. It is wary of rhetoric, which, from the depth of all language,
throws up its bewitching illusions and warps the woof of a text. It is a way
of speaking which thus remains completely sober because of its very indifference to style, which is to say, to writing. This sobriety surpasses that of
many modern interpreters who, moreover, are not always aware of the extent of this state of wakefulness. Accordingly, in none of the five "Talmudic readings" published here have we deleted the few prefatory sentences
that risk passing for an oratorical precaution, in which the speaker admits
or declares his stage fright; actually, these sentences reveal, in diverse ways,
his scruple, his humility, and the homage he renders to an utmost intelligence and subtlety.

Surely there are less cumbersome ways of approaching the Talmud. The
traditional approach would, in any event, require fewer excuses. The famous "study of the Torah" is, for Jewish piety, the fulfilment of a divine
will, as worthy as obedience to all the other commandments combined. It
has preserved Israel throughout the ages. It is certain of its course and of its
paths. These difficult and intricate paths require concentration, logical

This preface appears in Levinas's *Du sacré au saint: cinq nouvelles lectures talmudiques*
(Paris: Les Éditions de Minuit, 1977), which includes the last five commentaries in the present
volume.

vigor, and gifts of invention. Very natural as well is the other form of reading, adopted with rigor by historians and philologists, who would lean on science—still in its infancy in this area—and reconstitute the Talmudic heritage on the basis of its sources: They wait for anachronisms and contradictory moves to collide with each other in these pages, which are venerated by others but are approached by them head on.

But neither the certainty of Jewish piety nor the "certainties" of the "science of Judaism"—*Wissenschaft des Judentums*—guide the "Talmudic readings" proposed here. We are in less of a hurry than the historians and philologists to deconstruct the traditional landscape of the text, which for more than a millennium sheltered the soul of Judaism, dispersed and at one. Despite the variety of these most ancient epochs, in which the ground and the topography of its landscape were constituted and in which its horizons were outlined, the text was already unchangeable, invested by a spirituality that found its expression, its intellectual and moral archetypes and the reflections of its light, in its forms. The marvel of a confluence and the power of the current flowing from it equal the marvel of a single, contested source. But if, in loyalty to the "lived" and received text, we have not separated out the different strata of this sedimentation of history, we have, upon entering it, felt less called upon than does traditional study to make "practical decisions" proceeding from the Law and less given to—but perhaps also less gifted in—the speculative virtuosity of the great masters, whose sublime art nonetheless constitutes in the "houses of study"—the *yeshivot*—a very noteworthy aesthetic.

What matters to us is to ask questions of these texts—to which Jewish wisdom is tied as if to the soil—in terms of our problems as modern men. But this does not mean an immediate right to selection and to a pretentious separation of the out-of-date from the permanent. One must first take into account the nonrhetorical character of this Talmudic speaking and read it without neglecting its articulations, which may seem to be contingent but in which the essential is often hidden and in which one can almost hear its spirit breathing. It is to this preliminary task and *to the very idea of such a task* that our little book tries to contribute. Traditional study does not always expose the meanings that appear thus, or else it takes them for truisms that "go without saying," carried away as it is by the dialectic that overflows them; or else it states them in a language and in a context that are not always audible to those who remain outside. We strive to speak otherwise.

A word, finally, about content. We wished in these readings to bring out the catharsis or demythification of the religious that Jewish wisdom performs. It does this in opposition to the interpretation of myths—ancient or modern—through recourse to other myths, often more obscure and more cruel, albeit more widespread, and which, by this fact, pass for being more profound, sacred, or universal. The oral Torah speaks "in spirit and in truth," even when it seems to do violence to the verses and letters of the written Torah. From the Torah it extracts *ethical meaning as the ultimate intelligibility of the human* and even of the cosmic. That is why we have entitled the present book *From the Sacred to the Holy,* even though these words pertain, strictly speaking, only to the theme of the third reading of the series.

Judaism and Revolution

■ From the Tractate *Baba Metsia*, pp. 83a–83b ■

Mishna   *He who hires workers and tells them to begin early and finish late cannot force them to it if beginning early and finishing late does not conform to the custom of the place.*

*Where the custom is that they be fed, he is obligated to
feed them; where it is that they be served dessert, he must
serve them dessert. Everything goes according to the custom
of the place.*

*One day, Rabbi Johanan ben Mathia said to his son: Go
hire some workers. The son included food among the conditions. When he came back, the father said: My son, even if
you prepared a meal for them equal to the one King Solomon served, you would not have fulfilled your obligation toward them, for they are the descendants of Abraham, Isaac,
and Jacob. As long as they have not begun to work, go and
specify: You are only entitled to bread and dry vegetables.*

*Rabban Simeon ben Gamaliel said: It was not necessary
to say it, for, in all matters, one acts according to the custom
of the place.*

Gemara   *Doesn't this go without saying? If an employer were to pay a
higher wage, it would be possible to think that he is saying
to the workers: I agreed to pay you a higher salary assuming
that you would begin earlier and finish later. Thus, our text
teaches us that they can answer him: You have increased our
salary so that we work with more care.*

*Resh Lakish said: The hired worker is on his own time
going home; going to work is on his employer's time, for it is
written (Psalm 104:22–23): "When the sun rises, they leave
and go hide in their lairs; man then goes to his work, to his
labor until evening." But shouldn't we look at custom? In
question is a new city. Shouldn't one consider where they*

This reading was given in the context of a colloquium consecrated to "Youth and Revolution in Jewish Consciousness," held in March 1969. The proceedings were published in *Jeunesse et révolution: Données et débats* (Paris: P.U.F., 1972). Levinas's commentary appears on
pp. 59–80; there was no discussion.

come from? At issue is a population of diverse origins. And, if you wish, one can say: that is in the case in which he told them he was hiring them according to the law of the Torah.

Rav Zera taught (others say it was Rav Jose): It is written: "You bring on darkness and it is night." It is this world which is like night; "the night in which all beasts of the forest stir" (Psalm 104:20); those are the evil-doers in this world, who are comparable to the beasts of the forest. "When the sun rises, they go away and hide in their lairs" (Psalm 104:22). When the sun rises for the just, the evil-doers withdraw to hell, "they go away and hide in their lairs" (it must be read "in their houses," and it is the just who are spoken of here: there is no just man who does not have a home corresponding to his dignity). "Man then goes out to his work": the just will receive their reward. "To his labor until evening" (Psalm 104:23): he who knew how to continue his task until evening.

One day, Rabbi Eleazar ben Rabbi Simeon met a government official responsible for catching thieves. He said to him: How can you detect them? Are they not equal to brutes? For it is said: "In it, all the beasts of the night stir." According to others, it would have been another verse that he interpreted (Psalm 10:9): "He waits in a covert like a lion in his lair; waits to seize the lowly." And what if you caught a just man and let an evil-doer go? The police official answered: What can I do? It is the order of the king. Then Rabbi Eleazar ben Simeon replied: Come, I will show you how you should proceed. Around four o'clock (ten o'clock), go to the tavern; if you see a wine drinker holding a glass in his hand and dozing, inform yourself. If he is a scholar, he must have risen early to study; if he is a day laborer, he must have gone to work early; if he works the night shift, he could have been making needles. He did not go to work in the daytime but he worked at night; but if he is none of the above, he is a thief and you can arrest him. When this reached the king's ears, it was said: The reader of the message can serve as messenger. They looked for Rabbi Eleazar. And the latter arrested thieves. Hence, Rabbi Joshua bar Karhah relayed this to him: Vinegar, son of wine, how much longer will you deliver unto death the people of our God? Rabbi Eleazar conveyed this answer to him: I remove the thorns from the vineyard. The other retorted: Let the owner of the vineyard come and remove the thorns himself.

One day a laundryman met him and called him: Vinegar,

son of wine! Rabbi Eleazar said: His insolence is no doubt a sign that he is an evil-doer. He gave the order to arrest him. After having calmed down, he went to set him free but this was no longer possible. He then said about him (Proverbs 21:23): "He who guards his mouth and tongue guards himself from trouble." When they hanged him, he stood under the gallows and wept. They then said to him: Master, calm yourself. Right on the Day of Atonement, he and his son had illicit relations with the betrothed of another man. He put his hands on his own body and said: Rejoice, my innards, for if those who seem suspicious to us have come to this point, how much worse are those whose case is clear-cut! I am sure that neither worms nor decay will have power over you. But nonetheless he was not reassured. He was given a sleeping draught. . . .

The same thing happened to Rabbi Ishmael ben Rabbi Jose. One day, the prophet Elijah met him and said: How long will you deliver the people of our God to execution? He answered: What can I do, it is the order of the King. Elijah said to him: Your father fled to Asia; flee to Laodicea.

The Text

As always when I begin my Talmudic reading at this colloquium of intellectuals, I fear the presence in the room of people who know the Talmud better than I do. That is not a difficult feat but one which places me in a state of mortal sin, the sin of the student holding forth before his master. This year, in addition, one also has to contend with those who challenge Judaism. Since, in all likelihood, the latter are not the former, this makes for a lot of people to fear.

I have not indicated the title of my lesson. Maybe that of the colloquium as a whole will best suit my subject: "Judaism and Revolution." The meaning I intend to give to the conjunction joining the two title words will emerge in the course of the commentary. Commentary or interpretation? A reading of the meaning in the text or the text in a meaning? Obedience or boldness? Safety in proceeding or a taking of risks? In any case neither paraphrase nor paradox; neither philology nor arbitrariness.

We have before us a text which it would be wrong to label medieval. The Middle Ages have a beginning and an end (395–1453). The Mishna was edited at the end of the second century of our era. Our text is thus from the end of Antiquity, and the end of Antiquity is a venerable period. One of the eminent philosophers of our time assured me one day that, by the second century of our common era, everything had already been thought. Only the details remain to be specified. What follows my text—the Gemara—is of later origin; but at the beginning of the Middle Ages, many of the fine traditions of Antiquity were still alive.

The Worker That One Hires

He who hires workers and tells them to begin early and finish late cannot force them to it if beginning early and finishing late does not conform to the custom of the place.

Where the custom is that they be fed, he is obligated to feed them; where it is that they be served dessert, he must serve them dessert. Everything goes according to the custom of the place.

It is clear from the start that the Mishna affirms the rights of the *other person*, even if this person finds himself in the inferior position, which is dangerous to his freedom, of a worker for hire. This position is dangerous to his freedom because he runs the risk of losing his liberty without undergoing any violence; to be sure, the person is still acting willingly since he engages himself and stays within the interpersonal commerce of an exchange; but commerce is at the border line of alienation, and freedom easily turns into non-freedom. Our text teaches that not everything can be bought and not everything can be sold. The freedom to negotiate has limits which impose themselves in the name of freedom itself. It matters little that the limits formulated here are not the same as those demanded by modern trade unions. What matters is the principle of limits imposed on freedom for the greater glory of freedom. It is the spirit in which the limits are set: they concern the material conditions of life, sleep and food. Sublime materialism! The secretary who typed the translation of the page I am commenting on was not mistaken when she exclaimed: "But this is a trade union text!" A union text before the letter, certainly. For the nature of the limits imposed is fixed by custom and evolves with custom. But custom is already a resistance against the arbitrary and against violence. Its notion of a general principle is tribal and somewhat childish, but it is a notion of a general principle, the root of the universal and the Law. Sublime materialism, concerned with dessert. Food is not the fuel necessary to the human machine; food is a meal. No humanist eloquence comes to spoil this text, which really defends man. Authentic humanism, materialistic humanism. Hearts open very easily to the working class, wallets with more difficulty. What opens with the most difficulty of all are the doors of our own homes. Last May, we welcomed the disadvantaged mostly in the universities.

Our old text upholds the right of the person, as in our days Marxism upholds it. I refer to Marxist humanism,[1] the one which continues to say that "man is the supreme good for man" and "in order that man be the supreme good for man he must be truly man" and which asks itself: "How could man, the friend of man, in specific circumstances, have become the enemy of man?" and for whom the anomaly called alienation is explained by the structure of the economy, left to its own determinism. Our Mishna also wants to impose a limit on the arbitrariness of the economy and on this alienation. Let us underline one more detail of the context in which the Mishna places itself, which is typical of Jewish humanism: the man whose rights must be defended is in the first place the other man; it is not initially myself. It is not the concept "man" which is at the basis of this humanism; it is the other man.

An Infinite Right

One day, Rabbi Johanan ben Mathia said to his son: Go hire some workers. The son included food among the conditions. When he came back, the father said: My son, even if you prepared a meal for them equal to the one King Solomon served, you would not have fulfilled your obligation toward them, for they are the descendants of Abraham, Isaac, and Jacob. As long as they have not begun the work, go and specify: You are only entitled to bread and dry vegetables.

Here are some indications as to the extent of the other man's right: it is practically an infinite right. Even if I had the treasures of King Solomon at my disposal, I still would not be able to fulfil my obligations. Of course, the Mishna does qualify this. In question is the other man, who descends from Abraham, Isaac, and Jacob. But do not become alarmed. We are not in the presence of a racist idea here. I have it from an eminent master: each time Israel is mentioned in the Talmud one is certainly free to understand by it a particular ethnic group which is probably fulfilling an incomparable destiny. But to interpret in this manner would be to reduce the general principle in the idea enunciated in the Talmudic passage, to forget that Israel means a people who has received the Law and, as a result, a human nature which has reached the fullness of its responsibilities and its self-consciousness. The descendants of Abraham, Isaac, and Jacob are human beings who are no longer childlike. Before a self-conscious humanity, no longer in need of being educated, our duties are limitless. Workers belong to this perfected humanity, despite the inferiority of their condition and the coarseness of their profession. But, strange as it may seem, humanity is nevertheless not defined by its proletariat either. As if all alienation were not overcome by the consciousness that the working class may achieve from its condition as a class and from its struggle; as if revolutionary consciousness were not sufficient for disalienation; as if the notion of Israel, people of the Torah, people as old as the world and as old as persecuted mankind, carried within itself a universality higher than that of a class exploited and struggling; as if the violence of the struggle were already alienation.

The Descendants of Abraham

What else could descent from Abraham mean? Let us recall the biblical and Talmudic tradition relating to Abraham. Father of believers? Certainly. But above all the one who knew how to receive and feed men: the one whose tent was wide open on all sides. Through all these openings he looked out for passersby in order to receive them. The meal offered by Abraham? We know especially of one meal, the one he offered to the three angels—without suspecting their condition as angels; for to receive angels worthily, even Harpagon[2] would have bent over backwards. Abraham must have taken the three passersby for three Bedouins, for three nomads from the Negev Desert—three Arabs, in other words! He runs toward them. He calls them "Your Lordships." The heirs of Abraham—men to whom their ancestor bequeathed a difficult tradition of duties toward the other man, which one is never done with, an order in which one is never free. In this order, above all else, duty takes the form of obligations toward the body, the obligation of feeding and sheltering. So defined, the heirs of Abraham are of all nations: any man truly man is no doubt of the line of Abraham.

That is why Rabbi Johanan ben Mathia is so frightened by the engagement his son seems so happy with: I could never meet the obligations you have contracted. Even in offering the hired workers the meals of King Solomon, I would not be quit of my responsibilities toward them.

King Solomon in his magnificence is nothing to sneer at. The Bible describes how extraordinary were the meals King Solomon offered to his people by enumerating the number of cattle slaughtered to this end.

The Talmud goes even further (in the text closely following the one we are commenting on): the numbers in the Bible refer to the quantity of food each of the king's wives prepared each night in the hope of receiving him for dinner. Solomon had three hundred legitimate wives and seven hundred concubines. Let us calculate the budget for such a household. It would not suffice to provide food for one's hired workers, the descendants of Abraham. The extent of the obligation toward men who are fully men has no limits. One more time let us recall the word of the Lithuanian rabbi Israel Salanter:[3] the material needs of my neighbor are my spiritual needs.

But our text also alludes to something very important. All the splendor of King Solomon would not suffice to guarantee the dignity of the descendants of Abraham. There is more in the family of Abraham than in the promises of the State. It is important to give, of course, but everything depends on how it is done. It is not through the State and through the political advances of humanity that the person shall be fulfilled—which, of course, does not free the State from instituting the conditions necessary to this fulfilment. But it is the family of Abraham that sets the norms. This idea is worth what it is worth. It is suggested by the text. Let not the worshippers of the State, who proscribe the survival of Jewish particularism, be angered!

The Contract

Clearly contained in the lines we have commented on is that everything begins with the right of the other man and with my infinite obligation toward him. What is truly human is beyond human strength. Society according to man's strength is merely the limitation of this right and this obligation toward him. The contract does not put an end to the violence of the other. It does not abolish an order—or disorder—in which man is a wolf toward man. In the wolves' forest, no law can be introduced. But it is possible, when the other man is in principle infinite for me, to limit the extent of my duties to a degree, but only to a degree. The contract is more concerned with limiting my duties than with defending my rights. The descendants of Abraham are capable of perceiving this necessity and of coming to an agreement: they are ripe for a contract. This is why the father tells the son: Define the infinite which you have opened up right away. Set and determine the conditions. Hurry to establish the terms of the contract before the workers start to work. For once the work begins, I will find myself in debt until the end of my days.

You are only entitled to bread and dried vegetables.

The menu seems meager, to our taste, at least. Nevertheless, it contains the principle of variety: the conjunction *and*. For a little further on the Gemara will ask: "bread *and* dried vegetables" or bread *of* dried vegetables"? In Hebrew, only one letter—the *vav*—needs to be taken out to eliminate the conjunction. The expression would then mean "bread of dried vegetables" (like the one we ate during the war). The answer given is emphatic: "By God, the conjunction is necessary. This conjunction is as important here as the rudder is necessary to steer a ship in a dangerous river."

Without the conjunction, therefore, there is catastrophe. It is absolutely necessary—even when a contract limits the infinite of my obligations—that limitation itself have limits. To feed another is to keep food in its nature as a meal; it is never to transform it into subsistence fare. To a certain degree, when feeding another it is necessary to humor his fancy; otherwise, it is a shipwreck.

Custom

Here is the third paragraph in this first part of the Mishna:

Rabban Simeon ben Gamaliel said: it was not necessary to say it, for, in all matters, one acts according to the custom of the place.

Rabban Simeon ben Gamaliel thinks that the limits of obligations are always clearly indicated in custom. He apparently does not question the initial infinite of obligation. But he thinks that custom alone—the empirical, history, and consensus—establishes limits and limits limitation; he thinks that one cannot go beyond custom in human coexistence, that justice arises from the nature of things. Unless this insistence on custom bespeaks a conservative and counterrevolutionary traditionalism. For isn't revolution, beyond the violence and break in continuity by which people strive to define it, the refusal of the exegesis of customs, that is, of their renewal? No new wine in old bottles! Elimination of old bottles and old superstitions! Let us destroy the altars of false gods! Let us cut down the sacred groves! Let us not consecrate them to the true God. At the very most, we can explain the causes behind the customs, but let us rid humanity of them. Resh Lakish's intervention, a little further in the text, will become clear.

Let us now begin the Gemara.

> Doesn't this go without saying?

All that had seemed to us of such great import really goes without saying in practice, and so what is the use of the legislation of the Mishna? No! It does not go without saying. Here is one situation that can happen.

> If an employer were to pay a higher wage, it would be possible to think that he is saying to the workers: I agreed to pay you a higher salary assuming that you would begin earlier and finish later.

It is in fact possible to foresee a raise in salary which would force the worker to get up earlier and to go to sleep later; the employer becomes generous and wants to acquire additional labor taken from the leisure time of the worker. Isn't it possible to buy, if "price is no consideration," what the employer who pays a normal wage cannot buy because of a concern for what is human? Isn't is possible to buy the leisure time of workers on the black market? The Gemara would like the worker to answer the boss who becomes generous so as to obtain extra working hours thus: Sure, you have paid me more but that is so that I should work better. The quality of my labor I am willing to discuss, but I will not bargain about my human condition, which, in this particular case, expresses itself as my right to get up and go to sleep at the regular hours.

> Thus, our text teaches us that they (the workers) can answer him: You have increased our salary so that we work with more care.

Revolution

I do not seem to be keeping to my topic. I have not yet said much about revolution, only a word in relation to customs! What is the relation between this excerpt from the Talmud and revolution?

In contrast to many of today's speakers, I do not think that revolution should be defined in a purely formal manner, as violence or as the overthrow of a given order. I do not even think it is enough to define it as the spirit of sacrifice. There was much spirit of sacrifice in the ranks of those who followed Hitler. Revolution must be defined by its content, by values: revolution takes place when one frees man; that is, revolution takes place when one tears man away from economic determinism.

To affirm that the working man is not negotiable, that he cannot be bargained about, is to affirm that which begins a revolution.

Travel costs

Resh Lakish's intervention, which will now occur, seems to involve a purely practical matter: Who pays the traveling costs for the hired worker? Or, what amounts to the same thing: Is the travel time of the worker to be paid by the worker or by his employer?

> Resh Lakish said: The hired worker is on his own time going home; going to work is on his employer's time.

He must, of course, rise with the sun in order for this to occur. But although it is already day when he heads to work, and a workday is measured by the length of the day, traveling time to work is excluded from the workday; the return home will occur only at the onset of night. It is at the worker's expense. The conditions are harsh—he comes back at nightfall! Yes, we are far from the eight-hour day and farther yet from the forty-hour week and paid vacations. But the issue of travel time and the obligation to include it in the evaluation of a workday are already present. What matters is not numbers but the existence of non-negotiable limits. At the very least, it will be conceded that trade union rights have their history and that the future deproletarization of the proletarians is already present in the first affirmations of the inalienable rights of the worker.

But, why, in God's name, turn to the Psalms for something so self-evident? Isn't this proof of the famous sterility of the Talmudic method, which shocks the modern man (the man who knows everything)? Doesn't he denounce proofs produced by the association of ideas and the juxtaposition of texts having nothing to do with one another? Furthermore, what do psalms, which are poetry and in which the soul opens itself up before God, have to do with the problems of unions?

Psalms and the Length of the Workday

As little as I have ever understood the exact meaning of the expression "the opening up of the soul in its love of God," I ask myself, nonetheless, whether there isn't a certain connection between the establishment of working hours and the love of God, with or without the opening up of the soul. I am even inclined to believe that there are not many other ways to love God than to establish these working hours correctly, no way that is more urgent. A psalm is after all not such a bad text on which to found justice for the toiling man. Psalm 104 may be very beautiful and poetically perfect but you will not prove me wrong on this point, Memmi, you who are a goldsmith: verses 22–23 tell us the length of the workday:

"When the sun rises, they leave (that is, the beasts of the forest—wild animals) and go hide in their lairs; man then goes on to his work, to his labor until evening."

Resh Lakish was right to refer to Psalm 104. When the animals withdraw because the night is over, man gets up with the sun and performs his task until evening. The text is precise. The excellent master who taught me the Talmud taught me that it is proper to trust Talmudic references, if one is very cautious. I have already had occasion to bring this up before, without convincing anyone. This master taught that, beyond this or that verse, closely or remotely supporting what a Talmudic scholar is saying, it is by its spirit, that is, its context, that the verse conveys the proper tonality to the idea it is supposed to establish. We must therefore read Psalm 104 beyond verses 22–23. Psalm 104 is a psalm which praises the Eternal One, but in an unusual manner. That the creature should praise its creator is undoubtedly an old pious idea. In practice, the creature praises the Eternal One mostly when it does not see itself fully. The Eternal One is praised when one goes to the seashore or to the mountains and has time to contemplate the starry sky. When one is not on vacation or does not have the means to go on vacation, the creature praises the Creator much less. Psalm 104, however, is a psalm about the profound harmony that would rule within the creature—during vacations as well as during working days and months. It is the psalm of the perfected world:

Bless the Lord, O my soul! O Lord, my God, you are very great. You are clothed in glory and majesty, wrapped in a robe of light you spread out the heavens like a tent cloth. . . . You established the earth on its foundations, so that it shall never totter. You made the deep cover it as a garment; the waters stood above the mountains. . . . You set bounds they may not pass so that they never again cover the earth. . . . You make the grass grow. . . .

Work

The passage about the wild beasts who retreat to their lairs occurs toward the end. As soon as the day begins, nothing savage remains. Integrally human life is possible: work begins. In this psalm, work is not associated with misfortune, a curse, meaninglessness. The psalm seems to place the work of men amid the successes of creation. In Resh Lakish's reference to Psalm 104, beyond the technical problem of the length of the workday, from which we have mainly drawn a principle, we have an argument concerning the meaning of human work and thus a reason for the dignity of the worker: the rights of the worker are due to his function in the general economy of creation, to his ontological role.

The rights and dignity of man are derived from his condition as worker. Work belongs to the order of light and reason. The time of work, as Resh Lakish sees it, is not the time of frustration or alienation, is not cursed time. In a world in which work appeared as a mark of servitude reserved for the slave, Resh Lakish wants to see it as the perfection of creation.

But in that case Resh Lakish would not have a sacred love for revolution. For in his beatific reading of Psalm 104, he does not see how evil can enter the world through work. Our psalm has decidedly no feeling for dialectics and affirms, in short, that this is the best possible world. I think the Talmud has the same worries as we do. We will soon see another reading of Psalm 104. And we shall return to this very psalm after a digression which shall prove (if proofs are still necessary) that the Talmud is not a simple compilation—whatever some otherwise enlightened spirits might think— of folkloric memories in a contingent order, but that there is an inner movement in this text, that its arrangement is ordered by its meaning, that it is meaningful. I will come back to this later.

But, if the Talmud returns to Psalm 104 to read it differently, we should not lightly dismiss Resh Lakish's position. Maybe Resh Lakish was not at all blind to the imperfections of the creature; maybe the condition of the worker seems inhuman to him, but maybe he still thinks that the man who works is the only hope of the earth and that the tomorrows he prepares will be freed from the misery of a miserable condition. Have authentic revolutionaries always rejected the dialectic present within the condition of the exploited and canceled the time necessary for its movement? Resh Lakish, who seeks to base the length of the workday on a psalm verse, thus also finds himself grounding the rights of the worker on the very order of creation. No doubt he thinks that the biblical text is itself in agreement with the rational nature of things (because created) and in agreement with natural or rational law. Or he at least thinks that the natural law attached to the person of the worker and consecrated by the Torah guarantees better than custom the rights of the person. Perhaps

Resh Lakish is a revolutionary because he denounces custom in the manner we have specified above. We shall thus not be astonished by what follows. For the Gemara, in fact, asks:

> But shouldn't we look at custom?

The Gemara asks: Why does Resh Lakish think it necessary to draw a law from a biblical text when it was formulated with such clarity by the *Tanaim* in our Mishna: "One acts according to the custom of the place"?

The New Cities and the Torah

For Resh Lakish, custom in general is not an adequate order. Not that he wants an abstract justice, without traditions or customs. But Resh Lakish has enough imagination to perceive a society without customs, the so-called inhuman society which takes form, for example, in the mushroom cities of our industrial world. These men of the early Middle Ages already conceive of American cities! Everything has been thought. The limits of their concrete horizon do not prevent them from living in an intellectual horizon without limits and to perceive as something important the possibility that a society be without traditions:

> In question is a new city.

But, if it is a new city, don't its inhabitants come from somewhere? Yes, but from everywhere. The notion of an American or industrial society is thought out to the end.

> Shouldn't one consider where they come from? At issue is a population of diverse origins.

Cities rise from the void. They have no past. Within them, populations coming from everywhere are so mixed together and individuals so dispersed that all traditions are lost. Beings without history do exist. Does the fact of no longer having a history transform humans into inferior beings? Does being unable to claim descent from the great lineage of Abraham, Isaac, and Jacob—or to speak without symbols, does the fact of not belonging to a human community conscious of its history, organized and structured—make the rights of man inapplicable? Let us free humanity from traditionalisms. Let us no longer attempt to save it through patriarchal virtues of the group. Resh Lakish wants the law of the Torah to be independent of places and times: an eternal law attached to the person as such, even in his individualistic isolation. Modern society depends neither on history nor on its sedimentation. It discovers its order in human dignity, in the human personality. It is established in regard to the person. Away with customs and myths, all of Spinoza's knowledge of the first kind,[4] all those instruments of enslavement.

And the following very short paragraph specifies that only the law of the Torah is applicable, even in the case of those who do have a history and a tradition. Resh Lakish did not find a law on the length of the workday for those without a tradition, for the individualism of industrial society, in Psalm 104; he thought that it is always possible to hire workers outside custom, if it is done according to the Law of the Torah:

> And, if you want, one can say: that is in the case in which he told them he was hiring them according to the Law of the Torah.

According to just law, period. Without worrying about the local custom. It is not long historical tradition that counts. It is the personal nature of persons that counts.

Another Reading of Psalm 104

Let us now go back to Psalm 104, which earlier seemed to us to do away with revolution because it placed the law of work under the Law of the world created by God. Here we have Rav Zera reading Psalm 104:

> Rav Zera taught (others say it was Rav Jose): it is written: "You bring on darkness and it is night" (Psalm 104:20). *It is this world which is like night;* "the night in which all the beasts of the forest stir" (Psalm 104:22), *those are the evil-doers in this world, who are comparable to the beasts of the forest.*

The text, which seemed so harmonious before, so *one* in its meaning, to the point of excluding the necessity of change, appears to Rav Zera in a more ambiguous light. The night of wild beasts would be a mode of human existence. Evil is within the human. Creation is not already an order. Night must come to an end so that order can take the place of night. Evil must be eliminated, must have its hell, and the just must receive his reward.

> "When the sun rises, they go away and hide in their lairs." When the sun rises for the just, the evil-doers withdraw to hell, "they go away and hide in their lairs" (it must be read as "hide in their houses," and it is the just who are spoken of here: there is no just man who does not have a home corresponding to his dignity). "Man then goes out to his work": the just will receive their reward. "To his labor until evening" (Psalm 104:23): he who knew how to continue his task until evening.

The dialectic by which Evil can serve the Good, by which the Good can *objectively* be one of the forces of Evil, is confusion and night. A revolution to dissipate this confusion is needed. Good has to be Good and Evil Evil. Isn't that the true definition of the revolutionary ideal? It is true that our text says this in a pious language. But unless it is superstition, it is a way of speaking which, through symbolization or even sublimation, already includes what is authentic thought, already severs itself from opinion.

Curiously enough, the image of the rising sun is associated with details that have held the attention of our scholars. This is not accidental. For the end of night is not presented as an epoch in which universal love will reign and in which the just shall spend their time contemplating the harmony of the spheres. We are told that each of the just shall have his home. Isn't the proletarian condition, the alienation of man, primarily the fact of having no home? Not to have a place of one's own, not to have an interior, is not truly to communicate with another, and thus to be a stranger to oneself and to the other. After the world of night, after existence as a perpetual threat, after existence as wild beasts, not only threatening but also threatened, after fear and anxiety, what is announced here as the triumph of the just is the possibility of a society in which everyone has his home, returns home and to himself, and sees the face of the other. A second detail which is also not accidental: Rav Zera draws "receive his salary" from the part of the verse that says "Man goes to his work," as if work itself were salary, as if work were no longer cursed but free. We shall find this theme elsewhere in the Talmud. The reward of the just man is contained in his very labor. We have two notions at the same time. One is the general idea of the possibility of finding one's reward by participating in the divine order. Virtue's reward is virtue itself. But the other is the notion of work as vocation, of working as an artist.

"And he is just who performs his task until evening" (Psalm 104:23): he who knew how to continue his task until evening.

The perseverance of the just man in his justice, despite all the denials of an immutable idea of justice made in the ancient as well as the modern world. Once again, we come across a religious idea. In this commentary, by means of which I want to tear from a meaning at once one and infinite this or that aspect in isolation, no religious idea is abolished. "He who knew how to continue his task until evening": he who believed in a better world, in the efficacy of the good, despite the skepticism of men and the lessons of history; he who did not despair, who did not go to the tavern to free himself from the responsibilities of his service as a man (I have not introduced the word "tavern" here by chance). He who looked neither for distraction nor for suicide, who did not shirk the tension in which the responsible man lives, the one who perhaps best merits the name of revolutionary. If you have the patience to hear me out to the end, you will see that the rest of the text opposes itself to the idea that existence is a game, in the absolute sense of that word. This is contrary to the metaphysical tendencies prevalent today, according to which being is play, according to which freedom is not free enough because it drags along responsibilities. In the text, however, it is thought that being implies an extreme seriousness, that the responsibility stemming from freedom is not serious enough, that we are responsible beyond our commitments. In this sense, the task must be pursued until evening.

The Sources of Evil

The problem of the defense of man, of the bringing about of an order in which man will be defended, of revolution, takes us back to the central question: How is it that human order is eaten away by Evil? We begin with an anecdote: "One day Rabbi Eleazar ben Rabbi Simeon met an officer of the government responsible for catching thieves." Rabbi Simeon, father of the Rabbi Eleazar mentioned here, is the famous Rabbi Simeon bar Yochai, who has a special place among the *Tanaim*. He and his son spent thirteen years in a cave hiding from the Romans. Jewish mystical tradition attributes the Zohar to him. These facts are important. We will soon see his son, Rabbi Eleazar, at the opposite extreme from mysticism, a man very gifted in police work or politics (unless he brings us something else which we have to look for). In any case, from this anecdote about Rabbi Eleazar it is possible to conclude that the entire passage we are reading concerns the problem of collaborating with the Romans. The essence of great texts is not to arise outside history but to have a meaning beyond the situation which has evoked them. Are we sure that in today's theme—"Judaism and Revolution"—something else besides collaboration with the Romans is at stake? The text, even if it did arise as a result of cases of collaboration, opens up the entire problem of the relation between politics and Evil, the problem of the relationship of political struggle and Evil. That is, the text opens up an essential aspect of the problem of revolution. For a revolution does not destroy the State: it is for another political regime, but for a political regime nonetheless. Therefore:

> One day, Rabbi Eleazar ben Rabbi Simeon met a government official responsible for catching thieves. He said to him: How can you detect them? Are they not equal to brutes?

How does Rabbi Eleazar ben Rabbi Simeon know that thieves are equal to brutes? For a Talmudic sage, this is not a given of reason:

> For it is said: "In it (in the night) all the beasts of the night stir."

Once again it is our Psalm 104 which is made to serve. How does it shed light? Those who move about at night hide during the day: They are men who do not show themselves. Evil—or bestiality—is non-communication. It is being completely enclosed within oneself, to the point of not revealing oneself even to oneself!

According to others it would have been another verse that he interpreted (Psalm 10:9): "He waits in a covert like a lion in his lair; waits to seize the lowly."

What is the difference whether it is this verse or another? Aren't biblical texts redundant in their piety? Be careful! The second quotation is taken from Psalm 10. We should take a close look at the intent of Psalm 10. The Talmudists, in search of quotations, did not open a concordance to find indications of all the passages in the Bible in which wild beasts are mentioned. They have an admirable knowledge of the texts and of their nuances. They have fun passing themselves off as simpletons, but they know the texts and their issues perfectly well. Without any apparent brilliance, they know how to think quickly and allusively, so as to be understood among themselves, among people who are absolutely intelligent. In the Talmud—which some Jews allow themselves to deny while wishing to be Jews—are to be found all the articulations, all the knots of Jewish thought.

Psalm 10, in which Rabbi Eleazar ben Rabbi Simeon is supposed to have found a quotation as profound as that from Psalm 104, is the opposite of Psalm 104. It is a psalm about the absence of God. While everything in Psalm 104 sings the praise of the Creator and his fully evident presence in his creature, Psalm 10 says: "Why, oh Lord, do you stand aloof? Heedless in times of trouble? The wicked in his arrogance hounds the lowly." It is the poor and not the animals in the forest that are the issue. But God slips away, not fearing the scandal of non-assistance to a person in danger.

> The wicked man in his pride pursues the unfortunate. They are the victims of his plots. . . . The wicked man crows about his unbridled lusts, the grasping man reviles and scorns the Lord. The wicked, arrogant as he is, in all his scheming thinks: He does not call to account, God does not care. His ways prosper at all times. Your judgments are far beyond him; he snorts at all his foes. He thinks: 'I shall not be shaken, through all time never be in trouble.' His mouth is full of oaths. . . . (Psalm 10:2–7).

And there also,

> "he is like the lion in the forest, he sets secret ambushes to capture the poor man; he captures the poor man by drawing him in his net" (Psalm 10:9).

Police and Revolution

If the first quotation allowed a doubt to remain regarding Rabbi Eleazar's question, the reference to Psalm 10 reveals its meaning fully. Unquestionably, violent action against Evil is necessary. And we shall soon see that this violence takes on all the appearances of political action. But it is no less evident that this action must seek the nature and cause of Evil. It must understand the reason for the absence or silence of God or the meaning of

this silence. Rabbi Eleazar ben Rabbi Simeon, meeting the government official responsible for arresting thieves, does not just ask himself by what exte-
rior signs a thief is recognizable, but also asks himself what Evil is. Where
does it come from? How is it that Evil corrupts society? How is it that God
absents himself from the world? And apparently questioning the absolute
claim of politics, he asks: How can you act politically while ignorant of the
nature of Evil, while ignorant of its metaphysical and spiritual reason? Beyond your analysis of the immediate situation, what is the source of Evil
and of justice? Therein lies the difference between a police action at the
service of the established State and revolutionary action. It is not enough to
be against a cause, one must be in the service of one. I do not think that
revolutionary action is to be recognized by the massiveness of victorious
street demonstrations. The fascists knew more successful ones. Revolutionary action is first of all the action of the isolated man who plans revolution
not only in danger but also in the agony of his conscience—in the double
clandestinity of the catacombs and of conscience. In the agony of conscience that risks making revolution impossible: for it is not only a question
of seizing the evil-doer but also of not making the innocent suffer. In this
also is to be found the difference in Jewish thought between the police and
revolutionary politics.

And what if you caught a just man and let an evil-doer go?

The official—I think Rabbi Eleazar ben Rabbi Simeon associated with
officers of rank and not with mere policemen—said to him:

What can I do? It is the order of the king.

The police official does not have time to ask himself where the Good is
and where the Evil; he belongs to the established power. He belongs to the
State, which has entrusted him with duties. He does not engage in meta-
physics; he engages in police work. He cannot see how one can simultaneously serve the State and the Absolute. Is there in the Talmud an
incompatibility between the desire for the Absolute and revolutionary politics? Can they be reconciled if one stays within the category of non-Jewish
political thought? Is Judaism compatible with a revolutionary action
thought in terms of politics, as it emerged from the Greco-Roman State?

Then Rabbi Eleazar ben Rabbi Simeon replied: Come, I will show you how
you should proceed. Around four o'clock (according to Talmudic calculations,
this means ten in the morning) go to the tavern (here we have the reappearance
of the café of which I spoke earlier). If you see a wine drinker holding a glass in
his hand and dozing, inform yourself. If he is a scholar, he must have risen early
to study; if he is a day laborer, he must have gone to work early; if he works the
night shift, he could have been making needles (night shift workers already ex-

isted; their work consisted of making needles). He did not go to work in the daytime but he worked at night; but if he is none of the above, he is a thief and you can arrest him. When this reached the king's ears, it was said: The reader of the message can serve as messenger. They looked for Rabbi Eleazar. And the latter arrested thieves.

What happened? People at the king's court were dazzled by what they took to be Rabbi Eleazar's expertise in police matters. He has a wonderful system and he must apply it. To read the message correctly is, of course, to apply it. Let us beware of messengers of inapplicable messages or of messages "for others."

The Tavern

I have no doubt that Rabbi Eleazar was skillful. But I find his police wisdom a bit too concise. To go to the tavern and calmly arrest those who drink there if they are neither intellectuals, day laborers, nor night-shift workers. I pondered what this could mean for a long time. Is it already an anticipation of police inquiries that take place in bars in our modern capitals? In itself, this would not be much. Well, I think all this means that Rabbi Eleazar accepts the struggle with Evil on the State's grounds, in the Roman sense of the term "state," and that he accepts revolutionary action as political action. But Rabbi Eleazar shows us the source of Evil against which he will fight. This can be understood in two ways. He might have thought that those who do not work with their hands and those who do not study are the source of Evil. All the idle and useless ones. I suppose writers are included among those who study. All non-workers are Evil. Parasites are thieves, in the broader meaning of the term. Man must build the universe: the universe is built through work and study. Everything else is distraction. Distraction is Evil.

I think of yet another possible reading of our text. The two readings are linked, in any case. Rabbi Eleazar has discovered that the source of Evil is in the very institution of the tavern. The tavern, or the café, has become an integral and essential part of modern life, which perhaps is an "open life," especially because of this aspect! An unknown city in which we arrive and which has no cafés seems closed to us. The café holds open house, at street level. It is a place of casual social intercourse, without mutual responsibility. One goes in without needing to. One sits down without being tired. One drinks without being thirsty. All because one does not want to stay in one's room. You know that all evils occur as a result of our incapacity to stay alone in our room. The café is not a place. It is a non-place for a non-society, for a society without solidarity, without tomorrow, without commitment, without common interests, a game society. The café, house of games, is the point through which game penetrates life and dissolves it. Society without yesterday or tomorrow, without responsibility, without seriousness—distraction, dissolution.

At the movies, a common theme is presented on the screen; in the theatre, a common theme is presented on stage. In the café, there are no themes. Here you are, each at your own little table with your cup or your glass. You relax completely to the point of not being obligated to anyone or anything; and it is because it is possible to go and relax in a café that one tolerates the horrors and injustices of a world without a soul. The world as a game from which everyone can pull out and exist only for himself, a place of forgetfulness—of the forgetfulness of the other—that is the café. And here we come back to our first reading: not to build the world is to destroy it.

I am not waging war on the corner café—and I do not want to have all the café keepers of Paris rise against me. But the café is only the realization of a form of life. It proceeds from an ontological category, and it is this category that Rabbi Eleazar ben Rabbi Simeon perceived in the simple inns of his time: a category essential to Western being, perhaps to Eastern being as well, but rejected by Jewish being.

We must hurry now. I still have some rather difficult points to comment on in this text.

They looked for Rabbi Eleazar and the latter arrested thieves.

In the Service of the State

So Rabbi Eleazar is drawn into the struggle against evil-doers. He "collaborates with the Romans." And those readers eager to confer a certain documentary value, useful to the historian, upon the Talmud—so as to remove from it any doctrinal meaning all the more easily—will find in the following sentences a trace of the conflict between traditional Jewish society and those who thought possible the participation of Jews in the life of a State, of that State *par excellence* that was imperial Rome. However, even such a reading does not make it possible to ignore the existence of an underlying issue of doctrine in the Talmudic text. The "collaborator" is no common renegade but the very son of Rabbi Simeon bar Yochai! Perhaps all the acuteness of our contemporary dilemma is already present in our text: either to serve the ideal through an action concerned with preserving the framework of Judaism or to place oneself deliberately on the political level common to the men around us. This issue is not only present but discussed. The inner conflict arising from the contradictions of an action which, in order to fight against Evil, adopts the path of politics, the king's service, is already felt. And revolutionary action, which can go so far as to overthrow such a king, belongs to the service of the king—I think no one doubts this! Maybe this is why the sages of the fifth century of our era, who put the Gemara in writing, thought it useful to report the following exchange between Rabbi Eleazar ben Rabbi Simeon and Rabbi Joshua bar Karhah:

Rabbi Joshua bar Karhah relayed this to him: Vinegar, son of wine, how much longer will you deliver unto death the people of our God?

Vinegar, son of wine! Degenerate! You are the downfall of Judaism. Your father was wine. In you, this wine has turned to vinegar. Here you are, in the service of politics and, as a result, forced to participate in the work of the contemptible police! You have gone to the point of giving Jews up to the authorities!

Politics and Violence

To come to the point where one hands over Jews is certainly the utmost disgrace. Let beautiful souls be reassured concerning this statement of such petit-bourgeois racism and particularism. These sentences do not decide on Good and Evil on the basis of whether it is "good or bad for the Jews," a vulgar thought nevertheless proudly upheld, *mutatis mutandis,* by political men of all nations, who make of national loyalty their law and their highest morality. But those who shouted, a few months ago, "We are all German Jews" in the streets of Paris were after all not making themselves guilty of petit-bourgeois meanness.[5] German Jews in 1933, foreigners to the course of history and to the world, Jews, in other words, point to that which is most fragile and most persecuted in the world. More persecuted than the proletariat itself, which is exploited but not persecuted. A race cursed, not through its genes, but through its destiny of misfortune, and probably through its books, which call misfortune upon those who are faithful to them and who transmit them outside of any chromosomes. People of our God, in this very precise sense. It is of this people that Rabbi Joshua bar Karhah spoke to Rabbi Eleazar ben Simeon: Doesn't political action, be it revolutionary, turn against the people of God, against the persecuted, against the non-violence which it wishes for and for which a revolution is attempted? Doesn't political action turn against the non-violence which alone can end all persecution? Rabbi Eleazar answers:

I remove the thorns from the vineyard.

Rabbi Joshua bar Karhah retorts:

Let the owner of the vineyard come and remove the thorns himself.

This could mean many things. It is not up to you, in the name of universal politics, in the name of the king, to weaken moral laws. The concordance between Jewish destiny and the destiny of the world does not depend on human plans. The man who is integrally human is not to concern himself with politics. He must concern himself with morality. Vineyard—Israel. In the prophets, there is always a comparison between Israel and the vineyard. The vineyard of Israel belongs to its true and unique master—the Eternal One. Let the Eternal One resolve the conflict between morality and politics. A non-revolutionary interpretation, the interpretation of religious resignation. It is not up to us to punish our neighbors anyhow. God will take care of it. Taken to its ultimate conclusion, this would also mean: it is not up to us to build Israel. Let us wait for the Messiah. Unless, on the contrary, the text wanted to caution us against the confusion in which we live, in which Judaism is measured by its accord with progressivism, as though it did not indicate an autonomous and absolute order by which everything else is to be measured.

But the text can be read in yet another way. I refer to a commentator who made the following analogy, without drawing from it the conclusion that I propose to you (unless the analogy already meant this very idea for him and he did not see the need to insist upon it explicitly): "Vinegar, son of wine"—riff raff! The vineyard produced wine, in you this wine has turned to vinegar! You have betrayed the vine of the Lord that is Israel by associating it with the political activity of the Roman. Thus the meaning of Rabbi Eleazar's answer: If the wine became vinegar, it is because the vine is not as excellent as we think it is! The brambles which harm it must be removed. If I am violent, that is because violence is needed to put an end to violence. Rabbi Eleazar would then have been a revolutionary to the end: violence does not scare him. The vine's corruption has produced violence which, through violence, Rabbi Eleazar will bring to a halt. He will clean up society. By fire and steel; but then the only grapes there will be will be those that produce a wine which never turns into vinegar.

Beyond the Social Question

Rabbi Joshua bar Karhah's answer therefore keeps all its meaning: Let the proprietor of the vineyard come. Let him get rid of the thorns himself. It is not in political terms, with the unique alternative of the right and the left, that Evil must be dealt with, according to Judaism and according to which Judaism must itself be judged. While we recognize in Judaism, as in certain aspirations of the left, a defender of the human person—whose sacred rights are affirmed from the very first lines of our text, while we can admit that in extraordinary circumstances, violent action or a revolution imposes itself—we cannot identify the destiny of Judaism with the destiny of the proletariat. The Jewish cause is not exclusively a social cause. Doesn't anti-Jewish persecution aim at something else in Judaism, an intangible something? Someone here has said—I liked the expression very much—Judaism or responsibility for the entire universe, and consequently, a universally persecuted Judaism. To bear responsibility for everything and everyone is to be responsible despite oneself. To be responsible despite oneself is to be persecuted. Only the persecuted must answer for everyone, even for his persecutor. Ultimate responsibility can only be the fact of an absolutely persecuted man, having no right to a speech that would disengage him from his responsibility. We are a vineyard more complicated than a plot of land that is cultivated; only its owner, sublime particularism, is equal to the task of removing the thorns. In Rabbi Eleazar's acceptance of the political action in which revolution takes place, Rabbi Joshua bar Karhah saw a danger: the death of Judaism in revolutionary man. To what degree will revolution be fatal to Judaism, not because Judaism is a survival but because it is at the service of older, more delicate values than those at the disposal of socialism, because its endurance and its very patience are also at the breaking point? What values? This is not in the text I am commenting on. Outside of all political goals, my text affirms an obscurely perceived ideal, which prevents total assimilation and which exposes to persecution. In this persecution perhaps we see the dim recognition by everyone else of this irreducibility. People of God, in this sense. As if, beyond social and economic alienation, another alienation stalks man. As if only the owner of this secret garden could do that one thing that disalienates definitively, beyond any political disalienation. I think that a letter I will soon read you will bear witness to the fact that non-Jews can also feel this Jewish particularism. This adds to the acuteness of the tension between Judaism and universalism and confers upon Judaism a meaning beyond universalism, if one can express it thus.

A Letter

The author of this letter holds a prominent place in today's French literary world, if it could be said of a man like him that he holds a place without shocking him by all that the very idea of holding a place—even if it were sheer metaphor—evokes of the bourgeois and of comfort. I will not tell you his name. He participated in the May events in a total but lucid manner. He was deeply associated with them beyond the month of May. And suddenly he withdraws. In a letter which I did not expect, he wanted to give me his motives. He separated himself from his revolutionary friends when they opted against Israel. Here is the conclusion of his letter:

> No, I have always said that there was the limit beyond which I wouldn't go, but now I'd like to ask myself for a minute. . . . ask myself why these young people who are acting violently but also with generosity, felt they had to make such a choice, why they operated on thoughtlessness, on the usage of empty concepts (imperialism, colonization) and also on the feeling that it is the Palestinians who are the weakest, and one must be on the side of the weak (as if Israel were not extremely, dreadfully vulnerable). [The two Israels, I think: Mr. Israel and the State of Israel, for Israel is vulnerability itself.]
>
> But there is another reason, in my opinion. It is that in none of them is there any antisemitism, however latent, or even any idea of what antisemitism was.
>
> Thus it is not true that anti-Zionism is the antisemitism of today; that is

why the meaning of Israel itself, in its most obvious aspect, absolutely escapes them; I find this serious; it is as though Israel were put in peril by ignorance—yes, an innocent ignorance perhaps, but from now on gravely responsible and deprived of innocence—put in danger by those who want to exterminate the Jew because he is a Jew and by those who are completely ignorant of what it is to be Jewish. Antisemitism will now have as allies those who are as if deprived of antisemitism.

Isn't this a strange reversal, which proves that the absence of antisemitism is not enough?

Politics Questioned

Wasn't Rabbi Eleazar aware of this acute tension between political action and Jewish existence or, at least, wasn't he aware of the impossibility of understanding Judaism in terms of a political philosophy? Is it certain that Rabbi Eleazar enters into the service of the king, that he sees himself in a political capacity? The nature of the rest of the text makes us doubt this.

It is on a path of doubt and inner conflict that he finds himself. In any case, he never says "this is the order of the king" to justify the action that he undertakes from now on. This last expression recurs in the last section of our text—we already understand what it relates to—in the statement of Rabbi Ishmael ben Rabbi Jose, whom the prophet Elijah also reproaches with "handing over to death the people of our God." Rabbi Eleazar will know the unpopularity of daring and becomes open to being challenged: the doubt which Rabbi Joshua bar Karhah casts on the legitimacy of collaborating with the State nourishes the insults of the vulgar:

> One day a laundryman met him and called him: Vinegar, son of wine! Rabbi Eleazar said: His insolence is no doubt a sign that he is an evil-doer. He gave the order to arrest him.

Rabbi Eleazar senses crime beneath this insolence. (Do not interpret what I shall now say as analogous to contemporary events!) There is an abyss of difference between revolutionary protest and sheer verbal insolence. Sheer verbal violence is a symptom of criminality. A murderous insult is fatal to the one who makes it. Or, on a deeper level: the severing of the ties of language and the profanation of its internal laws increase criminality like a first breach in the wall of norms, like disobeying ritual laws.

And this is probably the meaning of the quotation that Rabbi Eleazar cites later from Proverbs, beyond the commonsense recommendation it contains. Insult and incontinence—this return to the scream, this scattering of the *logos*—set loose a disorder which from that moment onward becomes independent of good will. The verb keeps chaos chained. Grief to him who shatters language:

Rabbi Eleazar said: His insolence is no doubt a sign that he is an evil-doer. He gave the order to arrest him.

Rabbi Eleazar's anger cools, the forgiveness of the personal offense is not long in coming—and we see him, not recognizing the implacable sequence of events in the political order, trying to wrest free the man he had given over to this determinism. Unfortunately, the order—or disorder—of the law of politics is implacable. The man who has been given over to it cannot be regained.

After having calmed down, he went to set him free but this was no longer possible. He then said about him (Proverbs 21:23): "He who guards his mouth and tongue guards himself from trouble."

What follows is not to demonstrate that Rabbi Eleazar was a beautiful soul and that he felt remorse. He witnesses the execution of the man whose crime he had guessed beneath the insult received, but without being able to deduce the former from the latter. He cries over him as over an innocent man. Neither the respect for forms and their determinism nor simple intuition justifies the condemnation of a man in his eyes.

When they hanged him, he stood under the gallows and wept.

The Power of Man over Man

Rabbi Eleazar's infallible instinct is subsequently confirmed. Surely, it is only his instinct that justified his choice to enter politics, for he never derives support—like the police bureaucrat he replaced or like the scholar in our last paragraph—from the impossibility of challenging politics ("it is the order of the king"), the excuse which transforms the political man into a policeman.

Then they said to him: Master, calm yourself. Right on the Day of Atonement, he (the laundryman) and his son had illicit relations with the betrothed of another man. He put his hands on his own body and said: Rejoice, my innards, for if those who seem suspicious to us have come to this point, how much worse are those whose case is clear-cut? I am sure that neither worms nor decay will have power over you.

"The people of our God" is capable of all crimes then! No doubt the Talmud wants to remind us of this to put an end to so much mystifying and facile rhetoric! There are thorns in the garden of God. The disagreement between Rabbi Eleazar and Rabbi Joshua bar Karhah becomes even more pronounced. But something is said through its opposite which must also be understood. To condemn an innocent man—or even to condemn a guilty man without proof—is a fault that one cannot escape even in the grave.

There are deaths after death! This should not be seen as some sort of superstition. What is exposed here is the full range of the anxiety that comes with
the power of man over man.

> But he was nonetheless not reassured. He was given a sleeping draught. . . .
> (What follows in the text is a description of the ordeal to which Rabbi Eleazar's
> bowels are submitted and the discussion that arises from the ordeal's result.)

Uncertainty remains. Instinct, as sure as it can be, does not bear its own
justification within itself. That is why the ordeal, whose rather horrible details I spare you. Ordeal favorable to the instinct of Rabbi Eleazar and yet
debatable.

Between the position of Rabbi Eleazar and that of Rabbi Joshua bar
Karhah, what does one choose?

> The same thing happened to Rabbi Ishmael ben Rabbi Jose. One day, the
> prophet Elijah met him and said: How long will you deliver the people of our
> God to execution? He answered: What can I do; it is the order of the king.
> Elijah said to him: Your father fled to Asia; flee to Laodicea.

According to Talmudic tradition, the prophet Elijah, in the messianic
era, will resolve all antinomies. He makes his appearance in the last paragraph of the passage I am commenting on and seems to come back to the
thought of Rabbi Joshua bar Karhah. One must not hand over the children
of our God to the king. One must not enter the road of political violence to
combat Evil. It is possible to reject the political realm. One can flee to
Laodicea.

To go back to the private realm? To withdraw? To flee? To allow things
to go their own way? Do Elijah's words here have the full ring they will find
again at the time of the Messiah? And if they resound firmly against the one
who does not know how to question the order of the king, do they have the
same authority to stop "the one who wishes to weed the Lord's vineyard"?

NOTES

1. See the articles of Jean Lacroix and of Jacques d'Hondt in *Revue internationale
de philosophie* 35–36, consecrated to the crisis of humanism. See also the references
to Adam Schaff in Jean Lacroix's article.

2. Harpagon: title character in Molière's *The Miser*. Indicates a person who dem-
onstrates great avarice. (Trans.)

3. Rabbi Israel Salanter: the name of Israel Ben Ze'ev Wolf (1810–1883), founder
and spiritual father of the Musar movement, a moral movement based on the study
of traditional ethical literature. (Trans.)

4. In the *Ethics*, Spinoza distinguishes three levels at which the mind operates. Knowledge of the first kind, which Levinas refers to here, is belief or opinions, acquired by hearsay or by some arbitrarily chosen signs. Whatever ideas we form at this level are essentially images rather than thoughts, passive rather than active. (Trans.)

5. This colloquium was held not quite a year after the events of May 1968. "We are all German Jews" *(Nous sommes tous des juifs allemands)* was the cry taken up by demonstrators on May 22, 1968, when Daniel Cohn-Bendit, one of the leaders of the student movement, was refused permission to reenter France after having made a brief visit to West Germany. Cohn-Bendit is the son of German Jewish parents who emigrated to France in 1933. His background was used by people who opposed the May events to suggest that he was an outside agitator. The chanting of "We are all German Jews" was the student demonstrators' cry of solidarity with him. (Trans.)

THE YOUTH OF ISRAEL

- From the Tractate *Nazir*, pp. 66*a* and 66*b* -

Mishna   *Samuel was a nazirite, according to the words of Rabbi Nehorai, for it is said (1 Samuel 11): "And the razor (morah) will not touch his head." For Samson the word morah (razor) was said (Judges 13:5) and for Samuel the word morah (razor) was said. Just as the word morah in the case of Samson indicates the nazirate so it also indicates the nazirate in the case of Samuel. Rabbi Jose objected: Doesn't the word morah mean the fear inspired by creatures of flesh and blood? Rabbi Nehorai answered: But isn't it written: " 'How can I go,' said Samuel. 'If Saul hears of it, he will kill me' " (1 Samuel 16:2)? He thus, in fact, knew the fear inspired by a creature of flesh and blood.*

Gemara   *Rab said to Hiyya, his son: Snatch (the cup) and say grace. And, similarly, Rav Huna said to Raba, his son: Snatch the cup and say grace. Which means: greater is the one who says grace than the one who answers Amen. But don't we have a* baraita? *Rabbi Jose taught: He who answers Amen is greater than he who says grace. I swear that this is so, Rabbi Nehorai answered him. Know that it is the foot soldiers who begin the battle and that victory is attributed to the elite troops who appear as the battle is finishing. This problem was discussed among the Tanaim. There is a* baraita: *Both the one who says the blessing and the one who says Amen are included in the reward, but the one who blesses receives the reward first. Rabbi Eleazar said in the name of Rabbi Hanina: the disciples of the sages (talmide hakhamim) increase peace throughout the world for it is said (Isaiah 54:13): "All your children will be the disciples of the Eternal One; great will be the peace of your children."*

This reading was given in the context of a colloquium consecrated to "The Youth of Israel," held in October 1970. The proceedings were published in *Jeunesse et révolution dans la conscience jiuve: Données et débats* (Paris: P.U.F., 1972). Levinas's commentary appears on pp. 279–292; there was no discussion.

The Selection

The text which has been distributed to you has, on the surface of it, no connection to youth.

More serious still is the little connection that the various parts seem to have to each other. But their most suggestive teaching may lie in the underlying unity which they invite one to discover. That was one of my reasons for choosing it. There is, however, a less eccentric reason in its favor, which will not have escaped you. This text is about the *nazirate,* an institution explained in Numbers 6:1–21. The *nazirite* is a man who does not let his hair be cut: "throughout the term of his vow as nazirite, no razor shall touch his head." And the text of Numbers adds a justification to the prohibition, which, less contemporary than long hair itself, will certainly not convince everyone: "For the glory of his God is upon his head; as long as he wears this glory, he is consecrated to the Lord."

It is not in order to cut the verse in two and separate the law from the reasons adduced for it that I have chosen a text on the nazirate in regard to the youth of Israel. But while reading *Le Monde,* which knows everything, I was struck by the fact that long-haired youth wants to express, through its cumbersome hair style, its disagreement with the unjust society to which it nonetheless belongs. "We will not cut our hair until society changes," these young people say. Whether they want to or not, they are consecrated to the Lord! The second half of the verse reappears. It is here that we have the glory of God! I am convinced that the biblical text would never want a glory of God on the nazirite's head which did not mean or express before all else a demand for justice in the depths of his heart.

Acknowledging the Terms of the Text

But the institution of the nazirate, in the Book of Numbers, includes other rules. Let me set them forth before commenting on the text before you. It is indeed a pleasure for me to be able to say something precise in a talk on the essence of Judaism! These precise matters, apparently without mystery, are not least to yield precious suggestions. Of course, everything in the text is said in religious terms; but, in opposition to widespread prejudices about the particularism of Jewish religious thought, this language retains a quite rational and universal meaning, even for those who are sure— even absolutely sure—of their irreligion. An admirable certainty, let it be said in passing. To be sure of one's irreligion does not seem, to me, easier than to be sure of one's religious certainties. But let us leave that aside. The irreligious are people of firm beliefs. They do not doubt their freedom of thought.

Let us enter, then, despite our mistrust, into this religious language or imagery. Let us accept the givens of the text without devoting ourselves too soon to the psychoanalysis of its author—or authors—without suspecting anyone's intentions. Let us suppose that the text is sincere, and let us ask what it wants to say. Let us suppose that there is thought in the terms it makes use of and, consequently, that its words and representations can be transposed into another language and into other concepts. It is in this transposition that interpretation probably occurs. It would be impossible without a prior presentation of things, according to the very words of the text: "God," "consecrated to God," "glory of God." Let us not back away from these terms, but let us hope that from their very constellation in our text a meaning independent of any catechism will arise. Maybe we will even discover that the complex structures and unexpected meanings that our text teaches can only be said, in their multilateralness, in this religious language, from which interpretations—our own included—can only extract one aspect. Besides, I have never understood the radical difference one makes between philosophy and simple thought, as though all philosophies did not derive from non-philosophic sources. Often, all one needs to do is define an unusual terminology with words derived from Greek to convince the most difficult to please that one has just entered philosophy.

The Nazirate and Its Prohibitions

I come back now to the description of the nazirate. It is a condition the Israelite adopts for a set period as a consequence of a vow. Besides the promise not to cut one's hair, it includes two other prohibitions: during the entire period of the nazirate, the nazirite will drink no wine and will consume no product that comes from the vine: neither raisins nor the skin of grapes. Here, the text of the Bible itself extends the prohibition concerning wine to the products of the vine. As if the Law, in order to preserve from transgression, itself excluded anything which could, one thing leading to another, lead to transgression. As if the text of the Bible itself outlined the model for the "Fence around the Torah" to which the Rabbis' work will be devoted. It is to their work that countless prohibitions date back, prohibitions added to those stated in the Torah in order to ensure that the latter will be respected.

One last point: the nazirite forbids himself, during the period of the nazirate (which is a minimum of thirty days), all impure contact which is, *par excellence,* contact with the dead, or even being present in a room in which there is a dead person. It is certainly possible, through restraining one's will, neither to drink wine nor to consume any product of the vine. It is also fully within our power to keep our hair from a razor. Samson's hair, to be sure, was cut while he was sleeping; but the adventures that befell Samson do not occur frequently. It is obvious, however, that one can find oneself, without intending to, in a room in which a sudden death takes place. The nazirite can thus become impure despite himself. That, nonetheless, is enough to cut short his nazirate. He must then shave his head, offer a sacrifice called *Asham*, and begin the period of his nazirate again as he had established it when he made his initial vow.

This is the regulation of the nazirate, summarized in a very imperfect manner: besides the twenty-one verses of Numbers which institute it, a whole tractate of the Talmud—seventy double pages, one hundred thirty-two pages—are devoted to it. And at the end of these one hundred thirty-two pages are the thirty lines I have translated in order to comment on them.

But before going into my commentary, will you again allow me to guess at one of the 2,400,000 meanings that the prohibitions I have just summarized comprise? This no doubt assumes an infinitely greater knowledge than the one I possess but that certain orators imagine sufficient to exercise themselves on "Jewish thought." I hope that the Talmudists present here—and who at least know the extent of my ignorance in the matter—will forgive me for this attempt to explain. I consider it necessary so as not to disappoint the attentive gathering listening to me, which might be led to rebel against those eternal prohibitions with which every attempt to approach Judaism seems to end. What I am going to say will, therefore, be a way of understanding in conformity only with the little I have learned.

The Motivation

Why would contact with the dead render one impure? In Judaism, death is indeed a principle of impurity. It is even called the principle of principles or, according to a colorful but strictly technical expression, the grandfather of impurity: all spiritual impurity derives from contact with the dead. A mythological belief, you will say, and with the help of ethnography you will find it in other creeds. In the Jewish tradition, however, the impurity of the dead does not refer to the realm of the sacred and the profane. Contact with the dead is not a violation of a taboo. Death is the source of impurity because it threatens to take away all meaning from life, even when one has philosophically triumphed over death! For with each new contact with death, all meaning immediately risks being reduced to absurdity; the race to enjoy the moment, the *carpe diem*, may then become the only—sad—wisdom. Great engagements and great sacrifices are about to degenerate. Death is the principle of impurity.

Why the prohibition against wine? Because drunkenness is illusion, the disappearance of the problem, the end of responsibility, an artificial enthusiasm; and the nazirite does not wish to be deceived, or to be relieved of the weight of existence by forgetting Evil and misfortune. Lucidity, realism, absolute fidelity in a lucid state and not in drunkenness and exaltation.

Why long hair? What I will tell you about it later will justify somewhat the interpretation that I am attempting right now. Not to let one's hair be cut for the duration of the nazirate and the necessity of shaving one's head at the end of the nazirate, that is the Law. When the nazirite comes to the end of the period of his vow, he presents himself before the altar of the Temple, offers a sacrifice, has his hair cut, throws it in the fire, and drinks wine. But isn't letting his hair grow during the period of the nazirate a way of being "straightforward" [droit devant soi] without worrying about one's appearance? A way of being, "without a mirror": to be, without turning toward oneself? Anti-narcissism! Why is one obligated to shave one's head as soon as the vows of the nazirate are over? Perhaps to prevent the noble violence one has done to oneself from becoming sweet custom and the protest against institutions from becoming an institution. To let one's hair grow, not to look at oneself, not to come back upon oneself, not to be concerned with the effect one is having, not to measure the extent of one's daring—nothing is more beautiful, as long as purity and lucidity remain! But beware of audacity that has become a profession! Beware of the insolence practiced when all revolutionary consciousness has been extinguished. One must let one's hair grow, certainly, but at a certain point it must be cut. It threatens to become the uniform of the non-conciousness of self. Indifference toward self, contempt of appearance, undoubtedly, but also youth becoming a business firm and soon laying claims. Long hair worn as a uniform, that is the great scandal of long hair.

Here, then, is the possible motivation of several rites. The Talmud warns us against seeking for such motivations. Knowing the reasons for an imperative is sufficient to render it hypothetical, both in the Kantian and in the common meaning of the term. One immediately begins to think that the dangers warded off by the imperative surely threaten everyone in the world but me. This was, apparently, the misfortune of King Solomon: he was no doubt convinced that too many wives will make any man stray, as Scriptures point out, but thought himself above such contingencies. You know what became of him. I have thus committed a serious transgression in seeking reasons for the three prohibitions of the nazirite regulation. But at least I have given a glimpse of the loftiness of this condition, to which one can consecrate all of one's life, just as one can commit oneself to it for a limited time of at least thirty days.

Nazirate and Priesthood

The high priest is its model. Will what I have said about the nazirate rehabilitate, in the eyes of some, notions as suspect of clericalism as the Temple, the cult performed in it, and the priests consecrated to it? Whatever opinion one may have about the historicity of the institutions these suggest, one must read in their own language the books in which the norms expressing Judaism's vision of the world and its message are established, the books in which Judaism is being thought out. Before any history or sociology, one must decipher the texts' own language.

The high priest and the priests who are on duty—their turn comes periodically—are subject to the same prohibitions as the nazirites. They do not touch their hair for thirty days, do not enter the Temple if they have drunk wine. The commentators explain the violent death of the two eldest sons of the high priest Aaron, described in Leviticus 10, by the fact that they had gone into the Tabernacle without respecting this principle. Lastly, contact with the dead is permanently prohibited to the priests. Is the priest a permanent nazirite? Is the nazirite a temporary priest? The analyses of the Talmud shy away from such formulations, which are lacking in nuance. But doesn't the obvious analogy between the two sets of prohibitions and rituals provide an additional metaphor for expressing the loftiness connected to the nazarate, to the consecration to the Lord? The nazirite experiences the exceptional state of the priest penetrating the Temple, the metaphor for access to the Very High, and for a liturgy which one person alone performs for the collectivity, the peak of election: the service of one for all.

Lovable Youth

Where, in all this, is youth? After this morning's debate and what was said about it, particularly by Vladimir Jankélévitch and Mlle de Fontenay, youth appeared to us as a certain instability, if defined by age, as a notion insignificant in itself, dangerous when one recalls the usage which fascism made of it, using it to make people forget the real oppositions and conflicts of men.[1] And yet the attraction which the ideal of youth exercises on men is great, even if one refuses such definitions of it as youth-pride, youth-spontaneity, youth-denial of the past, youth-freedom, under the pretext that all these attributes have their other side of cruelty, barbarism, facileness. Nonetheless, youth is eminently desirable and eminently lovable in another. One could not speak of it in a pejorative fashion. When one contests youth one says that true youth is elsewhere. One is already using youth to attack youth.

Isn't the text to which I refer guided by a less dialectical concept of youth, less likely to allow the grace of youth to be parodied into egoism, and above all—and paradoxically—into the designation of that which is eminently perishable in human nature?

The Nazirite of Simeon the Just

Before getting to the text in front of you, I am going to start with another passage in the same tractate, page 4b. At issue there is a noble mode of existence, in which the phenomenon one can call youth appears. It is the story of an altogether unusual nazarate; many among you probably know it; it is a story that some of us, if not all of us, have been cradled by in our childhood: "Simeon the Just said. . . ." Simeon the Just is an extremely well known person. In the *Sayings of the Fathers*—in the *Pirke Avoth*, which you cited today, Mlle de Fontenay—right at the beginning, among the first "sayings" there is the one from Simeon the Just. "Simeon the Just was among the last sages of the Great Synagogue." A quite ancient scholar of the Law. He was the one who received Alexander the Great in Jerusalem. This makes us go back to rather out-of-the-ordinary relations; and Alexander the Great, who was no less a Greek for being Macedonian and who had Aristotle himself for a teacher, forms an opinion of traditional Judaism to which the young men of today, who think themselves profoundly Greek for having studied a bit of philosophy, do not always rise. Here, then, is what Simeon the Just says, according to page 4*b* of the tractate *Nazir* (without mentioning Alexander the Great, he makes us think of a Greek story): "Simeon the Just said: In my entire life, I have never participated in the meal accompanying the sacrifice of the nazirite who has become impure." The sacrifice referred to is that of the nazirite who has become impure through contact with a dead person, who is obligated to cut his hair before starting the period of his nazirate again; the sacrifice includes a meal in which the priest participates. And Simeon the Just was a high priest. He never in his life participated in such a meal. Why? The commentator explains: because he doubted that a nazirite whose nazirate had been interrupted could have the courage to begin the ordeal in its integrality again. He feared that the offered sacrifice would be without sincere intention, which would be a complete profanation of the sacrifices. Simeon the Just never wanted to participate in an act of profanation:

> In my entire life, I have never participated in the meal accompanying the sacrifice of the nazirite who has become impure, except for the meal accompanying the sacrifice of a young man who had come from the South. He had a nice appearance and beautiful eyes and hair falling in beautiful curls. I said to him: "My son, why did you decide to ruin such beautiful hair?" [Did he not, in fact, come to offer a sacrifice and to have his hair cut but, above all, would he not, in any case, have had to cut it at the end of his nazirate?] The young man then answered: "I was a shepherd in my village and watched my father's flocks. I would go to drink in the stream and, one day, I saw my image in it—my evil inclination. [Or my "instinct"? Or my "evil instinct"? Or my "person"? Or my "self"? The term used here, which I have tried to translate, is *Yitzri*, my *yetzer*, a noun which refers to the verb *Yatzor*, to create. *Yitzri*: perhaps "what there is of the creature in me."] And then, *yitzri* flew into a passion [or got drunk] and tried to chase me from the world [or from my world]. I said to it: 'Good-for-nothing, you derive pride from a world which isn't yours and in which you will finish as food for worms. By God, I will have your hair cut.'" Then [Simeon the Just adds] I got up, kissed the young man on the head and said to him: "Let nazirites like you be numerous in Israel; it is of you that Scriptures say: 'If a man expressly vows to be a nazirite, wanting to abstain in honor of the Eternal. . . .'"

And the Tosafist[2] comments: "From the start, this one's vow was dedicated to Heaven," was disinterested. Simeon the Just correctly understood that this one would not go back on his vows from having become impure through an unforeseeable contact with a dead person; but most nazirites make vows either when they are in trouble or to atone for a sin. The act of penance is thus considered by our commentator as an act done in self-interest. With the light shed by the Tosafist, this text reveals the meaning of the nazirate: disinterestedness. Not only in the exclusively moral sense of the term which disinterestedness without a doubt includes but in an even more radical sense. At issue here is a disinterestedness opposed to the *essence* of a being, which essence is precisely always persistence in essence, the return of essence upon itself, self-consciousness and complacency in self. As the young shepherd saw so well, it is not only a persistence but a growing old and dying. Self-consciousness, the forgetfulness of senescence, senseless pride! That is what the nazirite *par excellence*, which Simeon the Just met, resisted. It is that self-contemplation he shunned: what he objected to was not being beautiful but looking at oneself being beautiful. He rejected the narcissism which is self-consciousness, upon which our Western philosophy and morality are built. I say *our*. But the young shepherd of Simeon the Just rejected thought thinking itself, by which Aristotle's God is defined and with which Hegel's *Encyclopedia* and perhaps Western philosophy end. Did he feel that he was leaving the world, leaving the order that was his? Did he feel that in self-contemplation he was losing himself? His nazirate must be perceived at this level.

Engagement and Freedom

The text we are about to begin must be read as a continuation of what came before. It will teach us something new about the nazirate. It may bring out an idea about youth which is altogether different from the one our nazirite fought with when he felt himself triumphant but mad before his own image.

> Samuel was a nazirite according to the words of Rabbi Nehorai, for it is said (1 Samuel 11): "And the razor *(morah)* will not touch his head. . . .

The problem of the Mishna, which is very elliptically stated, is the following. There is a whole ritual through which the vows of the nazirate are taken. One is committed to them immediately; for one can die at any moment and find oneself unable to keep the commitment one has taken on. The future is present and cannot be deferred. (I cannot go into the meaning of this urgency here, which stands out in many of the discussions of the tractate *Nazir*.) But you can also take the vows by simply saying before a nazirite passing before you: "I want to be like this one." Can one become a nazirite by saying: "I want to be like Samuel?" (Samuel is the prophet Samuel, with whom 1 Samuel begins in the biblical canon.) Yes, if Samuel is considered a nazirite. It is precisely this that our Mishna discusses. In the biblical text, the word nazirite is not used in regard to Samuel. Rabbi Nehorai nonetheless thinks that Samuel was fully a nazirite. How does he know? For it is said: (1 Samuel 1:11): "And the razor (morah) will not touch his head."

What an odd nazirate! In the biblical text it is Samuel's mother who makes the vow: "The razor will not touch his head." Samuel himself has not yet been conceived when the promise is made. It is a vow which concerns only the hair. Not a word about impurity, not a word about the vine. But everything happens as though the vow made by the mother counted, as if personal engagement, freely undertaken—the guarantee of spirituality in our philosophical West—was not the supreme investiture of a vocation. As though, beyond the cult of youth, of newness, of the personal engagement which this liberalism contains, a high density of obligation could begin before our beginning, in the internal value of the tradition. That is at least what is at stake here.

To prove that Samuel is a nazirite, as if the problem at issue here were purely practical (does one become a nazirite when one says: "I want to be like Samuel?"), Rabbi Nehorai reasons by analogy:

> For Samson the word morah (razor) was said (Judges 13:5). Just as the word morah said in the case of Samson indicates the nazirate so it also indicates the nazirate in the case of Samuel.

Samson also is a nazirite engaged without having made a personal decision. It is not even his mother who pronounces the vows but a messenger of the Lord or an angel. And a vow which is God's command. Samson will be a nazirite by divine will. The nazirate of Samuel would thus be of the same kind as that of Samson. An angel of God utters the vows for you and, there you are, committed! Nothing is more scandalous to a consciousness for which everything must begin in a free act and for which self-consciousness, completing consciousness, is supreme freedom. But the biblical text about Samson explicitly calls him a nazirite, even before his conception. The angel says to Samson's mother: "Now be careful not to drink wine or any other intoxicant, or eat anything unclean. For you are going to conceive and bear a son; let no razor (morah) touch his head for the boy is to be a nazirite to God (to Elohim—God as God of strict justice) from the womb on" (Judges 13:4–5). And later on the angel—or the emissary of the Lord—as if referring to the regulation of the nazirite, forbids the mother to eat "what the vine produces" (Judges 13:14).

Would Samson of the long hair also be the prototype of the nazirite, just like Simeon the Just's young shepherd with the magnificent curls? Must Samuel, whom the tradition compares to Moses and Aaron, be recognized as a nazirite by analogy with Samson? For isn't it written (Psalm 99:6): "Moses and Aaron among His priests, Samuel among those who call on His name: when they called to the Lord, He answered them"? Both are dedicated to a vocation they had not chosen. But Samson is a youth. His whole tragedy is a tragedy of youth, made of the mistakes and loves of youth. That the loftiness of the nazirite could find a norm in the destiny of Samson leads us to question ourselves further about the possibilities of youth and about the essence of spirituality. We seem to be outside the meaning that Simeon the Just gives to the nazirate. Rabbi Jose's intervention is therefore fully understandable:

> Rabbi Jose objected: Doesn't the word *morah* mean the fear inspired by creatures of flesh and blood?

Fearless

Morah would mean "fear" and not "razor" if the Hebrew word is written with an *aleph* at the end instead of a *he!* "The razor will not touch his head" would become "Fear will never be above his head." Besides, one can find the same meaning in the verse, without substituting an *aleph* for a *he*, by deriving, according to the suggestion of the commentator Maharsha,[3] the word *morah* from *maruth*, meaning "power" and "lordship." The translation would then be: "And upon his head the power of another will never be exercised." And then, indeed, our text becomes very significant. The nazirite would be defined, according to Rabbi Jose, as the one who fears no one or, more precisely, as the one who does not fear power. Definition of the nazirite or definition of youth? They overlap in the person of Samson. Definition of youth which has not yet been attempted today. It is, in any case, better than the one, so vague, evoking "creativity," which is almost as irritating and as trite as the word "dialogue."

Unfortunately, the opinion of Rabbi Jose is contested:

> Rabbi Nehorai answered: But isn't it written: " 'How can I go,' said Samuel. 'If Saul hears of it, he will kill me.' " He thus, in fact, knew the fear inspired by a creature of flesh and blood.

Rabbi Nehorai's answer refers to the text of 1 Samuel 16:2. When Saul, going against the order given him by Samuel, spares Agag, king of Amalek, Saul's reign is virtually over in the Lord's eyes; God therefore sends Samuel to Bethlehem so that he can anoint as king the man who will be pointed out to him there. It will be David. But Samuel is afraid of this mission. If Saul were to find out about it, he would put him to death. And, strange text, the Lord shares this fear!

Would God not have enough power to ensure the security of his emissary? He prefers to teach Samuel a ruse. Samuel's coming to Bethlehem will be under the pretext of a local festival. Probably the Lord thinks that the government has some rights and some reasons for being. There is, in this text, a backing away from the revolutionary act. According to Rabbi Nehorai, at least, it is not in rash courage and in contempt of established power that the nazirate resides. If nazirate and youth go together, youth must not be reduced to the revolutionary spirit!

Nonetheless, I liked what Rabbi Jose said very much and I am sure his position appealed to everyone here. One can even suspect that it appealed a great deal to the sages of the Torah, who could have dispensed with reproducing a refuted opinion here. It is nevertheless reproduced. To challenge power in the name of an absolute is an unreasonable thing, but daring and noble. Should one say that because the nazirite is consecrated to God, he does not fear anyone, or is it because he does not fear anyone that he is consecrated to God? The two propositions are not equivalent! As for me, I do not seek the meaning of the term "God"—at once the most understandable and the most mysterious—in some theological system. I will try to understand it on the basis of a situation in which a man appears who truly does not fear anyone.

It is nonetheless Rabbi Nehorai who has the last word.

It is not, after all, courage and the challenging of power that define the nazirate and youth. With courage, one never knows exactly where one is going. There may be in that rash fearlessness and in its violence an element of pride and facileness: of cruelty, no doubt. A just violence: when, around us, all is pitiable creature! Think of the text of the tractate *Sanhedrin*, p. 93*b*, in which Ullah and Rabah and Rabbi Johanan[4] prefer not to experience messianic times so as not to witness the violence with which the triumph of absolute justice will have to be surrounded. Permanent theme. It is perhaps this that Rabbi Nehorai had in mind when he recalled the fear that Samuel experienced one day in thinking of King Saul's revenge, and when he recalled the Lord, our all-powerful God, who shared this fear, in order not to identify the nazirate with the end of the fear that human government can inspire.

Methodology

Rab said to Hiyya, his son: Snatch (the cup) and say grace.

I am now coming to the Gemara, where one would expect a commentary on the Mishna but where, to all appearances, something else is at issue. In fact, the entire Gemara of this last Mishna of the tractate *Nazir* seems to be made up of selected passages. The beginning of the text can be found in the tractate *Berakoth*, and the end of our text makes up the last part of three tractates: *Yebamot*, *Berakoth* once again, and *Nazir*, where we are. Would the Gemara be purely decorative here, ending a tractate of Halakhah with a few aggadic words to leave us pensive or to inspire us with pious thoughts? Such a way of reading should not be excluded; but it is not forbidden to be more demanding.

Let us ask ourselves what themes are broached in our Gemara. They are two: the first, concerning the merit one acquires by saying grace—grace over wine, in our example—is compared to the merit of answering *Amen* when hearing the blessing. Which is greater? Just think how important this is! Already, I can hear the outcry of short-sighted people, the famous "Let's be serious!" It permits you not to enter into the intention of your opponent when it makes you uneasy, especially when it is too lofty for the physical condition of your eyes. To know whether the merit of the person who blesses is greater than the merit of the one who answers *Amen* would in no way be a serious problem for a modern person who has read so many books. This remains to be seen.

As to the second theme evoked by the Gemara, it seems to be a pious thought and nothing more: the sages of the Talmud claim to make peace reign in the world:

> Rabbi Eleazar said in the name of Rabbi Hanina: the disciples of the sages increase peace throughout the world, for it is said (Isaiah 54:13): "And all thy children shall be taught of the Lord; and great shall be the peace of thy children."

Should we nonetheless ask ourselves whether there is something serious in this frivolous piety? Two problems arise: a) What does this Gemara mean? b) What is the intrinsic connection between the Gemara and our Mishna? There is even a third problem: the link between all this and youth. This last problem calls to account the one who has chosen this text to interpret to you.

What is the meaning of the text "Rab said to Hiyya, his son: Snatch (the cup) and say grace"? People are gathered together. A goblet of wine is brought so that a blessing can be said over it. Who is going to say this blessing? The father teaches his son: Grab the cup, say the blessing. That is worth more than saying *Amen* to a blessing said by another. And this teaching of the father to his son must be significant. Doesn't Rav Huna also say to his son: "Snatch the cup and say grace"?

From which we get the impossible conclusion of the Gemara, words hardly decent in their apparent egocentrism: "Which means: greater is the one who says grace than the one who answers *Amen*." But there is a problem. "Don't we have a *baraita*?" That is, a Mishna that has not been included in the collection of Rabbi Judah Hanassi, which states: "Rabbi Jose (the same Rabbi Jose who speaks in our Mishna) taught: He who answers *Amen* is greater than he who says grace." Rabbi Jose was thus in favor of a doctrine in which the merit of the one who says *Amen* surpasses the merit of the one who says the blessing. To which Rabbi Nehorai—this time in agreement with Rabbi Jose, who had contradicted him in our Mishna—added: "I swear that this is so. Know that it is the foot soldiers who begin the battle and that victory is attributed to the elite troops, who appear as the battle is finishing." This was, then, already known at the time: the poor soldiers get themselves killed; the officers attribute the victory to themselves!

But what is the connection between foot soldiers and the saying of grace, between elite forces and the *Amen?* Seemingly an altogether external connection: the one who comes last carries the day; thus the one who says *Amen* carries away the merit. What old wives' tales! What a foolish story! What strange logic, which goes from the realm of blessings to military images. This is not something to be taken seriously.

I am greatly assisted in getting out of this uncomfortable position by a commentator of the seventeenth century, whose texts, signed Maharsha, have great authority and are present, in the good editions, in the very text of the Gemara itself.

Here is his remark. His—religious—language must, to be sure, still be interpreted in order to reveal the additional, profane meaning it contains. But reading the Gemara is a permanent deciphering and, what is more, a deciphering without a code.

Saying Grace and the Third World

Saying grace would be an act of the greatest importance. To be able to eat and drink is a possibility as extraordinary, as miraculous, as the crossing of the Red Sea. We do not recognize the miracle this represents because we live in a Europe which, for the moment, has plenty of everything, and not in a Third World country, and because our memory is short. There they understand that to be able to satisfy one's hunger is the marvel of marvels. To return to a stage of indigence in Europe, despite all the progress of civilization, is a most natural possibility for us, as the war years and the concentration camps have shown. In fact, the route which takes bread from the earth in which it grows to the mouth which eats it is one of the most perilous. It is to cross the Red Sea. An old Midrash, conceived in this spirit, teaches: "Each drop of the rain which is to water your furrows is led by 10,000 angels so that it may reach its destination." Nothing is as difficult as being able to feed oneself! So that the verse "You will eat and be full and you will bless" (Deuteronomy 8:10) is not pious verbiage but the recognition of a daily miracle and of the gratitude it must produce in our souls. But the obligation of gratitude goes further. According to the Rabbis' way of speaking, saying grace arouses favorable angels, intercessors capable of fighting the evil spirits who place themselves between food and those who are hungry and who watch for and create any occasion for preventing bread from reaching the mouth. Isn't all this the form of a bygone rhetoric? But perhaps what we have here is a description of the charming society we live in, the society of free competition and capitalist contradictions.

If one agrees with this last proposition, the linking of the saying of grace with military combat is more understandable. But how will saying grace create champions of the good cause? Let us not stay within figures of speech! It is obvious that what is suggested to us here are peaceful struggles: the problem of a hungry world can be resolved only if the food of the owners and those who are provided for ceases to appear to them as their inalienable property, but is recognized as a gift they have received for which thanks must be given and to which others have a right. Scarcity is a social and moral problem and not exclusively an economic one. That is what our text reminds us of, through old wives' tales. And now we can understand that this internal and pacific war is to be waged not only by me, who in saying grace gives up possession, but also by those who answer *Amen*. A community must follow the individuals who take the initiative of renouncing their rights so that the hungry can eat. Very important, then, are these ideas of food and of struggle, all this materialism extending the laws of the nazirate.

The linking, apparently with so little basis, of our Gemara and our Mishna, is not due to some concern for piling up homiletic texts. Nor is it due to the fact that the protagonists of the Mishna are the same as the ones in the cited *baraita*. It teaches us that there must be a nazirate in the world—a source of disinterestedness—so that men can eat. To feed those who are hungry assumes a spiritual elevation. There must be a nazirate so that the Third World, so-called underdeveloped mankind, can eat its fill; so that the West, despite its abundance, does not revert to the level of an underdeveloped mankind. And, inversely, to feed the world is a spiritual activity.

Here, then, is a good reason for linking the theme of the nazirate to the theme of saying grace and the *Amen*. It does not matter whether the initiative of the individual who "snatches and says grace" carries more weight than that of the masses who imitate him or say *Amen* and follow him upon this path, which is the giving up of one's rights, the recognition of non-Roman property. This makes understandable for us the conciliatory but firm text which follows and which reminds us of the great antiquity of the problem:

> This problem was discussed among the *Tanaim*. There is a *baraita:* Both the one who says the blessing and the one who says *Amen* are included in the reward, but the one who blesses receives the reward first.

The Student of the Torah and Youth

A final problem remains: that which lies beyond this pacific struggle and is the condition for its success. To redeem the world through daring and renouncement, to redeem the world through goodness and struggle—to succeed in this, isn't it necessary to rise even higher? Is the nazirate to be limited to the vocations of priest, hero, or social reformer?

It is at this point that the types who hold the highest place in Judaism come into view: the *talmid-haham*, the student of the Torah, and the judge who has studied the Torah and applies it. There are the scholars of the Torah. And here again the commentator Maharsha has helped me a great deal. What is even more important than good will between men or, according to the words of Maharsha himself (and it is really a very beautiful language, probably much richer in meaning than the one I have extracted from it might lead one to suspect), what is more important than the creation of intercessor angels is the judge who reconciles men. Both Samuel and Samson were judges. We forget this about Samson; we always see in him the handsome fellow who rips apart the front gate of a city and who strikes down a crowd of Philistines with one stroke of an ass's jaw.

The Bible says: He was a judge in Israel for forty years. In order to be a judge in Israel, he must have known the Oral Law. At least that is how it must have been in the eyes of the sages of the Talmud. In the eyes of the sages, he must have been involved, anachronistically, in the future discussions of *Tanaim, Amoraim,* and *Gaonim.* In any event, in spirit and in truth, Samson must have been a *talmid-haham.* Beneath the youth who dares, beneath the youth of good will, is the youth of the one who studies the Torah and who judges.

Why youth? Because the text expresses itself thus: "All your children will be the disciples of the Eternal One." Children of Israel, children of the Eternal One. Youth is equivalent to the condition of a child, no matter what the age of the child! Youth is the state of receptivity to all that is permanent and quite the opposite of the "Oedipus complex." The children of Israel, students of the Torah, are youth *par excellence.* They are the ones who, in receiving the Torah, renew it.

The quotation of the verse from Isaiah 54:13, "All your children will be the disciples of the Eternal One; great will be the peace of your children," is followed in the tractates *Berakoth* and *Yebamot,* in which it is also evoked, by the following remark: "One must read, not 'banaik,' your children, but 'bonaik,' your builders." Great is the peace of your builders. To receive while building. To bring peace into the world by renewing it constructively, that is the youth of the nazirate, that is youth.

Older than Any Life and Younger than Any Youth

But a further step can be taken to rediscover this essence of a youth younger than any youth, in the peculiar arrangement of the text which juxtaposes the attachment to the Law of justice, in turn connected to the nazirate, to the idea of the nazirate referring to Samson and Samuel. Samson and Samuel had been "consecrated" before growing in their mother's wombs. These two nazirites did not begin their nazirate by their own decision, but on God's command and through the vow of a mother. It does not matter! They began their nazirate before birth. From which stems an idea which I personally find extraordinary and which I had an opportunity to present to the colloquium regarding another text: the attachment to the Good precedes the choosing of this Good.[5] How, indeed, to choose the Good? The Good is good precisely because it chooses you and grips you before you have had the time to raise your eyes to it. *Formally*, it thus challenges your freedom; but if no one is good through free choice, no one is a *slave* to the Good. Precisely because the other who commands us thus is the Good, he redeems, by his goodness, the violence done to the "freedom" before freedom. We thus arrive at the idea of a consecration—of a nazirate—older than the age at which we choose. The absolute nazirite is older than his life. Extraordinary old age! But also the absolute nazirite bears, throughout all his life, the mark of an unimaginable youth, of a youth before youth, of a youth which precedes all aging. The children of Israel are quite an anachronism! The nazirate is not the youth of beginnings; it is preteroriginal youth, before the entry into historical time. "The children of this tribe are counted for the census before they are of age, from their very presence in their mother's womb," the passage of *Midrash Tanhuma* concerning Numbers 3:15 tells us; this also appears in *Bereshit Rabba* 94:1. The passage is about the tribe of Levi, in which are born the priests and those consecrated to the Holy One. It is about their absolute youth, before the time of the world.

But that, ladies and gentlemen, is not just the youth of levites and nazirites. It is the youth of Israel.

NOTES

1. *Jeunesse et révolution dans la conscience juive. Données et débats* (Paris, P.U.F., 1972), pp. 230–242.
2. See note 3 in Levinas's Introduction to "Four Talmudic Readings." (Trans.)
3. See note 1 in "As Old as the World?" (Trans.)
4. See *Difficile liberté*, 2d ed., p. 107.
5. See "The Temptation of Temptation." (Trans.)

DESACRALIZATION AND DISENCHANTMENT

■ From the Tractate *Sanhedrin*, pp. 67a–68a ■

Mishna   *The seducer is he who says: Let us go and worship the stars.
The sorcerer, if he performs an act, is subject to penalties,
but not if he merely creates illusions. Rabbi Akiba, in the
name of Rabbi Joshua has said: Two people pick cucumbers:
one of them is subject to penalties, the other is exempt; the
one who performs the act is subject to penalties, the one that
gives the illusion of it is exempt.*

Gemara   *The seducer. Rav Judah declared in the name of Rab: "At issue here is a seducer in an unfaithful city (see Deuteronomy
13:14).*

    The sorcerer, if he performs an act, etc. There is a baraita:
*The text says "sorceress," whether it be man or woman; but
one says "sorceress" because the vast majority of women engage in sorcery.*

    How should they be executed?

    *Rabbi Jose the Galilean said: It is written (Exodus 22:18)
"You will not let the sorceress live" and there it is said
(Deuteronomy 20:16): "You will not let (live) a soul." As
there with a sword, so here with a sword.*

    *Rabbi Akiba has said: It is written here (Exodus 22:18):
"You shall not let the sorceress live," and it is written there
(Exodus 19:13): "Man or beast must be stoned; they shall
cease to live." As there through stoning, so here through
stoning.*

    *Rabbi Jose said to him: I draw my conclusion from equal
wording, "You will not let live," but you draw your conclusion from "You will not let live," which you compare to
"And he will cease to live" (unequal terms).*

This reading was given in the context of a colloquium on "The Jews in a Desacralized Society," held in October 1971. The proceedings appeared in *L'autre dans la conscience juive: Le
sacré et le couple: Données et débats* (Paris: P.U.F., 1973). Levinas's commentary appears on
pp. 55–74, and the discussion that follows on pp. 75–78.

Rabbi Akiba answered: I have drawn an analogy between two verses referring to Israelites, for whom Scripture decrees many modes of execution, while you have compared Israelites to idolaters, in whose case only one death penalty is decreed.

Ben Azai said: It is said: "You will not let the sorceress live" (Exodus 22:18), and right afterward: "Whosoever will have intercourse with an animal shall be put to death" (Exodus 22:19). The two matters are compared. Since he who has intercourse with an animal must be stoned, so must the sorceress be stoned.

Rabbi Judah replied: Is the fact that the two things are close together sufficient reason not to exempt the sorceress from stoning? Here is the real reasoning: Ov and Yidoni (necromancers and casters of spells) belong to the genre of sorceresses. Why were they mentioned separately (Deuteronomy 18:10)? To reason by analogy: just as Ov and Yidoni are punishable by stoning (Leviticus 20:27), so are sorcerers.

But the following objection can be made to Rav Judah: against Ov and Yidoni, two verses teach us the same thing. From two verses teaching the same thing, nothing can come. Rabbi Zechariah answered: This indicates that, according to Rabbi Judah, two verses saying the same thing can indeed teach us.

Rabbi Johanan said: Why is sorcery called Keshafim? *Because it challenges the Assembly on High (makhishin familia shel maala). "The Holy One is God; there is no other" (Deuteronomy 4:35).*

Rabbi Hanina said: This even concerns sorcery: the story of a woman who went to gather dust from under the feet of Rabbi Hanina. He told her: If you can, go and do it. For it is written: "There is no other" (Deuteronomy 4:35). How is this possible? Didn't Rabbi Johanan say: Why do we call it sorcery? Because it challenges the Assembly on High. For Rabbi Hanina it was otherwise because he had many merits.

Rabbi Aibu bar Nagri said, in the name of Rabbi Hiyya bar Abba: Done by the Latehem *(see, for example, Exodus 7:22), magical action is the action of demons; done by the La-hatehem, magical action is a matter of sorcery. Isn't it said (Genesis 3:24): "The blade of the fiery, everturning sword (lahat hasherev hamithapeshet)"?*

Abaye said: When the sorcerer insists upon exact paraphernalia, the magic is the work of demons; otherwise, it is simply sorcery.

Abaye said: the Halakhah on sorcery resembles the halakhah on the Shabbath. Some actions are punishable by stoning; some are not punishable, yet are forbidden; some are entirely permissible. He who performs an action is stoned— as in the one who picks cucumbers; he who creates an illusion is not punishable, yet he performs a forbidden action. Some actions are entirely permissible: like the one of Rabbi Hanina and Rabbi Oshaia, who, every Shabbath eve, studied the doctrine of creation, by means of which they created a calf one-third grown and ate it.

Rav Ashi related: I once saw Abhu of Karna blow his nose and balls of silk came from his nostrils.

Then the magicians said to Pharaoh (Exodus 8:15): "This is the finger of God." Rabbi Eleazar said: From this we learn that the demon cannot create a being smaller than a barleycorn in size.

Rav Papa said: By God! he cannot create a being even as large as a camel, but he can assemble him; but not those smaller than a barleycorn.

Rab was telling Rabbi Hiyya: I once saw an Arab cut a camel into pieces with his sword. Then he beat a drum before it and the camel came back to life. Rabbi Hiyya responded: Did you find blood and dung (after this performance)? It was only an illusion.

One day Ze'iri went to Alexandria, in Egypt, and bought himself an ass. When he went to give it something to drink, the spell broke and he found himself sitting on the boards of a gangway. Then the others said to him: If you weren't Ze'iri, we wouldn't give you back your money. For here no one buys anything without first testing his purchase by water.

One day Jannai came to an inn and asked for some water to drink. When a woman handed him shattitha, he noticed that her lips moved. He spilled some of it on the ground; they were scorpions. He then said to her: I drank of yours, drink of mine. When she had drunk, she changed into an ass. He got on the ass and rode out into the street. There, a friend of the woman broke the spell, and Jannai was seen riding upon a woman.

"And the frog came, and covered the land of Egypt" (Exodus 8:2). Rabbi Eleazar said: There was only one frog but it bred prolifically and filled all the land of Egypt. This was already a discussion among the Tanaim; Rabbi Akiba said: There was only one frog, which filled all the land of Egypt.

*Rabbi Eliezar ben Azariah said to him: Akiba, Akiba, why are
you meddling in Aggadah; stop what you are saying and turn
to problems of leprosy and tents. There was only one frog,
but it whistled for all the others and they came.*

*Rabbi Akiba said. . . . It was Rabbi Joshua, then, who
taught the matter to Rabbi Akiba. But we have a toseftah:
When Rabbi Eliezer became ill, Rabbi Akiba and his companions went to visit him. He stayed in his alcove, they in
the hallway. It was Shabbath eve. Hyrcanus, his son, came
in to remove his father's tefillin. Rabbi Eliezer became angry and his son went away, an object of his father's anger.
He then said to his companions: It would seem that my father has lost his reason. Rabbi Eliezer replied: It is the son
and the mother who have gone mad; they pay no attention
to the prohibition which can bring about stoning but preoccupy themselves with what is merely inappropriate for a
solemn day. When the sages of the Law saw that his mind
functioned fully, they entered and sat down four cubits
away.*

*He said to them: Why have you come? They answered: To
study the Torah. He said to them: And why have you not
come until now? They answered: We had no time. He said to
them: It would surprise me if you were to die of natural
causes! Rabbi Akiba said: And I?*

*He answered: Your lot is harsher than theirs. He put both
his arms on his heart and said: Woe unto you. My two arms
are like two scrolls of a sealed Torah. I learned much Torah
and I taught it much. I learned much Torah but I only took
from my masters what a dog takes when it is lapping the sea;
I have taught much Torah, but my students took from me
only what the tip of a brush takes away from a pot full of
paint. Moreover, I have taught three hundred teachings on
white leprosy and there was no one who asked them of me,
and I teach three hundred teachings—some say three thousand teachings—about the planting of cucumbers, and never
did anybody ask them of me, except Akiba, son of Joseph.
One day, we were going somewhere, and he said to me: Master, teach me about the planting of cucumbers. I said a word
and the field filled up with cucumbers. He said to me: Master you taught me their planting, teach me their uprooting. I
said a word, and they gathered in one spot.*

*Then they (the sages who had come to visit Rabbi Eliezer)
said: What is the law of a ball, a shoemaker's last, an amulet, a leather bag containing pearls, and a small weight? He*

answered: They become impure and must be purified as they are.

What of the shoe which is on the last? He said: It stays pure. And his soul departed in purity (as he was uttering the word "pure").

Rabbi Joshua arose and said: The prohibition is lifted, the prohibition is lifted!

At the close of Shabbath, Rabbi Akiba met the coffin of Rabbi Eliezer on the road going from Caesarea to Lydda. He beat his chest until the blood came. Before the line (of people in mourning), he spoke: My father, my father, the chariot of Israel and its horsemen! I have a lot of money but there is no money changer to change it for me.

It is therefore from Rabbi Eliezer that Akiba learned it. Yes, Rabbi Eliezer taught it to him, but he did not make the teaching clear to him. Then he learned it again from Rabbi Joshua, who made it clear.

But how could he have acted thus? Haven't we learned: he who performs the act is subject to penalties? It is different when it is in order to teach. The Master in fact said (Deuteronomy 18:9): "You should not learn to do abhorrent deeds." You should not learn to do them in order to practice; but you must learn to do everything in order to understand and to teach.

The Sacred and the Holy

> The earth hath bubbles, as the water
> has. . . .
>
> —Shakespeare, *Macbeth*, Act 1, Scene 3

I will not insist upon my incompetence before the texts I have to interpret. I very sincerely think that Jewish learning has grown much in France; Jewish thought is taught everywhere and consequently I am not at all sure I will be equal to the task that I have accepted out of tradition, the tradition of twelve colloquia. I beg you to be extremely indulgent with me.

I have also not had the possibility, as you can well imagine, of studying all Talmudic texts relating to the sacred. But what is more serious yet, the very one that I have chosen does not seem to refer to the sacred. It is in any event quite an unusual one, despite the euphemisms brought to bear on the translation before us. I do not know if Professor Baruk, who does us the honor of presiding at this session, will accept my way of commenting. It has in its favor the fact that the colloquium and some in the audience are used to it. Let the others not be shocked by it.

The Mishna does not speak at all of the sacred. In working this text, which is the best Talmudic text, of course—as the ones one is working always are—I nonetheless came to the conclusion that it could be quite suitable for today.

I have always asked myself if holiness, that is, separation or purity, the essence without admixture that can be called Spirit and which animates the Jewish tradition—or to which the Jewish tradition aspires—can dwell in a world that has not been desacralized. I have asked myself—and that is the real question—whether the world is sufficiently desacralized to receive such purity. The sacred is in fact the half light in which the sorcery the Jewish tradition abhors flourishes. The "other side," the reverse or obverse of the Real, Nothingness condensed to Mystery, bubbles of Nothing in things—the "as if nothing is happening" look of daily objects—the sacred adorns itself with the prestige of prestiges. Revelation refuses these bad secrets, a refusal testified to notably by pp. 67*a*–68*a* of the tractate *Sanhedrin*. These texts, through their definitions of sorcery—they suggest several—may perhaps allow us to distinguish the holy from the sacred, beyond the structural or formal resemblances evoked here this morning, when an attempt was made to denounce and deplore the degeneracy of the sacred in the modern world.

Sorcery, first cousin, perhaps even sister, of the sacred, is the mistress of appearance. She is a relative slightly fallen in status, but within the family, who profits from the connections of her brother, who is received in the best circles.

A truly desacralized society would then be a society in which this impure stratagem of sorcery, spreading everywhere, bringing the sacred to life rather than alienating it, comes to an end. Real desacralization would attempt positively to separate the true from appearance, maybe even to separate the true from the appearance *essentially* mixed with the true. It is within this perspective—I want no other introduction—that the text to be commented on touches closely on the topic of our colloquium.

Sorcery and Profits

In the Mishna I bypass the first sentence, which is not going to be developed in the translated passage, and which does not concern our subject. Let us start here:

> The sorcerer, if he performs an act, is subject to penalties. . . .

He is subject to penalties if the act of sorcery enters into the orbit of an activity having a goal that goes beyond the simple play of illusions, but not if he merely creates illusions. Rabbi Akiba, in the name of Rabbi Joshua, has said: Two people pick cucumbers: one of them is subject to penalties, the other exempt; the one who performs the act is subject to penalties, the one that gives the illusion of it is exempt.

The Mishna—which will acquire its full sense only through the way the Gemara will amplify the problem by the new questions its own questions will raise and by the non-spoken meanings that will appear in the meaning it expresses—distinguishes between the sorcery that procures illusions and the one that procures profit. In the example cited, our sorcerer is not very demanding: he does not speculate on a very expensive product; he is a poor sorcerer who produces cucumbers in a field. To stay at the level of illusion does not have great consequences, but if the sorcerer *picks* the cucumbers, if the illusion manages to fit itself within an economic process—and modern economic life is, after all, the place of preference for the harvesting of illusory cucumbers and for the heavy profits attached to such a harvest—sorcery becomes a criminal act. It is liable to sanctions. Which sanctions? This question pertains not to our curiosity as jurists but to the determination of the metaphysical rankings of sorcery and of the genre to which it belongs. This will be seen not in the nature of the sanction but in the way the Talmud discovers it. We shall see this immediately.

Why a Sorceress?

I am now coming to the Gemara. Let us bypass the first sentence relating to the little piece of the Mishna which does not pertain to our theme. The rest reads as follows:

> The sorcerer, if he performs an act, etc. There is a *baraita*: The text says "sorceress" whether it be man or woman; but one says "sorceress" because the vast majority of women engage in sorcery.

In the biblical verse condemning the person given to practicing sorcery, this person is named a sorceress (Exodus 22:18). This text from the Gemara cannot be taken literally. Sarah did not engage in sorcery, nor did Rebeccah, Rachel, Leah, Ruth, or Bathsheba. Rest assured of the dignity of the biblical woman. Rest assured of the dignity of the feminine in itself.

It is nonetheless true that wherever men dominate society, a certain ambiguity attaches itself to the humanity of woman. She is most particularly evocative of sexuality and eroticism, doubling in some fashion her human nature in an ambiguity—or in an enigma—of sublimation and depth, of modesty and obscenity. It is certainly possible to ask oneself whether this masculine domination is purely contingent and whether the emancipation of woman does not in the first place mean her entry—with no restrictions, of course—into a society in which men have nonetheless established the form of a universality more meaningful than sexuality and in which they have defined a sexually neutral human nature that does not repress the sexual. Let us leave these theoretical questions aside. In our society, as advanced as it may be, women go about made up and, in this case, the appearance is equivalent, quite consciously, to *being*. "Business meetings" are distinguished from those in which women are admitted as women; something there extends beyond the rigorous field of presence: the impossible offers itself as possible and the said unsays itself in saying itself; illusion—metaphor, euphemism, pun—associates itself with the Real and charms it.

Charm or latent sidetracking of meaning, birth of duplicity itself, of expression disowning thought: the grace of the face already changing into the horrible grin of the witches in their lairs in *Macbeth* and *Faust*, where words fuse, incapable of containing an identical meaning, and lose themselves in allusions, in rhymes without reason, in sneers, in the unsaid.

It is on the basis of a certain degradation of the feminine—but each essence is responsible for its own modes of degradation—that the charm of sorcery would function: appearance in the *very heart* of the real, dissolution of reality through the ungraspable resources of appearance, the non-real received in its unreality, as a trace of the surreal; equivocations perceived as enigmas; and, in the "fling" experienced as an ecstasy of the sacred, the law suspended.

Sorcerers must not be allowed to live! But through the deduction of the nature of the execution the sorcerers deserve, we shall find the modalities of the sacred which Emile Touati and his interlocutors spoke of this morning. By teasing *[en sollicitant]* the texts, of course, but these are texts which invite teasing *[sollicitent la sollicitation]*; without it, they remain silent or incongruous.

The Essence of Sorcery

How should they be executed?
Rabbi Jose the Galilean said: It is written (Exodus 22:18): "You will not let the sorceress live" and there (Deuteronomy 20:16): "You will not let (live) a soul." As there with a sword, so here with a sword.

In Deuteronomy and Exodus the same expression is in fact to be found: "You will not let live." An analogy of expression which would imply the same sanction. In the legislation of the Torah, however, the sages distinguish four methods of execution: by stoning, fire, the sword, or strangulation. Sensitive souls please forgive me, for these executions were rarely carried out. A Sanhedrin which would have put to death an accused man once in seven years would have merited the label of malevolent, says the tractate *Makoth* (p. 7a). Rabbi Eliezar ben Azariya said: "It would deserve such a label even if it agreed to such a sentence once in seventy years."

Rabbi Tarfon and Rabbi Akiba say: "During the entire time we sat on the Sanhedrin, no one was put to death."

But faults punishable by death do exist, and the same form of execution allows one to compare faults and to extract the essential meaning from the acts. Rabbi Jose the Galilean says that the sorcerer must perish by the sword. Why? Because in Deuteronomy the statement "You will not let live" concerns the notorious extermination by the sword of the Canaanite peoples, "vomited by the earth because of their abominations," according to the words of Scripture, in which the moral inspiration seems to me more certain than the historical testimony. These cruelties—stoning, fire, sword, strangulation—are hence only a language necessary for maintaining the difference which opposes Good and Evil and distinguishes between Evils. It must not disappear in the unctuous and "exalting" style of "to understand everything" and "to forgive everything," which resembles nothing so much as a purr. One must, therefore, execute sorcerers by means of the sword, according to Rabbi Jose the Galilean. Perhaps. What is much more interesting is the category under which sorcery is subsumed, according to this sage. And for us the category under which the sacred from which sorcery proceeds is subsumed: sorcery would pertain to the civilization of perverted peoples. (Historically perverted? It does not matter. In order to understand the meaning of the text I take the combination of givens as the text presents them.) Peoples perverted to such a degree that the earth vomits them. Sorcery, then, would be a phenomenon of perversion, absolutely foreign to Judaism itself. It is the sacred of others!

> Rabbi Akiba has said: It is written here (Exodus 22:18): "You shall not let the sorceress live," and it is written there (Exodus 19:13): "Man or beast must be stoned; they shall cease to live." As there through stoning, so here through stoning.

The gentle Rabbi Akiba, who, in the Sanhedrin, never condemned anyone to death! But the crux is in the comparison of texts: the opening of one moral site unto another, one landscape shedding light upon another. In Exodus 19:13, the Israelites, assembled at the foot of Mount Sinai and at risk of overstepping the limits within which they must stay at the moment of Revelation, are threatened with stoning.

As the expression in Exodus 22:18, "You will not let live," concerning the execution of the sorceress, resembles "They will cease to live," concerning the foolhardiness of the Israelites assembled at the foot of Mount Sinai and threatened with stoning, stoning should also apply to the sorceress. Rabbi Akiba demands a much crueler death for her than does Rabbi Jose. The gentle Rabbi Akiba! But the comparison of texts is instructive. It brings us a second interpretation of the profitable illusionism of the sorceress: it is not a foreign phenomenon but the temptation of the people called to the

Revelation. Sorcery is the fact of looking beyond what it is possible to see. It is to go beyond the limits within which one must stay when truth approaches, not to stop in time. It is the servants who see more than their mistresses. I am alluding to a Midrash in which the servant is proud to have seen the king, while the princess who passed by, leaning on the arm of the servant, has closed her eyes—but she had been much closer to the majesty of the king by this non-looking than had the servant who looked. Sorcery is the curiosity which manifests itself when the eyes should be cast down: indiscretion regarding the Divine; insensitivity to Mystery; clarity projected unto something the approach to which requires some modesty, certain forms of "Freudianism"; perhaps also certain claims of sexual education which show little concern for the unprecedented language such an education requires; and, finally, certain forms of the sexual life itself; perhaps even certain claims of "science for everyone."

Hence the polemic:

> Rabbi Jose said to him: I draw my conclusion from equal wording, "You will not let live," but you draw your conclusion from "You will not let live," which you compare to "And he will cease to live."

Indeed the analogy is not rigorous between the wordings of the two texts:

> Rabbi Akiba answered: I have drawn an analogy between two verses referring to Israelites, for whom Scripture decrees many modes of execution, while you have compared Israelites to idolaters, in whose case only one death penalty is decreed.

Rabbi Akiba acknowledges here that the meaning of his conclusion consists precisely in not understanding sorcery as a pagan perversion. It is a perversion of the holy people itself. Sorcery does not come about because of bad influences; it is the excess of knowledge itself, that which is beyond what can be borne in truth, the illusion which derives from the unbearable truth and which tempts from the very depths of the truth; a Jewish perversion, that is to say, the perversion of all those able to rise to the true, of all those who assemble at the foot of Mount Sinai.

> Ben Azai said: It is said: "You will not let the sorceress live" (Exodus 22:18) and right afterward: "Whosoever will have intercourse with an animal shall be put to death" (Exodus 22:19). The two matters are compared. Since he who has intercourse with an animal must be stoned, so must the sorceress be stoned.

Here, the proof is drawn not from the analogy between expressions but from the juxtaposition of the verses. Sorcery results from vice. It is neither perverse civilization nor unbridled curiosity. The scholars of the Law know that vice constitutes a category irreducible to any other evil, that it poses a special problem for mankind, puncturing the ground of universal solutions, mocking social justice. You no doubt know the strange Midrash of the tractate *Sanhedrin* that Rashi returns to in his commentary of Genesis 8:7: The raven that Noah sends out of the Ark to find out if the waters are decreasing on earth refuses to leave the Ark; he does not want to leave his female alone with Noah. Is a new world in which justice will reign possible at last? Someone in Noah's Ark doubts it. Will the justice that one can at least hope for from a revolution resolve the problem posed by vice?

> Rabbi Judah replied: Is the fact that the two things are close together sufficient reason not to exempt the sorceress from stoning?

Is it the voice of mercy we are hearing at last? Rabbi Judah seems to be saying: Are we going to stone a woman because two verses are close together? Let us not be optimistic: Rabbi Judah does not intend to spare the witch; he just needs a better reason to execute her. Or, rather, he seeks the essence of sorcery elsewhere.

> Here is the real reasoning: Ov and Yidoni (necromancers and casters of spells) belong to the genre of sorceresses. Why were they mentioned separately (Deuteronomy 18:10)? To reason by analogy: just as Ov and Yidoni are punishable by stoning (Leviticus 20:27), so are sorcerers.

Sorcery is a genus whose species we know, and the treatment inflicted upon the species—stoning—extends to the genus. That is for the formal side of the argument. What does it teach about sorcery? The species which informs us about the genus here includes the necromancers. We know them through the story of King Saul, who began purifying his kingdom according to the demand of Exodus by exterminating sorcery, including that of the necromancers. At the end of his reign, he found himself having to resort to their power; Saul's fall is marked by his recourse to the evil which he had himself conjured: A necromancer (a woman)—*Eshet baalat Ov* (1 Samuel 28:7) makes the prophet Samuel come from the kingdom of the dead, upon Saul's request, and the king questions him about the future awaiting him. Ov and Yidoni, doomed to be stoned, are therefore those who ask questions of the dead: the slaves of tradition. A new form of degradation of the sacred: the sacred of the intangible past. But perhaps in the search for presages, we have also the sacred of those who make tables turn and who ask for horoscopes; the most vulgar sacred, that of superstition and spiritism; spiritist spiritualism.

Power over Man

But hence there is a philosophical problem: How is degradation possible? How can holiness be confused with the sacred and turn into sorcery?

How can the sacred transform itself into enchantment, into power over human beings?

> Rabbi Johanan said: Why is sorcery called *Keshafim?* Because it challenges the Assembly on High.

Indeed if one were to write the expression "They challenge the Assembly on High" in Hebrew, *makhishin famalia shel maala,* one would find the letters *k, sh, f, m* forming the word *keshafim* (vowels are not taken into account!), which means sorcery. A comparison which no serious etymology could justify but, also, a formulation of an interesting idea: the meaning of sorcery would be to challenge the highest order. A challenge to the Absolute. The diabolical Luciferian *no.* The magician says *no* to the highest order. But how is this possible? Where would this *no* in the *yes* of the Absolute come from? Nothing is outside it to oppose itself to it. The idea of the sacred becoming degraded is crazy! It was never the Absolute but only its image! How could the supreme presence have distanced itself from itself? Spinoza does teach us how thought can lead back to God, but he was never able to show how God distances himself from himself so as to leave room for a knowledge of the first kind which replaces his idea.¹ But it could be that sorcery—the desacralization of the sacred—has some new mode of existence, between being and nothingness, in the madness of human minds. It is nothing for the person or the civilization that has reached the real sacred—holiness—the service of the Most High. It does not threaten them. It does not tempt them.

It is precisely this position that Rabbi Hanina defends.

There Is No Sorcery—

> Rabbi Johanan said (Deuteronomy 4:35): "The Holy One is God; there is no other."

There is no other God; there is no other of God, that is how the tradition has always read it: outside God there is nothing else. There is nothing else, God is the only reality.

> Rabbi Hanina said: This even concerns sorcery . . .

There is no sorcery!

> the story of a woman who went to gather dust from under the feet of Rabbi Hanina.

She wanted to have power over him through sorcery by gathering the dust under his feet, which would confer powers to her.

He told her (calmly): If you can, go and do it. For it is written: "There is no other."

That is to say: if you can do something against me, that is because the Most High wants it, and if he does not want it, you will not be able to do anything. I scoff at the dust that you gather from my feet.

But hasn't this position just been challenged by Rabbi Johanan?

How is this possible? Didn't Rabbi Johanan say: Why do we call it sorcery? Because it challenges the Assembly on High.

It is thus quite possible to challenge the Assembly on High. Why did Rabbi Hanina scoff at sorcery? Answer:

For Rabbi Hanina, it was otherwise because he had many merits.

—or It Comes from Human Weakness

The illumination and the reign of the Assembly on High penetrate the world only if they are received by human beings who spot this light and this power. The Absolute dispels the appearances of the absolute only for him who is fastened to the Absolute: in my full attention to the Most High, nothing can catch me by surprise. No traumatism is possible: the *no* slips into being only if my attention is relaxed. The diabolical inscribes itself within the possibilities of the man called to vigilance. That is the only way it is possible. It is not God who withdraws from the world. It is man who closes himself to God, if only when he blinks his eyes, thus interrupting with moments of black the continuous light of his vigilant gaze.

From this point on we shall see how the nothingness of sorcery inserts itself into the Real. The text we are presently commenting on seems decidedly to follow a plan, to be composed. It is not an alluvion of folk history.

Rabbi Aibu bar Nagri said, in the name of Rabbi Hiyya bar Abba: Done by the *Latehem* (expression found in Exodus 7:22), magical action is the action of demons; done by the *Lahatehem* (Exodus 7:11), magical action is a matter of sorcery. Isn't it said (Genesis 3:24): "The blade of the fiery, everturning sword *(lahat hasherev hamithapeshet)*"?

There are two aspects of magic: the magic practiced by the *Latehem* and the magic performed by the *Lahatehem*. In the course of eleven verses, the Book of Exodus, mentioning the way in which the magicians of Pharaoh, thanks to their own tricks, repeat the miracles through which Moses and Aaron intend to command respect from Pharaoh, sometimes designates these tricks by the word *latehem* and sometimes by the word *lahatehem*.

However, in Genesis 3:24, when the rotating sword at the gate of Paradise, from which Adam and Eve are expelled, is mentioned, the word *lahat,* meaning the blade of a sword, is used. The blade of a sword, weapon of this strange guard mounted without humans at the gate of Paradise, turned automatically. The effects obtained through *Lahatehem* belong to another type of magic and would indicate recourse to special paraphernalia.

> Abaye said: When the sorcerer insists upon exact paraphernalia, the magic is the work of demons; otherwise, it is simply sorcery.

Peculiar difference between sorcery as the work of demons and sorcery without any intermediary! Wouldn't the first indicate the one which inserts itself into technique: the sacred degenerating into the prestiges of technique? Beside a rational technique, at the service of human ends, there is a technique that is the source of illusion, a technique which allows the production and sale of cucumbers: the technique displayed by the beneficiaries of stock exchange speculations.

Interiorization and Magic

And the other magic? The one which does without instruments, the one of the mere murmur, of sheer breath? Maybe this is the magic of spiritualization, of interiorization, the possibility of overcoming conflicts by "interiorizing" problems, resolving them through appeal to good intentions, consenting to crime thanks to all the marvels of mental reservations! An interior magic with infinite resources: all is allowed in the inner life, all is allowed, including crime. The abolition of laws in the name of love; the possibility of serving man without making man serve; to abolish Shabbath² under the pretext that man is not made for Shabbath but that Shabbath is made for man. Is the Shabbath not the focal point of the challenge to the Law?

> Abaye said: the Halakhah on sorcery resembles the Halakhah on the Shabbath.

Sorcery and Sabbath

Rest assured that the comparison with the Halakhah on sorcery holds only for the legislation concerning Sabbath prohibitions. There are structural resemblances here. In the legislation concerning the Shabbath:

> Some actions are punishable by stoning; some are not punishable, yet are forbidden; some are entirely permissible.

There are three degrees: the permissible, the forbidden yet not subject to punishment, the forbidden and subject to punishment. It is the same in the case of sorcery.

He who performs an action is stoned—as in the one who picks cucumbers; he who creates an illusion is not punishable, yet he performs a forbidden action. Some actions are entirely permissible: like the one of Rabbi Hanina and Rabbi Oshaia, who, every Shabbath eve, studied the doctrine of creation, by means of which they created a calf one-third grown and ate it.

Were Rav Oshaia and Rav Hanina doing something permissible? It is permissible. If you know the mysteries of creation, you can, like the Maharal of Prague, make an object that looks supernatural. It is permissible. This daring text thus teaches us how ridiculous it would be to impose limits on human possibilities. Down with reactionary superstitions and fears of technical progress! As long as the illusion does not deceive us, we can dare anything, even the making of synthetic meat. It is not sorcery. Synthetic meat, yes, but it is meat for the Shabbath. This is not an insignificant detail. One is permitted to give being to even more daring dreams than that as long as the Shabbath remains: the sovereignty of man, capable of tearing himself away from the order of things, their necessity, and their cogwheels. The comparison between the laws which govern sorcery and the laws which govern the transgression of the Shabbath is therefore not merely structural. The law of the Shabbath marks the limit of technique and sorcery. Sorcery is, in a certain sense, the profanation of the Shabbath.

The structural resemblance nonetheless holds. The Shabbath day involves unconditional prohibitions; but, next to acts which are absolutely forbidden, are those which are not recommended, even if their performance does not bring punishment (laying *tefillin* on the day of Shabbath, for example), and acts which are generally forbidden but which, under certain conditions, are authorized, like all those necessary to the well-being of someone who is sick or in danger. When, in his youth, Hillel the Elder exposed himself to the cold on the roof of the house of study, in order to follow the lesson of Shemaya and Avtalion through a garret window, the Shabbath day was profaned so that all the necessary measures could be taken to warm him up. No one concerned himself with prohibitions. Just as Rav Hanina and Rav Oshaia did not bother with the prohibitions against sorcery when they made a calf one-third grown in order to have a roast on Shabbath.

I am always surprised to perceive, through the juridical discussions and the purely formal comparisons of the Gemara, meaningful glimmers which are probably what is essential! That sorcery could be compared to the transgression of the Shabbath—contrary to those who delicately called the rendezvous of witches a sabbath!—is quite remarkable. That the Shabbath is in the end *for the sake of man* but that it cannot be for the sake of man without an entire legislation that protects it from man and his abuses—and from his sorcery of interiorization, as we can now call the magic of murmurs—is even more remarkable.

Miscellaneous Items

We now come to a seemingly anecdotal section: miscellaneous deeds of sorcery, told by some old sages to divert themselves. But the banal conversation of the sages, *sihat hulin shel Talmidei hahamim,* has a meaning, however.

> Rav Ashi related: I once saw Abhu of Karna blow his nose and balls of silk came from his nostrils.

Referred to here are probably those who manipulate universes through the sheer play of handwriting; they buy and sell trainloads of wheat and tankers of oil on a corner of their desktop and dazzle our feeble eyes.

Another case but the same problem: Is there creation of any sort in sorcery? No, there is no creation in sorcery; sorcerers—I am not reading the text which follows but paraphrasing it slightly—are capable of creating neither the least significant nor the greatest of beings: they can only create already existing beings; they move things around. They have "tricks" to reassemble them when they are dispersed, to make them appear by making them come from elsewhere. Hullabaloo, movement, but nothing new:

Here it is:

> Rab was telling Rabbi Hiyya: I once saw an Arab cut a camel into pieces with his sword. Then he beat a drum before it and the camel came back to life. Rabbi Hiyya responded: Did you find blood and dung (after this performance)? It was only an illusion.

Of course, sorcerers have no power over the living. I recognize a whole literature of conflicts and emotional problems here, of paradoxical situations in which there is not a single teardrop, nor a single drop of warm human blood, not a single bit of real human pain. Ah, if at least a small amount of warm dung were left in the aftermath of all these dramas and crises! It was but a paper anguish.

Another story:

> One day Ze'iri went to Alexandria, in Egypt, and bought himself an ass.

Alexandria, in Egypt, that means a city of high civilization, a metropolis, one of our great capitals.

> When he went to give it something to drink, the spell broke and he found himself sitting on the boards of a gangway.

The ass was nothing but a wooden board. When he went to give it drink, the charm broke; water is indeed supposed to reduce the power of sorcery; water disenchants. Cold water, above all.

> Then the others said to him: If you weren't Ze'iri, we wouldn't give you back your money. For here no one buys anything without first testing his purchase by water.

The Modern World

Nothing is identical to itself any longer. That is what sorcery is: the modern world; nothing is identical to itself; no one is identical to himself; nothing gets said for no word has its own meaning; all speech is a magical whisper; no one listens to what you say; everyone suspects behind your words a not-said, a conditioning, an ideology.

A new anecdote whose meaning is similar:

> One day, Jannai came to an inn and asked for some water to drink. When a woman handed him some *shattitha,* he noticed that her lips moved. He spilled some of it on the ground; they were scorpions. He then said to her: I drank of yours, drink of mine. When she had drunk, she changed into an ass. He got on the ass and rode out into the street. There, a friend of the woman broke the spell, and Jannai was seen riding upon a woman.

Rashi adds: That is even why the text does not call Jannai Rav Jannai; it does not want the title of Rav to be granted to a man who appeared on the street on the back of a woman.

The last example: the famous frog who came to Egypt as the second plague. The text of Exodus says *tsfardea,* in the singular. Thus the question arises: Was there an enormous frog filling all of Egypt? That would have been terrible, but it would resemble Ionesco's *Amédée, or How to Get Rid of It.* Sorcery would then be the taking over of life by the waste products of life, the suffocation of culture under the archives of culture; continuation triumphing over every interruption and every beginning. The sacred in the very impossibility of desacralization! But the singular could indicate a monstrous proliferation of a single frog: proliferation of Evil or simply of fashion. Or—and this contingency is also touched upon by the commentators—one single frog was enough to make all the world's frogs come to Egypt. One frog or Evil—I do not know if the proletarians of all countries are uniting, but the criminals of all countries, despite their feuds, present a single front. Crime always has an international dimension. There had been only one frog; it whistled and immediately all of Egypt filled with frogs.

That takes care of the degeneration of the sacred in which the sacred abides. The sacred which degenerates is worse than the sacred which disappears. That is why the sacred is not sacred, why the sacred is not holiness.

The Scent of Holiness

What follows now is a contrast to these challenges. It is true that we can find only a hint, through the minutiae of the Law, of what animates the Pharisaic will, although it is a fairly expressive hint. What we find is separation from a world in which *appearance* falsifies *that which appears [l'apparence altère l'apparaître]* from the very dawn of its manifestation; in which desacralization is nothing but a new magic, augmenting the sacred, its degeneration into sorcery being one with its generation. In this bewitched world, that is, with no exit, for one cannot escape it without neglecting responsibilities, the *separation* of the Pharisees is put into practice. It is an absence from the immediacy of possessing by means of prohibitions and rules, a hope of *holiness* in the face of a *sacred* that cannot be purified, *Judaism as an irreducible modality of being present to the world.*

Our text gives us the epilogue of a Talmudic story whose prologue everyone knows. Page 59*b* of *Baba Metsia* is about some scholars of the Law who discuss a question of Halakhah, and in which Rabbi Eliezer finds himself opposing all his colleagues. The question discussed concerns purity and impurity. It is not a question of "inner" purity, which is so easy to discover and justify before or short of any action: Isn't it enough to proclaim that what counts is not what goes into but what comes out of the mouth of man? A claim that so spiritualizes purity that it risks making us drown in nihilist abysses of interiority, in which the pure and the impure become identified with each other. The sages of the Law discuss ritual purity, the one defined by external criteria. These rules of the external gesture must be there in order for inner purity to stop being merely verbal.

You know that in the Jewish tradition contact with the dead is the source of impurity. The text in *Baba Metsia* wants to find out whether the presence of a dead man, which confers impurity upon any object built as an open receptacle, also confers it in the particular case of a stove having a special shape, with whose details I do not wish to burden my presentation here.

According to Rabbi Eliezer, this stove can become impure. According to Rabbi Joshua and his colleagues, it remains pure. What a boring story! The discussion on a topic that may seem trifling to you—especially if the abysses of interiority do not make you dizzy, despite the threat hanging over a world about to be swallowed up by it—was so violent that it led to a split in the college of scholars! Rabbi Eliezer, in order to convince his opponents, had recourse to supernatural proofs. And it is precisely this aspect of the story which is very well known: A tree is uprooted all by itself, a river flows back to its source to support what Rabbi Eliezer says, but Rabbi Joshua does not allow that a debate stemming from a question raised by the Torah can be decided on the basis of a tree torn from its roots or of a river which goes back to its source.

Stop the miracles! Rabbi Eliezer invoked the testimony of the walls of the house of study in which the discussion was taking place. These walls, which undoubtedly had ears and which had heard so many rabbinic discussions, leaned and threatened to crumble so as to testify on behalf of Rabbi Eliezer, but Rabbi Joshua refused their testimony. What do walls have to do with a rabbinic discussion of the Torah! Torn between their respect for Rabbi Eliezer's proofs and their respect for Rabbi Joshua's argument, the walls remained inclined: crumbling and not crumbling, leaning for eternity. Then Rabbi Eliezer made a voice from heaven speak in his favor; but Rabbi Joshua refused this voice, claiming that the voice of heaven was not a proof, that the Torah, given to men who are on earth and who must act here below, is entrusted to human discussion and, for the necessities of action, to institutions. The majority then declared Rabbi Eliezer, the minority voice, anathema. It separated itself from this sage among sages and inflicted upon itself the penalty of no longer being able to profit from his teaching. And *Baba Metsia* tells us also that the prophet Elijah, questioned about the attitude of the Eternal by one of the Talmudic sages who had the good luck of running into him, told him the following: During this entire intellectual conflict, God, smiling, repeated: "My children have been stronger than I am! My children have been stronger than I am!"

The text we have before our eyes tells us about the end of Rabbi Eliezer. But the way we are led into it is very remarkable because of the strangeness of the association of ideas—or the logic—which determines its evocation. In the Mishna of a moment ago, we read that Rabbi Akiba, in the name of Rabbi Joshua, had said: "Two people pick cucumbers." But through the text which I still have left to comment on, you will learn that Rabbi Akiba received the famous teaching on cucumbers from Rabbi Eliezer. Our text, which is a quotation, figures here as an objection. The long tale which tells us of the last hours of Rabbi Eliezer—and you will, I hope, admire from many aspects the beauties of this story—is there only to decide whether it was Rabbi Joshua or Rabbi Eliezer who instructed Rabbi Akiba about the difference between a sorcerer who sells illusory cucumbers and a sorcerer who only makes them appear.

> Rabbi Akiba said. . . . It was Rabbi Joshua, then, who taught the matter to Rabbi Akiba. But we have a *toseftah:* When Rabbi Eliezer became ill. . . .

The Dying Rabbi Eliezer

In the quoted *toseftah,* we find Rabbi Eliezer at the end of his life.

> Rabbi Akiba and his companions went to visit him. He stayed in his alcove, they in the hallway.

The "anathema" still hangs over Rabbi Eliezer, and his colleagues do not allow themselves to go near him.

It was Shabbath eve. Hyrcanus, his son, came in to remove his father's *tefillin*.

As Shabbath approaches, Rabbi Eliezer, sick, in the alcove, still keeps the *tefillin*, which, it is recommended, are not to be worn on the day of Shabbath. His son comes to take the phylacteries from him so he can avoid wearing them on the day of the Shabbath, for although wearing them is, to be sure, not punishable, it remains forbidden.

Rabbi Eliezer became angry and his son went away, an object of his father's anger. He then said to his companions: It would seem that my father has lost his reason. Rabbi Eliezer replied: It is the son and the mother who have gone mad; they pay no attention to the prohibition which can bring about stoning but preoccupy themselves with what is merely inappropriate for a solemn day.

The son is wrong to worry about *tefillin*, the wearing of which on Shabbath does not carry any penalty, when his mother does not tend to the Shabbath lights or to the preparing and keeping warm of something to drink for the holy day. If she were forced to light the candles after nightfall or to heat water during Shabbath, she would be liable to stoning. It is Rabbi Eliezer who is right once again.

When the sages of the Law saw that his mind functioned fully, they entered and sat down four cubits away.

They came closer without going beyond the four cubits that must separate them from the person under anathema.

He said to them: Why have you come? They answered: To study the Torah. He said to them: And why have you not come until now? They answered: We had no time.

We were not free—which is true—because of the anathema.

He said to them: It would surprise me if you were to die of natural causes!

You deserve to die a violent death, to undergo torture. It is *knowledge* which is at stake. Not to go to the master is an irreparable fault. And the following lines are dedicated to the mastery of the master, and to the guilt of the disciple, who eventually fails his master.

Rabbi Akiba said: And I? He answered: Your lot is harsher than theirs.

Rabbi Akiba is the greatest. He is the greatest, thus the most responsible, most guilty toward the master. It is Rabbi Akiba who figures among the ten rabbinic sages who were tortured and executed by the Romans after the failure of the Bar Kochba revolt and who are commemorated in the *Yom*

Kippur liturgy. In this liturgy, their torture (that of Rabbi Akiba is the most horrible) is presented as the expiation of the unforgettable and hitherto unexpiated crime of the sons of Jacob, who had sold their brother. Or as the expiation of the eternal and invisible repetition of this crime against fraternity.

> He put both his arms on his heart and said: Woe unto you. My two arms are like two scrolls of a sealed Torah. I learned much Torah and I taught it much. I learned much Torah but I only took from my masters what a dog takes when it is lapping the sea. . . .

The master is someone's disciple. He has a feeling of guilt toward his masters. He too did not know how to take what they were offering. The disciple's respect for the master culminates in this guilt of the disciple as disciple, in the consciousness of his canine nature.

> I have taught much Torah, but my students took from me only what the tip of a brush takes away from a pot full of paint.

Here, there is no longer any comparison with a dog.

> Moreover, I have taught three hundred teachings on white leprosy. . . .

Always these teachings about external matters! Never anything on the "inner life"!

> And there was no one who asked them of me, and I teach three hundred teachings—some say three thousand teachings—about the planting of cucumbers, and never did anybody ask them of me, except Akiba, son of Joseph.

No doubt because Akiba had this insatiable desire to know, his fate during the tortures had been the harshest.

> One day, we were going somewhere, and he said to me: Master, teach me about the planting of cucumbers. I said a word and the field filled up with cucumbers. He said to me: Master, you taught me their planting, teach me their uprooting. I said a word and they gathered in one spot.

Thus, it is here that the quoted *toseftah*, contradicting the Mishna, teaches us that Rabbi Eliezer and not Rabbi Joshua gave Rabbi Akiba the teaching on cucumbers.

Statements of the Final Hour

And here our text, in its apparent attachment to questions of the ritual "to do" and "not to do," testifies, in my opinion, to a greatness that is precisely what brings incomprehension and scorn upon the Jewish tradition. The master is about to die. What is talked about during these moments? Eternal destiny? The inner life? Not at all. "What I must do" is more important than "what I am allowed to hope for":

> Then they said: What is the law of a ball, a shoemaker's last, an amulet, a
>
> leather bag containing pearls, and a small weight?

Sublime platitude! At issue are five objects made of leather which can be simultaneously considered receptacles and non-receptacles. Going back once again to the interrupted discussion on the impurity affecting receptacles in a room in which there is a dead man, the rabbinic sages want to wrest from the master a bit of the knowledge which he will carry to his grave. What does he think of the capacity of the five objects named to become or not to become impure? The five objects are not there by chance. Not that they are symbols. They have, in their very particularity, irreducible meanings. Leather plays a different role in each of them. It is quite a remarkable structuralist analysis.

In the case of the ball, the leather is part of the object; the leather is not merely the container for the dried herbs that fill it.

The last? At issue here is the leather frame on which a shoe is worked; it is therefore a solid object on which one places the shoe one is working on. Here, the leather receives the shoe by serving as its support. It is a way of receiving, but in a different way from that of the leather of the ball: here the object is *on* the form and not *in* the form.

And the amulet? It is a leather object in which a jewel is encased and which is worn as an ornament. What is the role of leather here? New category: neither simple container, nor part of the object, nor support. The leather encasing the jewel belongs in itself to the ornamentation of the ornament.

The leather bag containing pearls? Rashi says this was the pouch that was hung around the neck of sick animals in order to cure them. Sorcery? This aspect is not considered. Old wives' remedies to cure a cow, that is still medicine. Here, leather allows for something to be suspended. It is neither decoration, nor container, nor support.

Fifth and last category: the small weight. When it was made of metal, which crumbled easily, it lost weight easily. It was customary to enclose it in a leather pouch to preserve it from these losses. This time, the leather pouch is sheer protection against the crumbling away of the metal: it is neither part of the object, nor container, nor support, nor suspension.

Here, then, are five modes in which the leather object does not exclude the function of a container but, in which, it is, each time, engaged in another function. It is an analysis which indicates a curiosity about formal meaning in the Rabbis' casuistry.

He answered: They become impure and must be purified as they are.

As they are, that is, the whole object must undergo the rites of purification, not just the leather separated from the object. I cannot give the reason for it without risking starting over again Rabbi Joshua's and Rabbi Eliezer's discussion, whose results were so disastrous. Let us bow before the decision communicated by Rabbi Eliezer in his last hour. But his colleagues had yet another question:

What of the shoe which is on the last?

Indeed, the unfinished object cannot become impure. But if the shoe is finished, if it is a completed product, then it can become impure. While still on the last, the shoe is not finished, is not a thing, is still an object in the process of being made. Not being a thing, it cannot become impure; everyone knows this as well. But a completed shoe left on the last is on the thin line between that which is finished and that which is still being made. A situation created by minds seeking limiting cases.

He said: It stays pure. And his soul departed in purity.

He breathed his last in the purity of the shoe! But perhaps that is precisely what purity is. The care given not to the unfathomable purity of my intentions, but to the objective rules of purity, the purity of the shoe, and through it, to the purity at the limit of impurity.

If you tell a passerby, a journalist, for instance, knowledgeable about everything, that a great man of Israel died in purity because he stated that a shoe was pure, if you tell it without a context, and even if you tell it in the context of my interpretation, he will laugh at you and will publish your story in a boxed article in *Le Monde* in order to make the crowd of sneerers sneer.

Rabbi Joshua arose and said: The prohibition is lifted, the prohibition is lifted!

The Death of the Master

He is dead.

I will not comment much on the rest of the text, in which, without any commentary, you can feel the devotion to the master.

At the close of Shabbath Rabbi Akiba met the coffin of Rabbi Eliezer on the road going from Caesarea to Lydda. He beat his chest until the blood came. Before the line (of people in mourning), he spoke: My father, my father, the chariot of Israel and its horsemen!

He is the chariot, he is the horsemen and probably the driver of the chariot; he was both the master who leads and the debate to be conducted; the pilot and the skiff. Rabbi Akiba utters the words that the prophet Elisha uttered at the moment his master, the prophet Elijah—the man who did not know death—is taken from him in the storm.

I have a lot of money but there is no money changer to change it for me.

The death of the master, the end of questions, the end of answers, a knowledge that cannot be used. Supreme despair: Of whom can I now ask questions? And, then, the text, unmoved before its own account, comes back to cucumbers!

It is therefore from Rabbi Eliezer that Akiba learned it.

Didn't Rabbi Eliezer say: "On the way, he asked me how cucumbers are made"? It is therefore from him and not from Rabbi Joshua that Rabbi Akiba received the famous teaching with which our Mishna opened:

Yes, Rabbi Eliezer taught it to him, but he did not make the teaching clear to him. Then he learned it again from Rabbi Joshua, who made it clear.

That is why our Mishna says: in the name of Rabbi Joshua: Not understood, Rabbi Eliezer's lesson had thus not been a true teaching. No doubt, Rabbi Akiba had not had the time to ask all his questions!

There remains a last question, which you are asking yourself and which the Gemara asks itself: Did Rabbi Eliezer practice sorcery?

But how could he (Rabbi Eliezer) have acted thus? Haven't we learned: he who performs the act is subject to penalties? It is different when it is in order to teach. The Master in fact said: (Deuteronomy 18:9): "You should not learn to do abhorrent deeds." You should not learn to do them in order to practice; but you must learn to do everything in order to understand and to teach.

This last point is crucial: everything we have learned about this world of illusions and sorcery, about the decadence of the sacred in which the false sacred (or, rather, simply the sacred) maintains itself, all that must be known. The only relation the Jewish tradition grants to this sacred and its desacralization is knowledge of these abominations. The holiness it seeks owes nothing more either to the sacred world or to the desacralized world in which the sacred is always degenerating, nourishing itself through its very degeneration; the holiness which Israel is seeking owes nothing but knowledge to the realm of the mortal god of whose death the Jewish tradition has always been aware, having occurred, as far as it is concerned, millennia ago. The holiness it wants comes to it from the living God.

NOTES

1. See note 4 in "Judaism and Revolution." (Trans.)

2. Levinas spells Sabbath in two ways in this commentary. The more frequent spelling is that which is closer to the Hebrew pronunciation, "Shabbat." I have rendered this in English as "Shabbath," emphasizing its usage within the Jewish community. But Levinas also spells it "Sabbat," when it refers to the non-Jewish usage, specifically here "the witches' sabbath." In the latter case, I translated the word as "Sabbath." The distinction of the two terms has much to do with the distinction between holy and sacred, as Levinas develops it. I have therefore tried to emphasize the difference in spelling, at the price of some awkwardness. (Trans.)

AND GOD CREATED WOMAN

■ From the Tractate *Berakhot*, p. 61*a* ■

Rav Nahman, son of Rav Hisda, taught: Why, in "The Lord God made man" (Genesis 2:7) is "made," vayitzer, written with two yods? The Holy One, Blessed be He, created two in-clinations, the good and the bad.

Rav Nahman bar Isaac objected: If this is so, then it means that the animal which (he made), vayitzer (Genesis 2:19), where vayitzer is not written with two yods, does not have good and evil inclinations, though we can see that an animal can destroy, bite, and kick.

It must then be interpreted (the two yods must be inter-preted) as Rav Simeon ben Pazzi did; for Rav Simeon ben Pazzi said: Woe is me because of my Creator, woe is me be-cause of my own evil inclination. Or one must even inter-pret in the manner of Rav Jeremiah ben Eleazar, for Rav Jeremiah ben Eleazar said: Two faces did the Holy One, Blessed be He, create in the first man, for isn't it written (Psalms 139:5): "You hedge me before and behind; You lay Your hand upon me."

And the Lord God fashioned into a woman (literally: built into a woman) "the rib which he had taken from man" (Genesis 2:22). Rab and Samuel are talking. One said: It (the rib) was a face. The other said: It was a tail. For the one who said: It was a face, the text "You hedge me before and be-hind" presents no difficulties. But what does the one who maintains that it is a tail do with the text?

We must acknowledge that he thinks like Rav Ammi. For Rav Ammi said: "behind" means "the last one created," "be-fore" means "the first one to be punished."

All right as far as "the last one created" goes—for man

This reading was given in the context of a colloquium on "Ish and Isha or the Other *par Excellence,*" held in October 1972. The proceedings were published in *L'autre dans la con-science juive: Le sacré et le couple: Données et débats* (Paris: P.U.F., 1973). Levinas's commen-tary appears on pp. 173–186. There was no discussion.

was not created until Shabbath eve itself—but as far as "the first one to be punished," which punishment are you referring to? Would it be the one imposed after the story of the snake? Don't we have a toseftah: Rabbi said: In conferring honor, we start with the greatest, in cursing, with the least important. In conferring honor we start with the greatest, for it is written (Leviticus 10:12): "Moses said to Aaron, as well as to Eleazar and Ithamar, his surviving sons: 'Take the meal offering that is left over from the Lord's offerings and eat it unleavened beside the altar, for it is most holy.' " To curse, one begins with the least, for the serpent was cursed first, then Eve, and finally Adam. The priority of man in the matter of sanctions could then only refer to the Flood. For it is written (Genesis 7:23): "God wiped out all the creatures on the face of the earth, both man and cattle." First man, then the beasts.

He who says that rib means face is in accord with the two yods of vayitzer (Genesis 2:19); what does the one for whom rib means tail make of the two yods of vayitzer? He must follow the lesson of Rav Simeon ben Pazzi. For Rav Simeon ben Pazzi said that the two yods of vayitzer mean "Woe is me on account of my Creator, woe is me on account of my evil inclination."

He who says that rib means face is in agreement with the text that says: "Male and female he made them simultaneously" (Genesis 5:2). What does the one for whom rib means tail make of "male and female he made them simultaneously"? One must follow the lesson of Rabbi Abbahu. For Rabbi Abbahu objected: It is written: "He created them male and female" (Genesis 5:2), and it is written (Genesis 9:6): "Man was made in the image of God." How is it possible? He first had in mind to create two and in the end created only one.

He who said that rib means face can agree with the text (Genesis 2:21): "And he closed up the place with flesh." What does the one for whom rib means tail make of it? Rav Jeremiah and, according to others, Rav Zebid and, according to others, Rav Nahman bar Isaac taught: The flesh was necessary only at the place of the cut.

He who said that rib means tail can be in accord with the formulation (Genesis 2:22): "And the Lord God fashioned the rib that He had taken from the man into a woman." What does the one for whom rib means face do with it? Here one must follow Rabbi Simeon ben Menasia. Rabbi Simeon ben

Menasia taught: For the text "He fashioned the rib into woman," it has to be understood that the Holy One, Blessed be He, plaited Eve's hair into braids and took her to Adam, for in other countries the braid is called binyatha (building). *Another explanation: Rav Hisda said—and others said that it was taught in a* baraita: *The text teaches us that the Holy One, Blessed be He, made Eve like a granary. For just as the granary is narrow at the top and large at the bottom to hold the harvest, so woman is narrow at the top and large at the bottom to hold the child.*

"And he brought her to man" (Genesis 2:22). Rav Jeremiah ben Eleazar said: This teaches us that the Holy One, Blessed be He, acted as best man to Adam. Here the Torah wants to teach rules of behavior: a great one should act as "best man" for someone lesser without feeling any resentment.

According to those who say that rib means face, who walks ahead? (The feminine or the masculine aspect?) Rav Nahman ben Yitzhak said: It is reasonable to suppose that the man walks ahead, for there is a baraita: *A man does not walk behind a woman, even if it is his own wife on the road—and, even if he finds himself on a bridge with her, she should be beside him, and whoever walks behind a woman when crossing a river will have no part in the future world.*

There is a baraita: *If a man gives money to a woman from his hand to hers with the intention of looking at her, he will not escape the law of hell, even if he is full of Torah and of good actions, like Moses, our teacher. For it is written (Proverbs 11:21): Put your hand up! The evil man does not remain unpunished (literally: from hand to hand—the evil man will not remain unpunished); he will not escape the condemnation to hell that he deserves.*

Rav Nahman said: And Manoah was an am-haaretz (lacking in culture), for it is written: "And Manoah rose and followed his wife" (Judges 13:11). Rav Nahman bar Jose objected to him: Then Elkanah should be treated in the same fashion. Isn't it said: "And Elkanah followed his wife." And, similarly for Elisha. Isn't it written (2 Kings 4:30): "And he arose and followed her." It is not a question of following in the literal sense of the term, but "follow her words and her advice." Similarly for Manoah.

Rav Ashi said: Rav Nahman wanted to say that Manoah does not even go to beginners' school, for it is said in Genesis 24:61: "Then Rebekah and her maids arose, mounted the

> *camels, and* followed *the man." Followed, not* preceded,
> *the man.*
>   Rabbi Johanan said: Behind a lion and not behind a
> woman; behind a woman and not behind an idol worshipper;
> behind an idol worshipper and not behind a synagogue (on
> the side opposite the entrance) when the community is
> praying.
>   In any case, this last point is valid only for him that finds
> himself without a burden; if he bears a burden, it is not so.
> And this point applies only if there are no other doors; if
> there is another door, it is not so. And this applies only if he
> is not mounted on a donkey; if he is on the back of a don-
> key, it is not so. And this applies only if he is not wearing
> tefillin; if he wears tefillin, it is not so.

In beginning this lesson, I cannot avoid my usual confession of inadequacy. Under the ambitious title of Talmudic lesson, I have chosen as always
to interpret an aggadic text. I feel a very great responsibility concerning this
text before this gathering of so many authentic Talmudic scholars, whom I
should have asked to speak in my stead. I beg their indulgence.

The text will speak to us of woman. It opens with three statements
which concern the human apart from its division into masculine and feminine. From the start, the text is concerned with a certain duality in the human being and with an attempt to define what the human is. It is within
this context that the later discussion about the feminine and masculine
takes place.

I will reread the first statement.

The Two Inclinations

> Rab Nahman, son of Rav Hisda, taught: Why, in "The Lord God made
> man" (Genesis 2:7) is "made," *vayitzer,* written with two *yods?*

We seem quite removed from the problems so masterfully outlined for
us just a little while ago.¹ A question of spelling is suddenly asked. Why are
there two *yods* in the word *vayitzer,* which means "made"? At stake here is
the creation of man. The pious, proper thought of the right-thinking ones
no longer wonders about anything. Let them at least be prodded into thinking by a peculiarity of spelling. Is man created in the same way as a vase is
made? Listen to the first answer:

> The Holy One, Blessed be He, created two inclinations, the good and
> the bad.

I translated "two inclinations" according to custom: *yetzer* is translated as inclination. The word really means creature. The proof: Isaiah 29:6: "The creature *(yetzer)* said to the Creator he understood nothing." It is clear here that *yetzer* means creature and not inclination.

The first answer therefore means that the creation of the human being is extraordinary; to create a man was to create in one creature two. They were two in one. And this does not refer to woman. There will be no reference to woman until the end of these three initial statements. What is the human being? The fact that a being is *two* while remaining *one.* A division, a rupture in the depth of his substance or simply consciousness and choice: life at the crossroads, between two possibilities, between two tendencies which exclude or oppose each other. Consciousness and liberty would be the definition of man; in short, reason.

To which there is an objection in the second statement:

> Rav Nahman bar Isaac objected: If this is so, then does this mean that the animal which (he made), *vayitzer* (Genesis 2:19, where *vayitzer* is not written with two *yods*), does not have good and evil inclinations, though we can see that an animal can destroy, bite, and kick?

The argument must be filled out on the basis of what the commentators have given us. An animal can bite and kick, but it can also obey and provide labor. The animal, then, would already have consciousness and choice. Is it therefore possible to say that consciousness and reason define the human being? Here is another possible reading of the above objection, which goes further. If man is a reasonable animal—reason can in fact pin itself onto animality—there is no unbridgeable distance, no incompatibility between animality and reason. Reason can put itself at the service of bestiality and the instincts. The biblical verses about the alliance of God with all that lives could be understood in this manner. But must we not look elsewhere than to consciousness for the dividing line between what is human and the rest?

The second statement concludes, therefore, with a new definition of the human:

> The two *yods* must be interpreted according to Rav Simeon ben Pazzi; for Rav Simeon ben Pazzi said: Woe is me because of my Creator, woe is me because of my own evil inclination.

Obedience

The word *vayitzer*, broken down into *vay-yitzer* would mean "woe to the creature" (*vay,* an interjection like *alas!* is common in popular Jewish speech, notably in Yiddish): woe to the creature, woe when I obey my Creator (for in obeying my Creator I am constantly disrupted by my creaturely nature), but woe is to me also when I obey my essence as creature, my inclinations (for the idea of the Creator, that is, his Law, spoils my pleasure in sinning!). I am still torn, but this time not between the right and the left, as a sign of my freedom as outlined previously, but between the high and the low. The specifically human would be to be caught between my Creator, that is, the Law he gave me, and existence: the healthy desires of a creature that hungers, what Pascal called concupiscence, what we might call the erotic, in the very broad meaning of the word. The condition of creature is not a source of contentment, for man does not oblige it. The drama of existence is not only that existence is divided into choices between desires but that existence is also suspended between the Law that is given me and my nature, which is incapable of submitting to the Law without constraint. It is not freedom which defines the human being. It is obedience which defines him.

Between the Law and nature, between the Creator and the condition of creature, to be man remains as dramatic as the conflict between opposing passions. But here is the third paragraph:

Or one must even interpret in the manner of Rav Jeremiah ben Eleazar, for Rav Jeremiah ben Eleazar said: Two faces did the Holy One, Blessed be He, create in the first man, for isn't it written (Psalms 139:5): "You hedge me before and behind; You lay Your hand upon me."

Everything Is Open

The first man has two faces, without their being a head of Janus, as you shall see. It is striking that it has not occurred to Rav Jeremiah Eleazar to quote the beginning of Genesis, where it is said: "He created him man and woman," to speak of these two faces. The two faces of the human being have as yet nothing to do with the two faces of the couple! The sages of the Talmud prefer Psalm 139 here, from which they cite verse 5. This is the verse which would explain the unusual spelling of "he created" with two *yods*, when the word refers to the creation of man.

The method I have always used—I do not know whether it meets the approval of absolute Talmudists (I am only a very relative Talmudist)—consists in the following: each time a biblical verse is brought in as proof it is not likely that the sages of the Talmud are looking in these texts, squeezed every which way in spite of grammar, for a direct proof of the thesis they are upholding. It is always an invitation to search out the context of the quotation.

Psalm 139 is an admirable psalm.

Oh Lord, you have examined me and know me. You observe my walking and reclining, and are familiar with all my ways. There is not a word on my tongue but that You, O Lord, know it well.

And here are verses 5–10:

You hedge me before and behind; You lay Your hand upon me. . . . Where could I escape from Your spirit? Where can I flee from Your presence? If I ascend to heaven, You are there. If I descend to Sheol, You are there also. If I take wing with the dawn, to come to rest on the western horizon even there Your hand will be guiding me.

Always the hand of God grabs me and guides me. It is impossible to escape from God, not to be present before his sleepless gaze. A gaze which is not experienced as a calamity, in contrast to the terror felt by Racine's Phaedra!

Heaven, the entire universe is filled with my ancestors. Where to hide? Let us escape into the infernal night. But what am I saying? My father is there holding the fatal urn.[2]

In the biblical passage, certainly God's presence means: to be besieged by God or obsessed by God. An obsession which is experienced as a chosenness. Read the rest of the Psalm:

If I say, "Surely darkness will conceal me, night will provide me with cover," darkness is not dark for you; night is as light as the day; darkness and light are the same. It was You who created my conscience; You fashioned me in my mother's womb. I praise You, for I am awesomely, wondrously made.

In other words, man's humanity would be the end of interiority, the end of the subject. Everything is open. I am everywhere looked through, touched by the hand. Thus one can understand why Jonah could not escape his mission. This is what it means to have two faces. With only a single face, I have a place in the rear of the head, the occiput, in which my hidden thoughts and my mental reservations accumulate. Refuge which can hold my entire thought. But here, instead of the occiput, a second face! Everything is exposed; everything in me confronts [fait face] and must answer. I cannot, even through sin, separate myself from this God, who looks at me and touches me. Evil, the last recourse of those who wish to break off, the farthest recess of atheism, is not a break; Psalm 139 tells us that this hiding place is defenseless. God crosses the shadows of sin. He does not let you go or He catches up with you again. You are always exposed! But in this spirited psalm you are discovered with joy; it is the exaltation of divine proximity that this psalm sings: a being exposed without the least hint of shadow.

However, there is something else in this parable of the second face. Woman is not at issue yet. The feminine face will appear later, starting with this idea of a "continuous face," which, at the outset, signifies the sheer humanity of man. The meaning of the feminine will thus become clear against the background of a human essence, the *Isha* from the *Ish*. The feminine does not derive from the masculine; rather, the division into feminine and masculine—the dichotomy—derives from what is human. Complementarity has no concrete significance, is only a lazy turn of phrase, if one has not previously grasped, in the idea of the *whole*, the necessity and the sense of the division. I am not sure that our friend Jankélévitch wanted to express more than the formal notion of complementarity when he talked about interlockedness *[emboîtement]*.

The Other

Let us insist again upon the meaning we have discovered in Rav Jeremiah ben Eleazar's saying in light of Psalm 139. Let us free it from its theological forms. (In reading one should not stop at the form of the signs which speak to us—just as when reading the letter *A*, one should not stop at the roof shape that this letter forms.) What does this manner of being surrounded by God mean if not the very image which functions as its allegory? To be under the sleepless gaze of God is, precisely, in one's unity, to be the bearer of *another* subject—bearer and supporter—to be responsible for this other, as if the face of this other, although invisible, continued my own face and kept me awake by its very invisibility, by the unpredictability that it threatens. Unity of the *one* subject, irreplaceable in the impossibility to refuse responsibility for this other—closer than any proximity and yet unknown. Essential manner in which the human being is exposed to the point of losing the skin which protects him, a skin which has completely become a face, as if a being, centered about his core, experienced a removal of this core and, losing it, was "for the other" before any dialogue!

It is not in a dialogue that the human being could expose himself to such a degree. For this kind of exposure, the head with two faces is necessary. A human head, unique in its unity without synthesis or synchronicity, which marks my responsibility for the other, without the other and myself becoming, when we mutually recognize each other in each other's eyes, equivalent, interchangeable terms. But doesn't this strange duality of the non-interchangeable announce the difference between the sexes? Thus woman appears within the human. The social governs the erotic.

Side or Rib

I will continue reading the text:

And the Lord God fashioned into a woman

and, following the translation of the French rabbinate, which is the best and which gives a literal reading:

built into a woman "the rib which he had taken from man."

Here the discussion begins:

Rab and Samuel are talking. One said: It was a face (the famous rib was a face).
The other said: It was a tail.

A tail, that is to say, an appendage; not much—much less than a rib, one of the lower vertebrae of the spinal column, which no longer supports ribs, the last vertebra. The fact that a woman is not merely the female of man, that she belongs to the human, is an assumption shared by both disputants: woman is from the first created from that which is human. According to the first sage, she is strictly contemporary with man; according to the dissenter, to come into being, a woman required a new act of creation.

But where does the opposition between the two opponents lie? The one for whom the rib is a face posits a perfect equality between the feminine and the masculine; he thinks that all relations that bind them are of equal dignity. The creation of man was the creation of two beings in one but of two beings equal in dignity: difference and sexual relations belong to the fundamental content of what is human. What does the one who sees only a tail in the rib mean? He cannot ignore what has happened to the little piece of skin or bone taken from man; he knows that God went to the trouble of making it into a person. As a result, he too does not think that woman came into the world through natural evolution, from a lost bone of man; he knows that she came forth from a real act of creation. But he thinks that beyond the personal relationship that establishes itself between these two beings issued from two creative acts, the particularity of the feminine is secondary. It is not woman who is secondary; it is the relationship with woman which is secondary; it is the relationship with woman as woman that does not belong to what is fundamentally human. Fundamental are the tasks that man accomplishes as a human being and that woman accomplishes as a human being. They have other things to do besides cooing, and, moreover, something else to do and more, than to limit themselves to the relations that are established because of the differences in sex. Sexual liberation, by itself, would not be a revolution adequate to the human species. Woman is not at the summit of the spiritual life the way Beatrice is for Dante. It is not the "Eternal Feminine" which leads us to the heights.

I think of the last chapter of Proverbs, of the woman praised there; she makes possible the life of men; she is the home of men. But the husband has a life outside the home: He sits on the Council of the city; he has a public life; he is at the service of the universal; he does not limit himself to interiority, to intimacy, to the home, although without them he could no nothing.

Answerable for All the Others

Now here are some difficulties:

> For the one who said: "It was a face," the text "You hedge me before and be-hind" presents no difficulties. But what does the one who maintains that it is a tail do with the text?
>
> We must acknowledge that he thinks like Rav Ammi. For Rav Ammi said: "behind" means "the last one created," "before" means "the first one to be punished."

To maintain that woman as woman is not one of the poles of spiritual-ity, that love, although it dominates our poetry and literature, is not equiva-lent to the Spirit, is to deny that verse 5 of Psalm 139 makes any reference to woman. Rav Ammi interprets it in agreement with the thesis we have just examined: man is the last creature, the last to come into the world, the rear guard of the creature. This world is therefore not what man would have planned or wanted. It is not even what man has seen the beginning of. It has not come about as a result of man's creative freedom. Man has come into an already-made universe. Man is the first to receive punishment. It is he who answers for what he has not done. Man is responsible for the uni-verse, the hostage of the creature. Beyond the realm attributable to his free-dom, he is pressed from his front and rear: He is asked to account for things which he did not will and which were not born from his freedom.

Rav Ammi's interpretation thus situates the human in the responsibility "for all others." It is in perfect agreement with the thesis which upholds that woman, in her sexual particularity, was born from a minor joint of man or of the human being. In the relationship with another person, the preposition "with" changes into the preposition "for." I am "with the others" means I am "for the others": responsible for the other person. Here the feminine as such is only secondary. Man and woman, when authenti-cally human, work together as responsible beings. The sexual is only an accessory of the human.

These are not mere subtleties. What is challenged here is the revolution which thinks it has achieved the ultimate by destroying the family so as to liberate imprisoned sexuality. What is challenged is the claim of accom-plishing on the sexual plane the real liberation of man. Real Evil would be elsewhere. Evil, as psychoanalysis discovers it in sickness, would already be predetermined by a betrayed responsibility. Libidinous relations in them-selves would not contain the mystery of the human psyche. It is that which is human that would explain the acuteness of conflicts knotted into Freud-ian complexes. It is not the acuteness of libidinous desire that, in itself, would explain the soul. As I see it, this is what my text shows. I am not taking sides; today, I am commenting.

All right as far as "the last one created" goes—for man was not created until Shabbath eve itself—but as far as "the first one to be punished," which punishment are you referring to? Would it be the one imposed after the story of the snake? Don't we have a *toseftah:* Rabbi said: In conferring honor, we start with the greatest, in cursing with the least important. In conferring honor we start with the greatest, for it is written (Leviticus 10:12): "Moses said to Aaron, as well as to Eleazar and Ithamar, his surviving sons: 'Take the meal offering that is left over from the Lord's offerings and eat it unleavened beside the altar, for it is most holy.' " To curse, one begins with the least, for the serpent was cursed first, then Eve, and finally Adam. The priority of man in the matter of sanctions could then only refer to the Flood. For it is written (Genesis 7:23): "God wiped out all the creatures on the face of the earth, both man and cattle." First man, then the beasts.

Let us explain the literal meaning of the text. The quoted *toseftah* seems to challenge the priority of human responsibility. Isn't the snake the first one to be cursed after the original sin? Certainly, one could concede that punishment is inflicted upon the least worthy (first to the serpent, then to Eve, finally to Adam), and reward is given to the most worthy. When Aaron and his sons are promoted to the priesthood, Moses names Aaron first. But this distinction between positive and negative sanctions still challenges the principle according to which man would be the first to answer. That is why the Gemara replies that punishment is inflicted upon man first in circumstances such as those of the Flood, in which, according to Genesis 7:23, man is named first.

But let us look closely at the nature of the acts in the three examples cited.

The merit which is the reason for Aaron's elevation to the priesthood and the fault which brings the curse on the serpent are merit and fault only in regard to the Eternal. Such is not the reason for the Flood! Rabbinic tradition and the biblical text agree: the causes for the Flood were injustice and the sexual perversion of men and animals. Ethical evil from which the other person suffers. But also confusion of what is human and what is animal. Evil gnawing at the creature in this confusion of human and animal. For this perverted universe, man answers first. This humanity is defined, not by liberty—do we know whether Evil began with man?—but by a responsibility prior to all initiative. Man answers for more than his freely chosen acts. He is the hostage of the universe. Extraordinary dignity. Unlimited responsibility. Man does not belong to a society which bestows limited responsibility upon its members. He is the member of a society of unlimited responsibility.

But what did Rabbi want to teach us?

Where the Spirit Is

Some other aspects of our responsibility: When a fault committed does not involve another person, it is proper to invoke extenuating circumstances. In exalting merit, one must respect the contingencies of rank, give back to society what is its due.

But beyond this point, the obligation to answer for the other takes on the full strictness of unconditionality.

> He who says that rib means face is in accord with the two *yods* of *vayitzer* (Genesis 2:19); what does the one for whom rib means tail make of the two *yods* of *vayitzer*? He must follow the lesson of Rav Simeon ben Pazzi. For Rav Simeon ben Pazzi said that the two *yods* of *vayitzer* mean "Woe is me on account of my Creator, woe is me on account of my evil inclination."

Let us explain this language: the opinion according to which the rib extracted from Adam for the creation of woman was an aspect of the human—a face—will no doubt interpret the two *yods* from the word *vayitzer* as an allusion to the original duality of masculine and feminine in Adam. But what meaning would the two *yods* receive from the one for whom the rib is an insignificant appendage of the human (which we have translated as tail)? The answer: He will follow the interpretation given by Rav Simeon ben Pazzi, whose opinion we have interpreted above: man is torn between his nature as creature and the Law, which comes to him from the Creator. To acknowledge that the sexual relation itself is only incidental to the human is to locate the spiritual life of humanity in a concern for balancing an existence torn between nature and Law. To put it even more broadly: culture is not determined by the libido.

But the division of the human being into feminine and masculine, in its relation to man's humanity, opens yet other perspectives.

> He who says that rib means face is in agreement with the text that says: "Male and female he made them simultaneously" (Genesis 5:2). What does the one for whom rib means tail make of "male and female he made them simultaneously"? One must follow the lesson of Rabbi Abbahu. For Rabbi Abbahu objected: It is written: "He created them male and female" (Genesis 5:2), and it is written (Genesis 9:6): "Man was made in the image of God." How is it possible? He first had in mind to create two and in the end created only one.

If the rib means "side," the feminine face, in the first man, equals the masculine face. We then recognize the meaning of "Male and female he created them simultaneously." Is it possible that woman's creation from a minor joint of man could be worth as much as the marvelous notion of woman equal to man from the outset, of woman as the "other side" of man? In this questioning, the issue is not how two verses could both be possible; it is not a matter of concordances between texts, but of a train of thought in its multiple possibilities. The problem, in each of the paragraphs we are commenting on at this moment, is in reconciling the humanity of men and women with the hypothesis of a masculine spirituality in which the feminine would not be an equal term but a corollary. Feminine specificity or the difference between the sexes which it manifests would not be, from the outset, on the same plane as the oppositions which constitute Spirit. Daring question: how can the equality of sexes stem from the priority of the masculine? This, let us note in passing, removes us from the simple notion of complementarity.

Hierarchy or Equality

Our text asks itself, however, in what way the idea of two equal beings—man and woman—in the first man is "the most beautiful idea." Does the image of God mean from the outset the simultaneity of the male and the female? Here is the answer of Rav Abbahu: God wanted to create two beings, male and female, but he created in God's image a single being. He created less well than his original idea. He would then—if I may venture to say so—have willed beyond his own image! He wanted two beings. In fact, he wanted that from the beginning there should be equality in the creature, no woman issuing from man, no woman who came after man. From the beginning he wanted two separate and equal beings. But that was impossible; this initial independence of two equal beings would no doubt have meant war. It had to be done not strictly according to justice, which would demand two separate beings. To create a world, he had to subordinate them one to the other. There had to be a difference which did not affect equity: a sexual difference and, hence, a certain preeminence of man, a woman coming later, and as woman, an appendage of the human. We now understand the lesson in this. Humanity is not thinkable on the basis of two entirely different principles. There had to have been a *sameness* that these *others* had in common. Woman was set apart from man but she came after him: *the very feminity of woman is in this initial "after the event."* Society was not founded on purely divine principles: the world would not have lasted. Real humanity does not allow for an abstract equality, without some subordination of terms. What family scenes there would have been between the members of that first perfectly equal couple! Subordination was needed, and a wound was needed; suffering was and is needed to unite equals and unequals.

> He who said that rib means face can agree with the text (Genesis 2:21): "And he closed up the place with flesh." What does the one for whom rib means tail make of it? Rav Jeremiah and, according to others, Rav Zebid and, according to others, Rav Nahman bar Isaac taught: The flesh was necessary only at the place of the cut.

How can we speak of the flesh which was created to fill the empty space if the rib from which woman was made was but an appendage? Would the family be born without any wounds to tend? If the rib was a face, one un-

derstands that the separation of the two faces is already a separation between beings, that it leaves a wound, a gaping scar, and that flesh is needed
to close the wound. Rav Jeremiah teaches us that the size of the wound is
not the determining factor. It is enough that there was a sundering.

Appearance

However, there is in woman, this equal, this companion, some essential
aspects apart from the face.

> He who said that rib means tail can be in accord with the formulation (Gen-
> esis 2:22): "And the Lord God fashioned the rib that He had taken from the man
> into a woman." What does the one for whom rib means face do with it? Here
> one must follow Rabbi Simeon ben Menasia. Rabbi Simeon ben Menasia taught:
> For the text "He fashioned the rib into woman," it has to be understood that
> the Holy One, Blessed be He, plaited Eve's hair into braids and took her to
> Adam, for in other countries plaiting is called binyatha (building).

In the feminine, there is face and appearance, and God was the first hair-
dresser. He created the first illusions, the first make-up. To build a feminine
being is from the outset to make room for appearance. "Her hair had to be
done." There is in the feminine face and in the relation between the sexes
this beckoning to the lie, or to an arrangement beyond the savage straight-
forwardness of a face-to-face encounter, bypassing a relationship between
human beings approaching each other in the responsibility of one for the
other.

> Another explanation: Rav Hisda said—and others say that it was taught in a
> baraita: The text teaches us that the Holy One, Blessed be He, made Eve like a
> granary. For just as the granary is narrow at the top and large at the bottom to
> hold the harvest, so woman is narrow at the top and large at the bottom to hold
> the child.

Something beyond the face which everyone forgets! Beyond sexuality,
the gestation of a new being! The relation with the other person through
the son.

It is thus not in terms of equality that the entire question of woman can
be discussed. From now on our text will seek to show the importance of a
certain inequality, be it only a matter of custom. But it is getting late. I will
pass over the text quickly now.

Which of the two faces, the masculine or the feminine, leads? Here
equality would end in immobility or in the bursting apart of the human
being. The Gemara opts for the priority of the masculine. A man must not
walk behind a woman, for his ideas may become clouded. The first reason
stems perhaps from masculine psychology. It assumes that a woman bears

the erotic within herself as a matter of course. If a man overtakes a woman on a bridge—bridges used to be narrow spaces—the man must strive to walk beside the woman on this bridge, even when this woman is his own wife. It is forbidden to cross a river behind a woman because in crossing a river a woman will show something of her underthings; the interhuman relation will be soiled by concupiscence. A man must not give money to a woman directly. Not even when it is altogether proper and honorable, for he may thus seek an occasion to look at her. The principle is healthier than this outmoded rigorism. Relations between equal beings should not become pretexts for ambiguity. "Even if the man who does this is full of Torah and of good actions like Moses, he is bound for hell." The theme of the priority of the masculine is emphasized without putting into question, in the relationship between man and woman, the relationship of man to man. Question: Manoah, the father of Samson, is called an ignoramus and uncivilized because it is said in scripture: "And Manoah walked behind his wife." But didn't the prophet Elisha follow the Shunamite woman? Answer: to follow can mean to take advice. Essential point: in the interhuman order, the perfect equality and even superiority of woman, who is capable of giving advice and direction. According to custom, it is the man who must nevertheless, regardless of the goal, indicate the direction in which to walk.

The Order of Dangers

At this point the relationship with the woman as woman must be placed within other human relationships:

> Rabbi Johanan said: Behind a lion and not behind a woman; behind a woman and not behind an idol worshipper; behind an idol worshipper and not behind a synagogue (on the side opposite the entrance) when the community is praying.

A very commonsense prohibition, to be sure. But we are talking of extreme situations. If there are only two paths, and if a lion walks on one and a woman on the other, which path to choose? Rabbi Johanan said: It is better to walk behind the lion. A woman and an idol worshipper? Follow the woman. To walk behind an idol worshipper or to be behind a synagogue on the side opposite the entrance? Walk behind the idol worshipper.

To walk behind the lion: to live life, struggle, and ambition. To experience all the cruelties of life, always in contact with lions or, at least, with human guides who can suddenly turn around and show you their lion face. To walk behind a woman, to choose the sweetness of intimacy, perhaps the dove coos removed from the great upheavals and the great shocks which scan the Real? What peace there is in the intimacy of love! The text of the Gemara prefers the danger of the lions to this intimacy. The feminine has been much defended today as if the relationship with the feminine were only the meeting of the other *par excellence,* with all the excellences of such a meeting. What of evasions, of all the ambiguity of the famed love life (even when it claims to rise above pleasure)? What of all the abysses, the betrayals, the perfidiousness, the pettinesses?

But our text still prefers the sentimental road to that of idolatry. Idolatry, that is no doubt the State, the prototype of idolatry, since the State adores being an idol; idolatry, that is also the cult of the Greek gods and hence all the appeal of Hellenism. It is probably because it evokes Greece that idolatry can still be preferred to something else! But idolatry also encompasses all the intellectual temptations of the relative, of exoticism and fads, all that comes to us from India or China, all that comes to us from the alleged "experiences" of humanity which we would not be permitted to reject.

The fourth thing is the worst; worse than the enthusiasm for idolatry. Isolation within Judaism, a *no* uttered to the community. To be outside a synagogue filled with people, that is the extreme apostasy; to say: that does not concern me, that concerns the Iranians and not the Israelis, that concerns immigrant Jews and not French Jews. Here the condemnation is beyond recall.

But there are circumstances which permit four exceptions.

> In any case, this last point is valid only for him that finds himself without a burden; if he bears a burden, it is not so. And this point applies only if there are no other doors; if there is another door, it is not so. And this applies only if he is not mounted on a donkey; if he is on the back of a donkey, it is not so. And this applies only if he is not wearing *tefillin;* if he wears *tefillin,* it is not so.

At what point is the man isolated in front of the synagogue doomed? When the man behind the synagogue full of people, isolated by the side with no doors, bears no burden; if he finds himself behind the synagogue with a burden, he deserves to be treated with indulgence. One indeed does not enter the synagogue with a sack of wheat. But the exception means more than that. A person may rebel against the synagogue because of the unbearable burden he carries. Let us forgive this revolt!

Second exception: the man finds himself on a donkey: one cannot enter a synagogue on a donkey: one cannot always find a parking space. But the donkey is also what carries you along, an influence under which you have fallen, a current of opinions or ideas, not necessarily intelligent but very stubborn. Forbearance! Forbearance!

The third exception concerns the one who finds himself on the side opposite to the entrance of the synagogue, but where there is another door. His revolt against the synagogue is possibly a quest for another door. He isolates himself from the collectivity of Israel the better to enter it. His case is not desperate.

Last exception: the case of the one who although far from any entrance, still puts on *tefillin*. He preserves, despite the revulsion he feels toward Judaism, the minimal rites. Through this, he is not lost.

You see: the feminine is in a fairly good position in this hierarchy of values, which reveals itself when choices become alternatives. It is in second place. It is not woman who is thus slighted. It is the relation based on sexual differences which is subordinated to the interhuman relation—irreducible to the drives and complexes of the libido—to which woman rises as well as man. Maybe man precedes—by a few centuries—the woman in this elevation. From which a certain—provisional?—priority of man. Maybe the masculine is more directly linked to the universal, and maybe masculine civilization has prepared, above the sexual, a human order in which a woman enters, completely human.

But who is the man who finds himself behind the synagogue where there is no other door, the man more lost than an idol worshipper? I am asking myself whether it is not the one who, outside the rituals and the laws, which are only the *letter*, believes himself to be "in spirit and in truth" in the most intimate intimacy of Being. Here he is thrown into the shoreless abysses of interiority. It has never given back those it has succeeded in seducing.

NOTES

1. See *L'autre dans la conscience juive: Le sacré et le couple: Données et débats.* (Paris: P.U.F., 1973), pp. 159–172.

2. "Le ciel, tout l'univers est plein de mes aieux. Où me cacher? Fuyons dans la nuit infernale. Mais que dis-je? Mon père y tient l'urne fatale." Racine, *Phèdre,* act 4, scene 6.

DAMAGES DUE TO FIRE

• From the Tractate *Baba Kama*, p. 60a–b •

Mishna   *If someone brings on a fire which consumes wood, stones, or earth, he would be liable, as it is written (Exodus 22:5): "If fire breaks out and catches in thorns so that the stack of corn, or the standing corn, or the field is consumed, he who starts the fire must make restitution."*

Gemara   *Raba said:* Why did the Merciful One write thorns, stacks, standing corn, *and* field? *They are all necessary. For if the Merciful One had written only thorns, one might have said that it was only in the case of thorns that the Merciful One imposed liability because fire is often found among them and carelessness in regard to them is frequent, whereas in the case of stacks, which are not often on fire and in respect of which negligence is not usual, one might have held that there is no liability. If again the Merciful One had mentioned only stacks, one might have said that it was only in the case of* stacks *that the Merciful One imposed liability, as the loss involved there was considerable; whereas in the case of thorns, where the loss involved was slight, one might have thought there was no liability.*

   But why was standing corn necessary? To teach that just as standing corn is in an open place, so is everything which is in an open place subject to the same law. But why, then, for Rabbi Judah, would standing corn be mentioned, since Rabbi Judah thinks that one is responsible for damages that fire causes even to goods we cannot see? To include anything which stands (which is attached to the earth). How, then, is the responsibility for anything that stands deduced by the sages? They derive it from the conjunction or (or the standing corn). What does this or *mean for Rabbi Judah? He needed it to divide (to make payment for damages obligatory*

This reading was given in the context of a colloquium consecrated to the topic of war, held in September 1975. The proceedings were published in *La conscience juive face à la guerre* (Paris: P.U.F., 1976). Levinas's commentary appears in pp. 13–26, and the discussion that follows on pp. 27–29.

even when it is a matter of only part of the enumerated damages). What permits dividing according to the Rabbis? The second conjunction or *(or the fields of another).*

What does Rabbi Judah do with this second or? *According to him, it would be the counterpart of the* or *of the standing corn. But why was the field mentioned? To include (in the payment for damages) the case in which fire lapped a ploughed field and grazed stones.*

Couldn't the Merciful One have written field *and dispensed with all the rest? The rest is necessary. If He had written only* field, *one might have thought that for the products of the field one owes reparation, but for other things not. That we are responsible also for all the rest, that is what we are meant to understand.*

Rabbi Simeon bar Nahmani in the name of Rabbi Johanan: Calamity comes upon the world only because there are wicked persons in the world, but it always begins with the righteous, for it is said: "If fire breaks out and catches in thorns." When does fire break out? When it finds thorns; but it begins by consuming only the just, for it is said: "and the stack of corn is consumed"; it does not say: "When it consumes the stack" but: "When the stack is consumed," which means that it is already *consumed.*

Rav Joseph taught: It is written (Exodus 12:22): "And none of you shall go outside the door of his house until morning." As soon as freedom is given to the angel of extermination, he no longer distinguishes between the just and the unjust; moreover, he even begins with the just, for it is written (Ezekiel 21:8): "I shall wipe out from you both the righteous and the wicked." Then Rav Joseph wept: And such a verse to top it all! Those (the just) count for nothing. Abaye said to him: That is a favor to them, for it is said (Isaiah 57:1): "Good men are taken away before disaster strikes."

Rav Judah stated in the name of Rab: It is a rule: One must enter an inn when it is full daylight and leave it when it is full daylight, for it is said (Exodus 12:22): "None of you shall go outside the door of his house until morning."

There is a baraita: If there is an epidemic in a city, keep your feet from entering it, for it is said: "None of you shall go outside the door of his house until morning"; and then it is said (Isaiah 26:20): "Go my people, enter your chambers, and lock your doors behind you. Hide but a little moment, until the storm passes"; and besides it is said (Deuteronomy

32:25): "The sword shall deal without; within, there shall be terror."

Why this besides? *One might have thought all of this applies to night and not to day. That is why it is said: "Go, my people, enter your chambers and lock your doors behind you." But one might have thought that this holds only if inside the house (within) there is no terror and that, if inside there were terror, it would be better to join with people in one group. That is why it is said: Outside, the sword will make victims. Even if inside there is terror, outside the sword shall make victims. Raba used to keep the windows (of his house) sealed during the time of the epidemic, for it is said (Jeremiah 9:20): "For death is come up unto our windows."*

There is a baraita: *If famine is in the city, disperse (broaden) your steps, for it is said (Genesis 12:10): "There was famine in the land, and Abram went down to Egypt to sojourn there." Furthermore, it is said (2 Kings 7:4): "If we decide to go into the town, we shall die there." What is the purpose of this* furthermore? *It might be thought that this is valid only when there is nothing life-threatening where one is going, and that it is invalid when emigration leads to danger; that is why it is said: So let us cast ourselves upon the Assyrian camp: if they let us live, we will survive.*

There is a baraita: *If the angel of death is in the city, one should not walk in the middle of the road, for the angel of death moves about in the middle of the road: benefiting from the liberty granted to him, he walks about publicly. If the city is at peace, one should not walk at the sides of the road, for not being granted liberty, the angel of death slinks along in hiding.*

There is a baraita: *If there is an epidemic in a city, one should not go the house of prayer alone, for it is there that the angel of death keeps his implements; this is true, however, only in the case where schoolchildren do not read Scriptures there and where there are not ten people to pray (together).*

There is a baraita: *If the dogs howl, that is because the angel of death has entered the city; if the dogs are happy, Elijah has come into the city. But that is on the condition that there is no bitch among them!*

Rav Ami and Rav Assi were sitting before Rabbi Isaac, the blacksmith. One asked him to treat of the Halakhah and the other of the Aggadah. When he began a Halakhah, he was

prevented by the latter; when he began an Aggadah, he was
prevented by the former. He then said to them: I will tell
you a parable. This can be compared to a man who had two
wives, one young and the other old. The young one tore out
his white hair, the old one his black hair, so that he became
bald on both sides. He then said to them: I will tell you a
story which will please you both. If a fire breaks out and
catches in thorns and progresses of itself, then the one who
set the fire has to pay. The Holy One, Blessed be He, said: I
kindled a fire on Zion, as it is said (Lamentations 4:11): "He
kindled a fire in Zion which consumed its foundations," and
I will rebuild it one day with fire, as it is said (Zechariah
2:9): "And I myself will be a wall of fire all around it and I
will be a glory inside it." Thus, the one who set the fire has
to pay. The Holy One, Blessed be He, said: It is incumbent
on me to make restitution for the fire which I have set. A
Halakhah: one begins with a compensation one is obliged to
make because of what belongs to you, and one concludes by
a compensation due for damages caused to the very person,
in order to teach you that the damage caused by fire is to be
compared to the damage caused by an arrow.

We will begin by distributing the text. It is the moment when I tremble most, not that I fear that the text does not contain things as clever as those you have just heard but that I always feel inferior to my text. This is not a purely rhetorical statement or false modesty but the acknowledgment, once again, that these texts contain more than what I am able to find in them. Strangely enough, Jewish wisdom maintains the style of its master, Moses, who was "slow of speech and slow of tongue." It is not a personal defect which thus perpetuates itself. It is the objective style of a thought which fails to embrace the forms of rhetoric. It is the way inspiration inspires in contact with harsh and complex and contradictory realities. A sermon without eloquence.

Destructive Fire

Mr. President, ladies and gentlemen, here then is the text, which, in addition to its jerky and awkward rhythm, is rapidly and poorly translated. At first glance, it is not about war. This page 60 of the tractate *Baba Kama* speaks of the damages caused by fire and of the liabilities they imply. It does not refer to war but to destructive fire and, later, to epidemics, to famine— all of this causing damages and death. These are also the effects of war. Is it possible to deduce the *essence* of war from this starting point? Or to deduce what is more war than war? Perhaps this is where our reading will, in fact, take us.

Seen in its effects, war will be approached here above or outside its positive political or social conditions. At first, we seem to stray from the subject. But the very fact of a discussion about the liabilities a destructive fire implies challenges the fatality of destruction. In a sense, we seem to come close to the thesis about the rationality of war, of which Robert Misrahi[1] spoke earlier. Never will this rationality be put into question, to be sure; but, born of human relations, violence remains at the edge of an abyss into which, at a certain moment, everything can founder, including reason. We leave war to return to its ultimate source, which is Auschwitz, and into which it risks reverting. The very reason of war would come from a madness and would risk sinking back into it.

The Structure of the Text

Second characteristic of the text chosen: it is original. Not because, as with all Talmudic texts, it is inimitable. It is original in its structure. It is, in fact a Halakhah, that is, a lesson which states a *behavior* to be observed, which states a law. But in the text itself, the Halakhah, *without calling into play the interpretation of the reader*, is transfigured into an Aggadah, into a homiletic text, which, as you perhaps know, is the way philosophical views, that is to say, the properly religious thought of Israel, appear in Talmudic thought. (I do not regret having brought together philosophy and religion in my preceding sentence. Philosophy, for me, derives from religion. It is called into being by a religion adrift, and probably religion is always adrift.[2]) And this aggadic interpretation of a Halakhah concerning fire will end with a new Halakhic teaching: the text thus goes from Halakhah to Aggadah, and from Aggadah to Halakhah. That is its original structure, very remarkable in its stylistic rhythm, but not indifferent to the question preoccupying us. So much for preliminary remarks.

The Extent of Liabilities

The text begins with the Mishna. That is the name given to the lessons attributed to the authority of rabbinic sages called *Tanaim*, holders of the Revelation referred to as Oral Law and which, according to Israel's faith, has been transmitted from masters to disciples ever since the epiphany at Sinai.[3] The Oral Law would be independent of Scriptures, although it refers itself to them and directs their interpretation. It was given written form toward the end of the second century of our era (the time of the last *Tanaitic* generations) by Rabbi Judah Hanassi. Our Mishna states the responsibility incurred by someone who is the cause of a fire in a field.

If someone brings on a fire which consumes wood, stones, or earth, he would be liable, as it is written (Exodus 22:5): "If fire breaks out and catches in thorns so that the stacks of corn, or the standing corn, or the field is consumed, he who starts the fire must make restitution."

The text seems clear. But, for three-quarters of a page, it is commented on by the Gemara, which will draw the diverse categories of goods requiring compensation from it. It will justify the use of each word, and even parts of speech will signify teachings to it. Let us first recall what the word *Gemara* means. It is the putting into writing of discussions about the Mishna among the generations of rabbinic sages who followed the *Tanaim* and who are called *Amoraim*. In their hermeneutic, they refer particularly to *Tanaitic* traditions excluded from the code of Rabbi Judah Hanassi and, for that reason, called *baraitot* (outside). Our Gemara proceeds by pretending to be astonished at the apparent prolixity of the text quoted from Exodus 22:5 and by accounting for it step by step.

> Raba said: Why did the Merciful One write *thorns, stacks, standing corn,* and *field?* They are all necessary. For if the Merciful One had written only thorns, one might have said that it was only in the case of thorns that the Merciful One imposed liability because fire is often found among them and carelessness in regard to them is frequent, whereas in the case of stacks, which are not often on fire and in respect of which negligence is not usual, one might have held that there is no liability. If again the Merciful One had mentioned only stacks, one might have said that it was only in the case of stacks that the Merciful One imposed liability, as the loss involved there was considerable; whereas in the case of thorns, where the loss involved was slight, one might have thought there was no liability.

First, what is the meaning of the word Merciful *(Rakhmana)*, which comes back constantly in this text? It means the Torah itself or the Eternal One, the Eternal One who is defined by Mercy. But this translation is altogether inadequate. *Rakhamim* (Mercy), which the Aramaic term *Rakhmana* evokes, goes back to the word *Rekhem*, which means uterus. *Rakhamim* is the relation of the uterus to the *other*, whose gestation takes place within it. *Rakhamim* is maternity itself. God as merciful is God defined by maternity. A feminine element is stirred in the depth of this mercy. This maternal element in divine paternity is very remarkable, as is in Judaism the notion of a "virility" to which limits must be set and whose partial renouncement may be symbolized by circumcision, the exaltation of a certain *weakness* which would be devoid of cowardice. Perhaps maternity is sensitivity itself, of which so much ill is said among the Nietzscheans.

Why is the verse quoted by the Mishna so wordy then? The Gemara explains the usefulness of the word *thorns*, which indicates a type, and of the word *stacks*, which indicates another, irreducible to the first. This generalization or even formalization of Scriptural terms is a procedure characteristic of Talmudic exegesis. It is in the same spirit that the mention of *standing corn* is justified.

> But why was *standing corn* necessary? To teach that just as standing corn is in an open place, so is everything which is in an open place subject to the same law.

One is responsible, in case of fire, for all things one can see. But here the discussion gets more complicated, for, according to another tradition represented by Rabbi Judah, liability extends even to damage caused to goods that one cannot see. Let us note the appearance here of a responsibility concerning that which escapes perception and consequently the precautions and powers of the one who has caused the harm. The text from Exodus must now be justified both by the rabbinic sages, who understand responsibility as being limited to what can be seen, and by the one who understands it in a broader sense.

> But why, then, for Rabbi Judah, would standing corn be mentioned, since Rabbi Judah thinks that one is responsible for damages that fire causes even to goods we cannot see?

Answer:

> To include anything which stands (which is attached to the earth)

even trees and animals.
But what about the others? How do they deduce compensation for things that stand?

> How, then, is the responsibility for anything that stands deduced by the sages? They derive it from the conjunction *or (or the standing corn)*.

There would be an extension of the notion in this *or:*

> What does this *or* mean for Rabbi Judah? He needed it to divide. . . .

This *or* implies division: one is responsible not only when the misfortunes enumerated in the verse happen simultaneously but also if each happens separately.
What then permits "dividing," according to the Rabbis, since they have already used *or* for the things that stand?

> The second conjunction *or (or the fields of another)*.
> What does Rabbi Judah do with the second *or?* According to him, it would be the counterpart of the *or* of *the standing corn*.

Consequently, Rabbi Judah does not give it any special meaning. Thus, the text can be read both according to the hypothesis of Rabbi Judah and according to the hypothesis of the sages.

> But why was the *field* mentioned? To include the case in which fire lapped his neighbor's ploughed field and grazed his stones.

Finally:

> Couldn't the Merciful One have written *field* and dispensed with all the rest? The rest is necessary. If He had written only field, one might have thought that for the products of the field one owes reparation, but for other things not. That we are responsible also for all the rest, that is what we are meant to understand.

Here then is a rigorously Halakhic text. Its general meaning is clear: It affirms responsibility for damages caused by a disaster, due, to be sure, to human freedom, but which, as fire, immediately escapes the powers of the guilty party. Fire, an elementary force to which other elementary forces will add themselves, multiplying damages beyond any rational conjecture! The wind adds its whims and violences to it. And yet responsibility is not diminished. Rabbi Judah extends it to concealed goods, which we cannot attempt to salvage because they are out of our sight. But are we speaking of war? Are we not in a time of peace? Aren't the courts there? Don't the judges gird their sashes? Isn't everything in its place? Isn't there justice? But perhaps the elemental force of fire is already the intervention of the uncontrollable, of war. It does not annul responsibilities!

The Rationality of the Irrational

But here the text—without the fantasy of a modern interpreter seeking paradoxes—transforms its juridical truths into religious and moral ones.

> Rabbi Simeon bar Nahmani in the name of Rabbi Johanan: Calamity comes upon the world only because there are wicked persons in the world, but it always begins with the righteous, for it is said: "If fire breaks out and catches in thorns." When does fire break out? When it finds thorns; but it begins by consuming only the just, for it is said: "and the stack of corn is consumed"; it does not say: "When it consumes the stack" but: "When the stack is consumed," which means that it is *already* consumed.

"Calamity comes upon the world only when there are wicked persons. . . . " That is war. That is morality as it is commonly preached. If the Talmud brought us only such proverbial truths, one could do without it. But Rabbi Samuel bar Nahmani, who interprets the biblical verse allegorically, draws something more from it. "Trials begin only with the just." This is a little less banal.

But isn't the image of thorns instructive? "When does fire break out? Only when it finds thorns." Thorns—that is what prickles! The wit of "cultivated minds," the paradoxes of intellectuals searching for new ideas, could these be the cause of violence? But maybe the thorns are simply evil people. Injustice within society would give rise to external armies. It is an old idea of the rabbinic sages, which Professor Henri Baruk took over in his own way when he admired the biblical expression "Lord of Hosts," the very one that had scandalized Simone Weil (the philosopher). Mr. Baruk thinks that the "Lord of Hosts" is a sublime name of God! Through it the Divine signifies that social evil already contains within itself the uncontainable forces of war.

But fire starts by consuming only the righteous. For it is said, "and the stack of corn is consumed." It does not say: "When it consumes the stack," but that the stack of corn *is consumed.* Fire breaks out because of the thorns; it just gets started but the stack of corn is *already* consumed. Is this the irra-tionality of war? The turning upside down of order through the intervention of the elemental and uncontrollable? Do we have here the favorite theme of the prophet Ezekiel, as the rabbinic sages read him, and which we shall find again later on: the righteous are responsible for evil before anyone else is. They are responsible because they have not been righteous enough to make their justice spread and abolish injustice: it is the fiasco of the best which leaves the coast clear for the worst. But, if this were so, there would still be reason in the very irrationality of war: the justice of history. And, in this case, we would perhaps still be dealing with an occurrence not entirely free of the will of rational beings. This would agree with the political rationalism of Robert Misrahi, whose chances of being right we must never dismiss![4]

But the parable of the thorns and the stacks of corn can be understood in another way: evil people bring war about. To be sure. Those who could stop it would have been its first victims. A rationality is still unfolding in the events of war but no longer finds a Reason capable of unraveling it. The reason of war would end in unreason.

Another reading: it is the righteous who pay for the wickedness of Evil. Here again we have a violence which is not chaotic: the righteous are yet distinct from the wicked. Our text would not be completely pessimistic. The priority of the righteous would be upheld: the priority of the righteous would be due to his laying himself open to sacrifice. Good is the non-resis-tance to Evil and the gift of atonement.

But perhaps in the end, the *reason* of war consists in the very *turning upside down* of Reason. According to the Talmudic tractate *Berakhot*, Mo-ses reserves for the moment of his supreme intimacy with God the question which must have mattered to him the most. It was: "Why are the righteous sometimes prosperous, sometimes not, and the unrighteous sometimes prosperous, sometimes not?" He did not ask: "Why do the righteous suffer and the wicked prosper?" A rigorously upside-down order would certainly be diabolical, but it would still attest to a *governed* world. Moses is afraid only of an absolutely contingent world! According to the last reading of the thorns and the stacks which we proposed, there would still be a direction in Creation: an order. Order, whatever it is, gives Reason back its place.

Beyond All Reason?

We shall now go a step further. We are entering the realm of total disorder, of sheer Element, no longer in the service of any thought, beyond war. Or perhaps we are entering the abyss from which all these uncontrollable forces emerge. An abyss that yawns during exceptional periods. Unless it is always ajar, like a madness which sleeps with one eye open in the heart of reason.

> Rav Joseph taught (Exodus 12:22): "And none of you shall go outside the door of his house until morning!" As soon as freedom is given to the angel of extermination, he no longer distinguishes between the just and the unjust; moreover, he even begins with the just, for it is written (Ezekiel 21:8): "I shall wipe out from you both the righteous and the wicked." Then Rav Joseph wept: And such a verse to top it all! Those (the just) count for nothing.

To the angel of extermination freedom is given. The term "extermination" *(hamashkhit)* is very expressive in the text. But amid the arbitrariness of extermination is Ezekiel's theme—the priority of the just—still maintained? A semblance of reason?

Let us listen to the commentators. Maharsha says:[5] In speaking, one term always has to come before the other. Can one deduce from the impossibility of terms being simultaneous a teaching on the chronological priority of the events they designate? This deduction would be justified here. Indeed, when Abraham, praying for Sodom, protests against the confusion of the righteous with the unrighteous, the righteous are also named first, but it is the preposition *im* (with), which is used; while in Ezekiel 21:8 we find the conjunction *v* (and). It would allow, within the arbitrariness of extermination, the tragic priority of the righteous to be preserved. This possibility is important, for it maintains the permanence of the question: does the ultimate reason of the violence of war sink into the abyss of an extermination coming from beyond war? Or does the madness of extermination retain a grain of reason? That is the great ambiguity of Auschwitz. That is the question. Our text does not resolve it. It underlines it. Our text does not resolve it because the answer here would be indecent, as all theodicy probably is.

The Insignificance of the Righteous

Rav Joseph wept when thinking of Ezekiel's verse: "And such a verse to top it all! The righteous count for nothing!" Maybe Rav Joseph believes himself to be righteous and weeps because he recognizes his less than enviable situation. But his thought can be rethought another way, and his tears can be spilled more nobly. The righteous could still hope that their death would save the world. But, here they are, dying first, and the unjust perish with them. Holiness serves no purpose, then. It is completely useless, completely gratuitous; gratuitous for those who die as a result of it, certainly; but gratuitous, above all, for the world whose sin this death was to atone for. Useless sacrifice!

It is at this point that Abaye intervenes.

Abaye said to him: That is a favor to them, for it is said (Isaiah 57:1): "Good men are taken away before disaster strikes."

Abaye consoles Rav Joseph: the saints and the righteous, being the first to disappear, will not see the evils coming upon the world. A relative consolation, last echo of rationality in the half-open abyss. But this consolation is adequate to the righteousness of the righteous and takes into account the injustice lurking in the depths of their justice. It takes into account the insufficiency of all personal perfection of private righteousness. A punished righteousness, but punished with righteousness. The texts of Ezekiel take aim at the impossibility of private righteousness; of the righteousness of the righteous who save their own selves, who think of their own selves and their own salvation. The existence of evil people by their side attests, in fact, to the defect in their righteousness. They are responsible for the evil that remains. A homiletic thought, but homily is not rhetoric. Saints, monks, and intellectuals in their ivory tower are the righteous subject to punishment. They are the Pharisees, in the non-noble meaning of the term, which the Jewish tradition is the first to denounce. The righteous subject to punishment may also be the Jewish people when it closes itself off in its community life and contents itself with its synagogue, like the Church, satisfied with the order and harmony which reign within its precincts.

Will Abaye's consolation—that the righteous will have a negative reward—stop the tears of Rav Joseph if Rav Joseph suffers for others? Not to see the suffering of the world is not to bring this suffering to an end. Abaye, who grants the saints the ignorance of the sufferings of others, is perhaps as pessimistic as Rav Joseph, who weeps.

We are, in this punishment of the righteous and in their reward, quite far from the anthropology of the West, quite far from its insistence upon the perseverance in being, upon the famous *conatus* describing the *essence* of man. To be human is to suffer for the other, and even within one's own suffering, to suffer for the suffering my suffering imposes upon the other. This is the paradoxical anthropology animating the small book of Haim of Volozhin,[6] *Nefesh Ha'haim*, in which the *human* appears as a rupture of *being* and *perseverance in Being*, and only as a result of this rupture, as a relation with God.

Night

The theme of extermination without justice is followed by a text which seems to be linked to it only by its reference to the same verse of Exodus (12:22). My efforts as a commentator, however, are based on the hypothesis that the Talmud is not a mere compilation. Moreover, I am convinced of this, despite the appearances to the contrary, and I always attribute my difficulties in finding this coherence and this profound logic of Talmudic speech to the poverty of my means. Perhaps nothing should ever be published under the title "Jewish thought" as long as this logic has not been rediscovered.

> Rav Judah stated in the name of Rab: It is a rule: One must enter an inn when it is full daylight and leave it when it is full daylight, for it is said (Exodus 12:22): "None of you shall go outside the door of his house until morning."

The suspension of justice, the hour of the exterminating angel, is night. The separation of light from darkness is mentioned at the very beginning of the Bible. The Hebrew term used by Rav Judah speaking in Rab's name, and which I have translated by "full daylight," is the expression *ki tov* of Genesis 1:4, a term following immediately upon the creation of light and affirming its excellence. One must neither leave his home nor seek refuge at night. Rav Judah states: it is the rule. Interhuman relations require the clarity of day; night is the very danger of a suspended justice among human beings. Would a distinction have to be made between daytime wars, which conform to the political philosophy of Robert Misrahi, and those which extend into and enter night, where reason is no longer mistress over the powers that have been unleashed? Would there not be wars which extend and end with the "holocaust," in which the exterminator appears and in which justice is no longer in control? Curiously, in the Bible, the ones chosen by the Eternal One rise early when they go to accomplish their mission. "And Abraham rose early in the morning. . . . " "And Moses rose early in the morning." And Joshua wanted to stop the sun so that he could end his war in the light. Even though they were going to fulfil a divine commandment, these men took the precaution of leaving in the morning. Even more should this be the case for the rest of us, who enter into a relation with the other man without having an incontestable mission. But the opinion of Rav Judah, who does not ignore the confusion of night, is therefore comforting in reminding us of the barrier established from the first day of creation between Day and Night.

Night in Broad Daylight

What follows now is more anxiety producing. There is infiltration of night into day. Fire is no longer spoken of; the subject is epidemics. The struggle of doctors against an epidemic is less clear-cut than that of fire-fighters against fire. The elemental, the uncontrollable, is beyond the war which is still visible: an epidemic is everywhere, its frontiers are not circum-scribed. And how many contradictions, leaving no way out of the situation, do we see in the passage below?

> There is a *baraita:* If there is an epidemic in a city, keep your feet from entering it, for it is said: "None of you shall go outside the door of his house until morning"; and then it is said (Isaiah 26:20): "Go my people, enter your chambers, and lock your doors behind you. Hide but a little moment, until the indignation [storm] passes"; and besides it is said (Deuteronomy 32:25): "The sword shall deal death without; within, there shall be terror."

First of all, we find the idea, already stated, of that moment in which the exterminator can do anything. But here the reference is no longer exclu-sively to the verse of Exodus, in which the advice not to go outdoors is given at the supreme hour of Israel's liberation from the Egyptian yoke, and in which the "beyond war" is perhaps only the terror of revolutions. Here, Isaiah 26:20 is cited, in which the storm is sheer menace: one must go back home. Assuming that one has a home. You will see the entire problem of present-day Israel appear, with all the difficulties of the return. One must withdraw into one's home. "Go home until the storm passes." There is no salvation except in the reentry into oneself. One must have an interiority where one can seek refuge, in which one is able to stop participating in the world. And even if "at home"—in the refuge or in the interiority—there is "terror," it is better to have a country, a house, or an "inwardness" with terror than to be outside. If the Americans call this "splendid isolation," they are lucky. It can be quite splendid for them, for it is without terror within!

These contradictions are emphasized in the text which follows:

> Why this *besides?* One might have thought all this applies to night but not to day. That is why it is said: "Go, my people, enter your chambers and lock your doors behind you." But one might have thought that this holds only if inside the house (within) there is no terror and that, if inside there were terror, it would be better to join with people in one group. That is why it is said: Outside, the sword will make victims. Even if inside there is terror, outside the sword shall make victims. Raba used to keep the windows (of his house) sealed during the time of the epidemic, for it is said (Jeremiah 9:20): "For death is come up unto our windows."

Why this *besides?* Why this accumulation of verses? It is because there is no longer any difference between day and night, between outside and in-side. Do we not smell here, more strongly than a while back, beyond all violence which still submits to will and reason, the odor of the camps? Violence is no longer a political phenomenon of war and peace, beyond all morality. It is the abyss of Auschwitz or the world at war. A world which has lost its "very worldliness." It is the twentieth century. One must go back inside, even if there is terror inside. Is the fact of Israel unique? Does it not have its full meaning because it applies to all humanity? All men are on the verge of being in the situation of the State of Israel. The State of Israel is a category.

No Exit

While outside it is the sword, inside it is terror. But one must go back inside. "Raba used to keep the windows (of his house) sealed at the time of the epidemic, for it is said: 'For death is come up unto our windows.' " He closed not only the doors but also the windows to the outside world. He wanted to forget the outside completely. He sealed the windows because the outside world was intolerable. That inside in which there is fear is still the only refuge. It is the no-exit. It is the no-place, the non-place.

This, for me, is the central passage of the entire text on which I am commenting: the no-exit of Israel is probably the human no-exit. All men are of Israel. In my way, I would say: "We are all Israeli Jews."[7] We, that is, all human beings. This interiority is the suffering of Israel as universal suffering.

Speaking to the Enemy

No exit and no entrance! Another solution arising from despair is pitted against the recommendation to prefer terrified interiority to dangerous exteriority: escape toward the danger of exile, escape toward "plenty"; at issue here is not fire, not an epidemic, but famine.

> There is a *baraita:* If famine is in the city, disperse (broaden) your steps, for it is said (Genesis 12:10): "There was famine in the land, and Abram went down to Egypt to sojourn there."

The commentators, in their great piety, make an essential distinction here: They contrast an absolute, exterminating famine, forcing even an Abram to leave the Promised Land, to the going out of the Promised Land of Elimelech (Ruth 1:2), who emigrated during a famine which was still bearable. As if he had gone to seek his fortune in America! A blameworthy emigration which is at the origin of the destruction of Elimelech's family (whence the beauty of Ruth's conversion—conversion or return, return of the one who never had to leave or come back—the reversal of things or possibility of the Messiah).

> Furthermore, it is said (2 Kings 7:4): "If we decide to go into the town, we shall die there."

The text which begins with this *furthermore* tells the famous story of Samaria, encircled and starved: Lepers excluded from the community ask themselves whether they should go into the enemy camp, to the Assyrians besieging the city, to find some scraps there, as they can expect nothing from the besieged city dwellers, who are themselves in the throes of starvation. What is this reference to Samaria doing here? That is precisely the text's question:

> What is the purpose of this *furthermore?* It might be thought that this (fleeing from hunger) is valid only when there is nothing life-threatening where one is going, and that it is invalid when emigration leads to danger; that is why it is said: So let us cast ourselves upon the Assyrian camp: if they let us live, we will survive.

As you know, matters resolved themselves without the Assyrians. When the lepers enter their camp, the Assyrians are no longer there. They had already fled! The famished lepers first throw themselves on whatever they find but immediately afterward they say to themselves, lepers though they are, that it is not right not to announce the good news to the city and to exclude from the booty its non-leprous dwellers. You know this beautiful text, which I need not defend. What matters here is the solution of "escape toward danger" at the time of extermination: at the time of external menace and internal terror. Go, even to the Syrians! Israel's experience through the centuries. We may have here, though, an indication of a way out in the direction of human beings, an idea: even if they are enemies, more can be hoped for from men than from that *elemental* thing—or from that Nothing—which famine symbolizes. Is this a position favorable to the thesis of Robert Misrahi or even to those who extol peace at any price, even if one is the only party seeking it? I do not know. The lepers succeeded in obtaining it because they found themselves alone in their enemies' empty camp.

Extermination Has Already Begun

But here we have a conception in absolute contradiction with the rationality that would be stronger than exterminating violence:

> There is a *baraita:* If the angel of death is in the city, one should not walk in the middle of the road for the angel of death moves about in the middle of the road: benefiting from the liberty granted to him, he walks about publicly. If the city is at peace, one should not walk at the sides of the road, for not being granted liberty, the angel of death slinks along in hiding.

Here you have the ubiquity and the omnitemporality of the violence which exterminates: there is no radical difference between peace and war, between war and holocaust. Extermination has already begun during peacetime. Even if the angel of death is not publicly acknowledged, is not recognized and named as such! It is the very thesis of those who link war and destitution to holocaust. Social injustice and all the forms of exploitation would be only a euphemism for murder, the thesis of those who, in the end, say, with Professor Baruk, that God is really the Lord of Hosts. Everywhere war and murder lie concealed, assassination lurks in every corner, killings go on on the sly. There would be no radical difference between peace and Auschwitz. I do not think that pessimism can go much beyond this. Evil surpasses human responsibility and leaves not a corner intact where reason could collect itself.

But perhaps this thesis is precisely a call to man's infinite responsibility, to an untiring wakefulness, to a total insomnia.

The Peace of Synagogues

Is this the logical link with what follows? No escape into isolation! Watch out for the peace of private worship! Beware of dreams in an empty synagogue!

> There is a *baraita:* If there is an epidemic in a city, one should not go to the house of prayer alone, for it is there that the angel of death keeps his implements; this is true, however, only in the case where schoolchildren do not read Scriptures there and where there are not ten people to pray (together).

But also use your judgment to feel what is in the wind! Follow the impulse of your instincts!

> There is a *baraita:* If the dogs howl, that is because the angel of death has entered the city; if the dogs are happy, Elijah has come into the city. But that is on the condition that there is no bitch among them!

Not to seek refuge in the artificial peace of synagogues and churches! We have already spoken about this. Except if life is not absent from them, if children are learning Scriptures there and if prayer proceeds there from a collectivity. No lull in solitude. I do not know what Clausewitz would think of the thesis that arms are stored in synagogues which do not engage in public worship and in holy places which are not also schools. But that is undoubtedly where ideologies, oppositions, and murderous thoughts are born. If there are children who read the Scriptures, the murderous engines of the inner life lose their explosive force.

If dogs howl, says the last quoted text, that is because the angel of death has entered the city; if mean dogs are happy, that points to Elijah—the precursor of the Messiah! But only if there are no bitches among them!

The first statement is affirmed unconditionally: The dogs howl—instinctive, irrational forebodings; dogs are the first to sense that the angel of death is here. But, when youth is in rapture and when there is optimism on the boulevards, that does not at all prove the coming of the Messiah. Let us not confuse eroticism and messianism! Those dogs, pleased by the presence of a bitch, point to one of the deceptive aspects of salvation through youth. For youth, animated by pure vital impulse, which is not always the equivalent of a pure impulse, messianic times are always near. Beware of the quality of joy! You can see that the Talmud is a subtle and lofty and gay science.

Halakhah and Aggadah

What remains is the last section. It is a reversal of the very mode of the text. The Aggadah, in which we find ourselves since the fable of the thorns and the stacks of corn, turns again—consciously—into Halakhah to become Aggadah again and to finish as Aggadah.

> Rav Ami and Rav Assi were sitting before Rabbi Isaac, the blacksmith. One asked him to treat of the Halakhah and the other of the Aggadah. When he began a Halakhah, he was prevented by the latter; when he began an Aggadah, he was prevented by the former.

Rabbi Isaac is a blacksmith. He knows the peaceful handling of fire. Certainly, he is not here by accident. You will also see that there is a link between what was said earlier about youth and the remainder of our text:

> He then said to them: I will tell you a parable. This can be compared to a man who had two wives, one young and the other old. The young one tore out his white hair, the old one his black hair, so that he became bald on both sides.

I know that baldness is not a debasement. It is only a laying bare of the skull. When the skull is full of intelligence—as sometimes happens to it—one forgets about the baldness, but sometimes baldness disfigures.

There is Aggadah and Halakhah. Aggadah and Halakhah are, in this text, compared to youth and old age. I defined them completely differently when I said: Halakhah is the way to behave; Aggadah is the philosophical meaning—religious and moral—of this behavior. It is, however, not certain that the two definitions contradict each other. The young obviously think that the Halakhah is gray hair, mere forms: forms which have lost their color. The young woman plucks them out: the young interpret to the point of uprooting the roots of terms. The old woman is the traditional point of view: orthodoxy which reads the texts literally. She preseves them in their decay. For her, there is no text to rejuvenate; the white hairs still stand. They count. In contrast to the young woman, she plucks out the black hair, which are harbingers of all the vitality, all the impatience of innovative interpretation. At issue is the very division of the community of Israel, its splitting apart into youth and non-youth. Everywhere, from that moment, there is violence.

This division into young and old, this separation into revolutionaries and traditionalists, is condemned. The text is against the cult of the traditional and against the cult of the modern! The spirit loses its sovereignty in such cults. The one group wants to renew to the point of rediscovering a religion of dances and shows; the other group, because of its respect for white hair, sees frivolity everywhere. But the spirit is not bigamous! What is terrible is this bigamy of the spirit which the two wives, old and young, represent, maturity as conservatism and youth as a search for novelty at any price.

Rabbi Isaac, the blacksmith, supplies a solution:

He then said to them: I will tell you a story which will please you both.

In other words, I will give you a Halakhah which is an Aggadah, an Aggadah which is a Halakhah.

If a fire breaks out and catches in thorns and progresses of itself, then the one who set the fire has to pay.

But the Halakhah is immediately transposed into Aggadah or, more exactly, linked to an Aggadah read as Halakhah:

The Holy One, Blessed be He, said: I kindled a fire on Zion, as it is said (Lamentations 4:11): "He kindled a fire in Zion which consumed its foundations," and I will rebuild it one day with fire, as it is said (Zechariah 2:9): "And I myself will be a wall of fire all around it and I will be a glory inside it."

The Blacksmith's Lesson

Besides teaching us about the ambiguity Halakhah-Aggadah inherent in every Halakhah and in every Aggadah, what does Rabbi Isaac teach us about the compensation due for damages caused by fire, he who is an expert in the peaceful use of destructive forces?

Thus, the one who set the fire has to pay. The Holy One, Blessed be He, said: It is incumbent upon me to make restitution for the fire which I have set. A Halakhah: one begins with a compensation one is obliged to make because of what belongs to you, and one concludes by a compensation due for damages caused to the very person, in order to teach you that the damage caused by fire is to be compared to the damage caused by an arrow.

If the damage is caused by objects belonging to you, it is up to you to compensate. That is the law. But the fire, far from lessening this responsibility, aggravates it: It is compared to damage "caused by an arrow that is shot." It is the designation of a special category. The arrow is not merely something that belongs to you, like a shingle off the roof of your house which injures a passerby. It supposes a destructive aim; it is aimed at someone. We know from elsewhere, however, that the person who shoots the arrow owes compensation for the destruction of material goods. To be sure. But there are four other things to pay for: the care given to the injured, the unemployment into which he is forced, the physical pain which was caused him, the moral suffering of the shame or of the social diminution which results from his disablement. Does Jewish law anticipate Social Security? In any case, it knows the weight and the value of the other person.

This is a curious way of establishing identities! The release of elementary and anonymous forces is made equal to the intention that aims at a precise mark, that of the archer! The creativity of a fire that restores is reduced to its defensive function! The blacksmith, who knows the peaceful use of elemental forces, extends responsibility, pushed to its extreme, to the chaos of war, and no doubt, to the National-Socialist holocaust. Robert Misrahi can be pleased: that is certainly the idea he put into his ideal of *democratic socialism*,[8] a term which should be dear to us if only because, under Hitler, it was styled the abstraction of degenerated Jewish intellectuals. Encouraged anew by the blacksmith-rabbi, we should dare to use this term and to throw it out as a challenge. We must also say: Yes, war criminals do exist! Those hours when all cats are grey, in which everything seems possible, without impunity, must be paid for.

That is what the text teaches to our failing memory. And I should have ended with this if our text did not also announce to us—something that matters a great deal to us at the present moment, and without which the war criminals would never have paid—that Zion will be rebuilt.

Consuming Fire and Protective Wall

Rabbi Isaac deduces an Aggadah from a juridical principle linked to the image of a shot arrow. An Aggadah promises the reconstruction of Jerusalem in its glory, a reconstruction by the very means which were used to destroy it, precisely through fire, become protector. But where is the glory of His presence among us, if not in the transfiguration of consuming and avenging fire into a protective wall, into a defensive barrier?

NOTES

1. See *La conscience juive face à la guerre* (Paris: P.U.F., 1976), pp. 3–9.
[Levinas's commentary often makes reference to Robert Misrahi's talk "Essai d'analyse philosophique de la guerre," which immediately preceded Levinas's own. The following short paraphrase will give some idea of Misrahi's position:

Misrahi maintains that there is a rationality to war, in the first place, because war is always fought for political, that is, self-interested ends, that require the use of the intelligence in order for these ends to be pursued. As a result, no war can be a total war, as it is limited by the parties' desire to attain their ends. This also means that since war is an enterprise that calculates ends, the intellect which calculates them can be appealed to to reach these ends outside war.

Another point that Misrahi makes is that there is an underlying principle, the principle of reversibility, which operates in human relations. The aggressor in war has forgotten that what applies to him also applies to the other. Wars come into being because he who is attacked reciprocates. Thus, there is a mechanism, transparent to reason, with a logic of its own, that limits aggression and eventually restores true reciprocity, peace.

Misrahi's comments draw heavily on the work of the Prussian general Karl von Clausewitz (1780–1831), who is considered the most original and most influential writer on the subject of war. Levinas makes a passing reference to Clausewitz toward the end of this commentary. (Trans.)]

2. There is a play on words here between *dériver* (to derive) and *être à la dérive*, (to be adrift). "La philosophie *dérive* pour moi de la religion *en dérive* et toujours probablement la religion est *en dérive* (Trans.)

3. Leibnitz, who had read Maimonides and admired him, knows the doctrine of the Oral Law: "Moses did not make the doctrine of the immortality of souls part of his laws: it was consonant with his views, *it was taught from hand to hand"* (Gerhardt edition, vol 6, p. 26). It is we who have [italicized] the last seven words of the quotation.

4. See note 1. (Trans.)

5. See note 1 in "As Old as the World?" (Trans.)

6. Haim of Volozhin (1749–1821): rabbi and educator, leading disciple of Rabbi Elijah ben Solomon Zalmon, the Gaon of Vilna. Rabbi Haim was the acknowledged spiritual leader of the non-Hassidic Russian Jewry of his day. Levinas has written about him on several occasions. See, for instance, "A l'image de Dieu d'après Rabbi Haim Volozhiner," in *L' au-delà du verset;* and also his Preface to *L'âme de la vie,* by Rabbi Hayyim de Volozhine (La Grasse: Éditions Verdier, 1986). (Trans.)

7. See note 7, on "We are all German Jews," in "Judaism and Revolution." "We are all Israeli Jews" is a reference to that prior statement. (Trans.)

8. Robert Misrahi, in the same talk to which Levinas has been referring frequently in the course of this commentary, had linked the traditional Jewish vision of peace and messianic times with that of democratic socialism. He claimed that this was more than an idealist dream but something that could be achieved here and now. (Trans.)